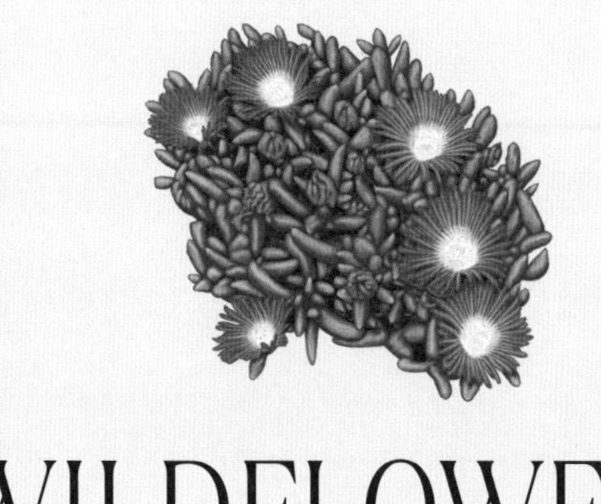

WILDFLOWERS

WILDFLOWERS

Wild garlic
(*Allium ursinum*)

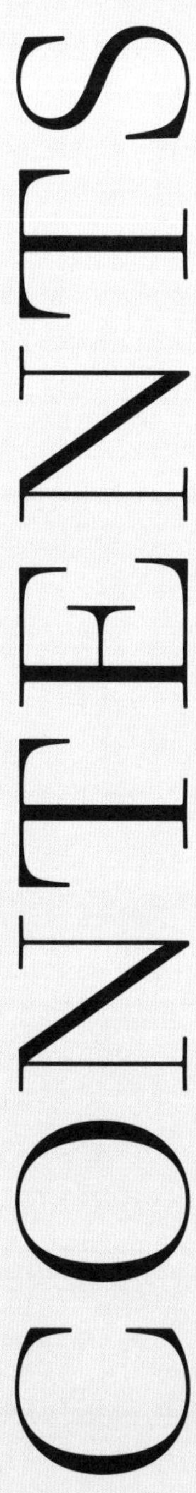
CONTENTS

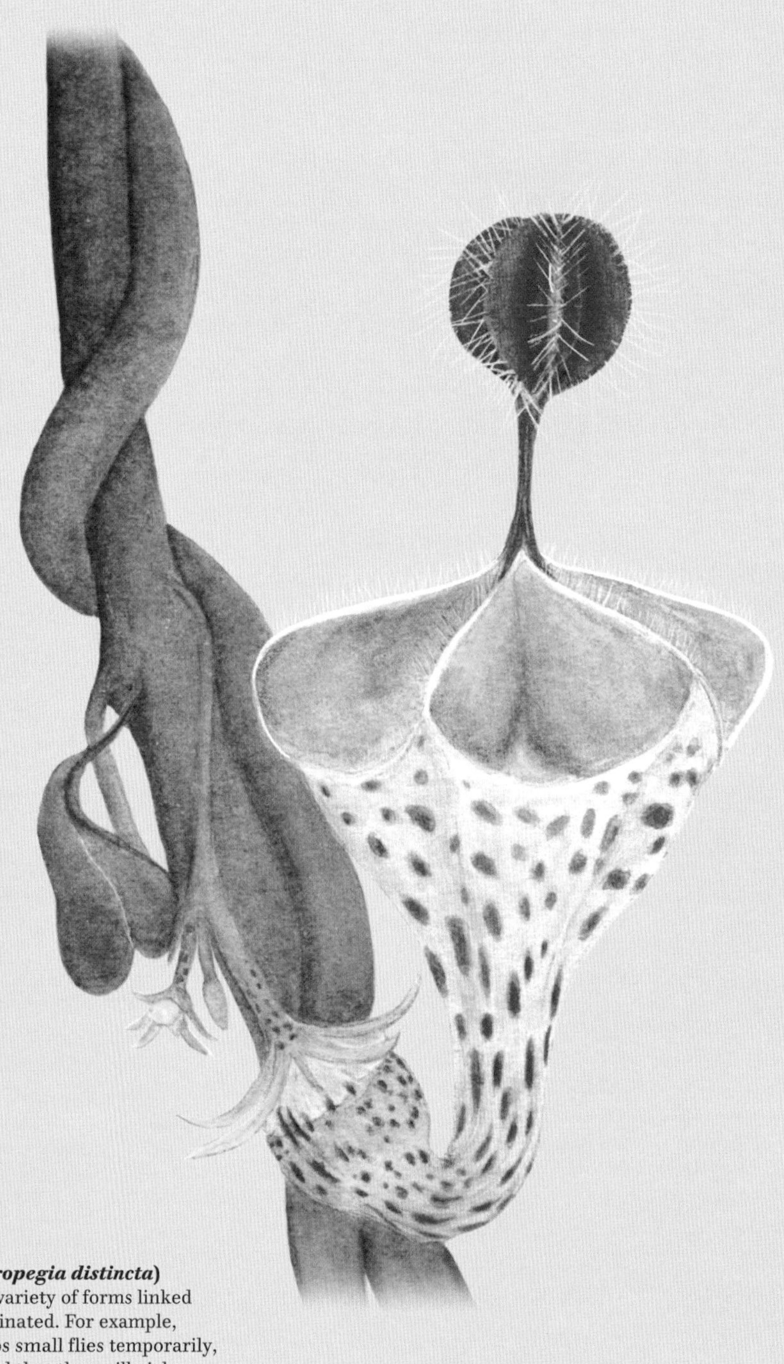

Parachute flower (*Ceropegia distincta*)
Wildflowers come in a variety of forms linked to the way they are pollinated. For example, this “pitfall flower” traps small flies temporarily, increasing the likelihood that they will pick up and deliver pollen.

Wild plants energize the planet, and have over thousands of years been a source of food and medicine for people. The lives of humans have always been intertwined with wildflowers; they are fundamental to our existence.

WILDFLOWERS

We share the planet's biosphere—the thin layer of life that we call home—with about 400,000 different types of wild vascular plant (plants that have specialized tissues for transporting water and nutrients). They exist in almost every terrestrial habitat on Earth, from Arctic tundra and hillsides to shallow seas and deserts.

First things first: what is a plant? The ancient philosophers classified as plants all living things that were not animals, including fungi and algae (pp.18–21). Today we define the Plant Kingdom (or Kingdom Plantae) as encompassing all green algae and the land plants—a group including spore plants, such as mosses, liverworts, and ferns, and seed plants, including gymnosperms and flowering plants. The last are the focus of this book. Together, wild plants range from microscopic single-celled organisms to towering trees.

Most plants obtain their energy from sunlight, using chloroplasts. Chloroplasts evolved from an endosymbiotic cyanobacterium—a free-living cyanobacterium that entered and became engulfed by another cell. Chloroplasts produce sugars from carbon dioxide and water, using the pigment chlorophyll. Chlorophyll is what makes plants green. But there are exceptions, as we shall see. Parasitic plants, many of which lack chlorophyll, obtain their carbon from other plants and fungi (pp.58–59), and some "plant predators" (pp.90–91) "hunt" animal prey.

Wildflowers have evolved an arsenal of adaptations to cope with the challenges they face in nature—and that's why they exist in such a bewildering diversity of forms.

TECHNICAL TERMS Scientists use special words to talk about wildflowers, and many of these are included in this book. Check the glossary on pages 274–275 for a simple explanation of key terms.

WHAT IS WILD?

A wildflower is a plant that grows in a natural environment—rather than one that was planted intentionally. "Wildflower" is a very broad term that typically encompasses a variety of life forms—from trees to herbaceous plants—and lineages, from spore plants (including mosses, liverworts, and ferns) to angiosperms (the flowering plants). Indeed, when considering where wildflowers came from (see Chapter 1), it is necessary to consider the spore plants (mosses, for example), because they preceded the evolution of flowering plants.

Wildflowers include native species—those occurring naturally in an area—as well as aliens or exotics—those that have been introduced from elsewhere and have naturalized in a given place. Some of the latter may be invasive (meaning they outcompete other plants). It is often difficult to ascertain whether a wildflower is native or not, and in any case, some have been naturalized in a particular location for centuries or longer.

Plants have been domesticated for food, medicine, and ornament for thousands of years. Along the way, people have created many hundreds of thousands of cultivars (a plant produced by selective breeding), for example vegetables and such showy garden plants as roses and dahlias. These plants are excluded from the definition of wildflowers.

This book features several hundred species of wild plant, with a focus on flowering plants, especially those that are most conspicuous or most likely to be encountered in many parts of the world. The aim is to cover as many of the major taxonomic groups as possible.

Bladder senna (*Colutea arborescens*)
This shrub is native to dry hillsides in the Mediterranean. Where it has been planted as an ornamental in Northern Europe, however, it has escaped to roadsides, where it grows as an alien exotic.

Netted iris (*Iris reticulata*)
This small bulb and its relatives are familiar spring-flowering potted garden plants; however, in the wild they typically grow in large numbers on exposed, stony slopes.

Harebell (*Campanula rotundifolia*)
This species, in nature, grows in cool temperate grasslands.

PLANTS AND PEOPLE

Plants and people have evolved together. In fact, human history is inseparable from that of plants; we have always been dependent on them. This legacy can be seen today in the form of plant crops that are cultivated for food and fiber, medicine, and energy, as well as the prominence of plants in art, culture, and religion the world over. The anatomy of ancient humans (hominids) reflects the plants they ate thousands of years ago. Since then, there has been a cultural shift from hunter-gatherer behavior to agriculturally fueled societies. But, while we are as dependent on plants now as we have ever been, our way of life threatens the very existence of many species. Two in five of the world's wild plants are threatened with extinction today.

Solutions to many of the greatest challenges we face as a species rely on plants and the biodiversity they support. It is becoming increasingly clear that our well-being is underpinned by plants and nature. Yet many people scarcely notice, let alone appreciate, plants: a phenomenon known metaphorically as "plant blindness." If we are to tackle plummeting biodiversity and thrive as a species ourselves, we must find new ways to coexist with nature. An appreciation of the plants and wildflowers with which we share our existence is fundamental to tackling this challenge.

Desert hyacinth (*Cistanche deserticola*) This wildflower has been used by people for millennia in traditional herbal medicine, especially in China and West Asia. Today, in a warming climate, it has increasing potential as a food plant in arid regions, where it could be grown without the need for irrigation or fertilizers.

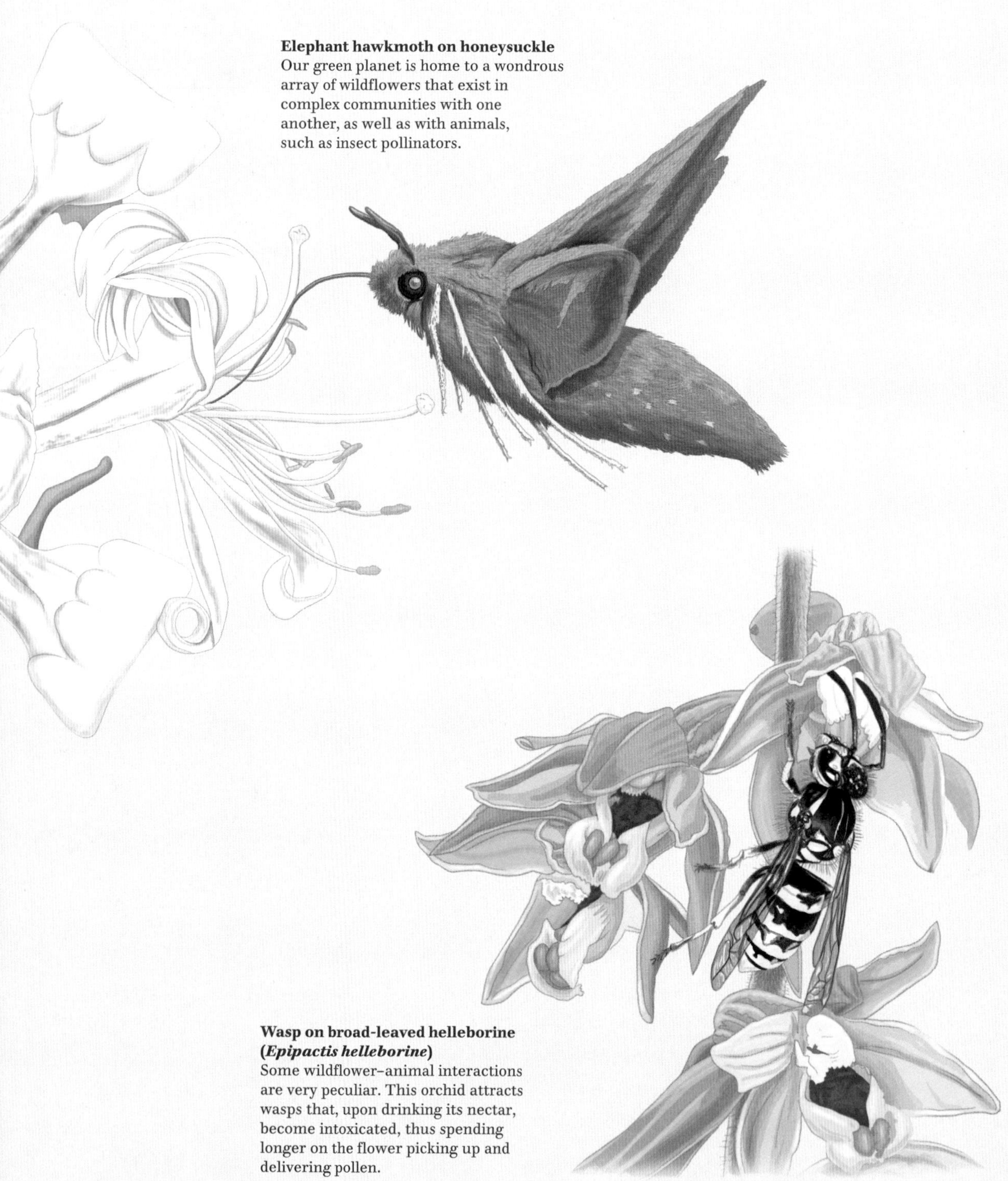

Elephant hawkmoth on honeysuckle
Our green planet is home to a wondrous array of wildflowers that exist in complex communities with one another, as well as with animals, such as insect pollinators.

Wasp on broad-leaved helleborine (*Epipactis helleborine*)
Some wildflower–animal interactions are very peculiar. This orchid attracts wasps that, upon drinking its nectar, become intoxicated, thus spending longer on the flower picking up and delivering pollen.

OUR GREEN PLANET

Plants fuel the world's ecosystems, configure the air and climate, and provide food and habitats for other organisms. Grains, vegetables, and fruits have been domesticated from wild plants for thousands of years, and today plants are also used in biotechnology in ways we could never have imagined.

But where did plants come from? How did they evolve to conquer the land? To answer this, we must first step back into a land before trees, when mosses first carpeted the Earth (pp.22–23); then we will walk through fern prairies and flowerless forests, and gaze up at colossal trees that towered over the dinosaurs (pp.24–27). These fossil forests precede the emergence of a great dynasty: the flowering plants (pp.30–31). They were to change planet Earth indefinitely.

Today our world is ruled by a dazzling diversity of wildflowers that possess myriad different forms and coexist in complex communities (pp.54–55). They communicate with one another (pp.86–87) and have evolved complex and sometimes downright bizarre interactions with animals (pp.80–85).

This book is a celebration of wildflowers: how they came to be, what they are, what they do, and how they have shaped our green planet. But why do they matter? Well, today—more than ever before—it is clear that we could not survive on Earth without wildflowers.

Aristolochia grandiflora

DISCOVER

CHAPTER I

WHEN THE FIRST PLANTS EVOLVED, they changed our planet forever. By examining fossils and the DNA of living plants, scientists have pieced together the jigsaw of how plants conquered the land one green dynasty at a time, from mosses and their relatives, to flowering plants. Today we live among a dazzling diversity of plant species.

It's difficult to picture our planet without plants. But more than 500 million years ago Planet Earth was devoid of vegetation. Then the forerunners of plants evolved, and they were to form the basis of life on Earth as we know it.

THE RISE OF PLANTS

Plants made the journey onto land 470 million years ago, when the planet became cool and hospitable enough to support them. The first plants to appear were algae, and these were followed by cushion-like or ground-hugging plants, such as mosses and liverworts. It wasn't until about 150 million years later that plants evolved complex "plumbing" systems to transport water, and were able to form the first forests. There were still no flowers at this time; the plant kingdom was ruled by strange trees called lycophytes, and then ferns. All these plants reproduced by spores, dustlike reproductive particles that spread far and wide, but which usually needed wet places to thrive.

Dinosaurs usually spring to mind when we think of our prehistoric planet. But in order to understand the evolution of extinct animals, we must also consider the plants on which some of them fed. Herbivorous dinosaurs, such as stegosaurs, fed on plants including ferns and cycads, and, given their size, they would have consumed great quantities of them. Perhaps this provided space for other, fast-growing plants to evolve.

A BLOSSOMING PLANET More than 100 million years ago flowering plants evolved, changing the face of the planet forever. Flowers enticed a proliferation of insects for cross-pollination, and that, in turn, enabled all sorts of other animals to prosper. The plants we see today—from algae, ferns, and conifers, to flowering plants—are a snapshot of the many millions of species that have existed over evolutionary time.

The first flowers
According to the fossil record, the first flowers may have resembled the magnolias we see growing today, which belong to a very ancient group of plants. They may have been pollinated by beetles, just as many are still.

Living things are classified into groups called genera, families, and orders. These are based on their genetic relatedness. Scientists have used DNA analysis to figure out how plants evolved and conquered the land, one dynasty at a time.

PLANT DYNASTIES

It wasn't easy for plants to make the shift from the water to land and, after that, just about every terrestrial habitat imaginable. First, they needed a protective layer to prevent them from drying out. Then they required special water-conducting tissues called xylem. A strange mosslike plant called *Zosterophyllum* was one of the first to develop veins for transporting water. This was a step forward in the rise of plants, preceding the next dynasty: the lycopods.

Lycopods are still around, but the small specimens that exist today are a shadow of their evolutionary forebears. Extinct lycopods were some of the first to evolve roots, stems, and leaves similar to those we see in living plants. Some 350 million years ago these plants towered over the land. *Sigillaria* is a fossil lycopod that, from the Devonian to the Permian period (388–254 million years ago), formed great forests that grew rapidly out of the warm, wet earth. The remains of this monstrous plant formed peat, which eventually turned to coal.

These early plant dynasties paved the way for the evolution of ferns, then the seed plants, and eventually flowering plants, like those we see today.

THE RISE OF LARGE LEAVES

About 350 million years ago plants turned over a new leaf. Megaphylls were a new form of larger, flatter, more complex leaf, with many veins. The dynasty of large-leafed plants would alter Earth's atmosphere profoundly, influencing all other life. *Eophyllophyton*—now extinct—is thought to be one of the first plants to have evolved megaphylls.

FROM WATER TO LAND

ZOSTEROPHYLLUM

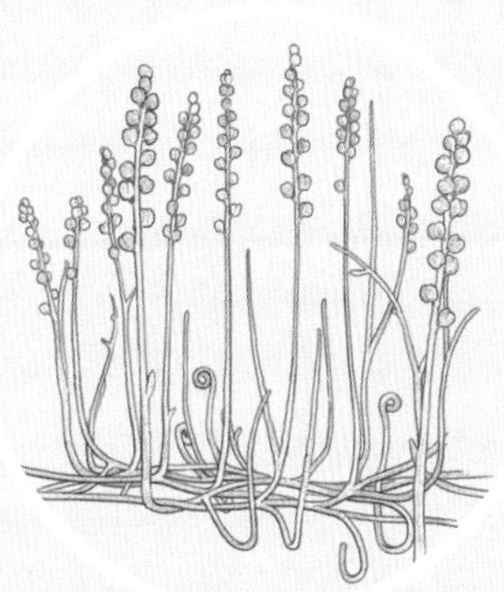

1.

Plants evolved a protective layer to prevent them from drying out on land.

2.

Plants evolved special vessels for transporting water from the soil, and symbiotic relationships with fungi.

SIGILLARIA

3.

Plants evolved roots, stems, and leaves, enabling them to soar upward into the canopy.

4.

As plants conquered the land, great forests formed and laid down peat, which eventually turned to coal.

5.

Spore plants diversified, filling new niches on land.

6.

Dynasties of spore plants paved the way for the evolution of seeds and, ultimately, flowers.

Ancient algae
Rinistachya is an extinct green alga, the fossil of which was discovered in a shale deposit in South Africa in 2018. Although this plant existed 370 million years ago, it still resembles the living freshwater green algae we see today, suggesting that they have diverged little from their long-lost ancestors during this time.

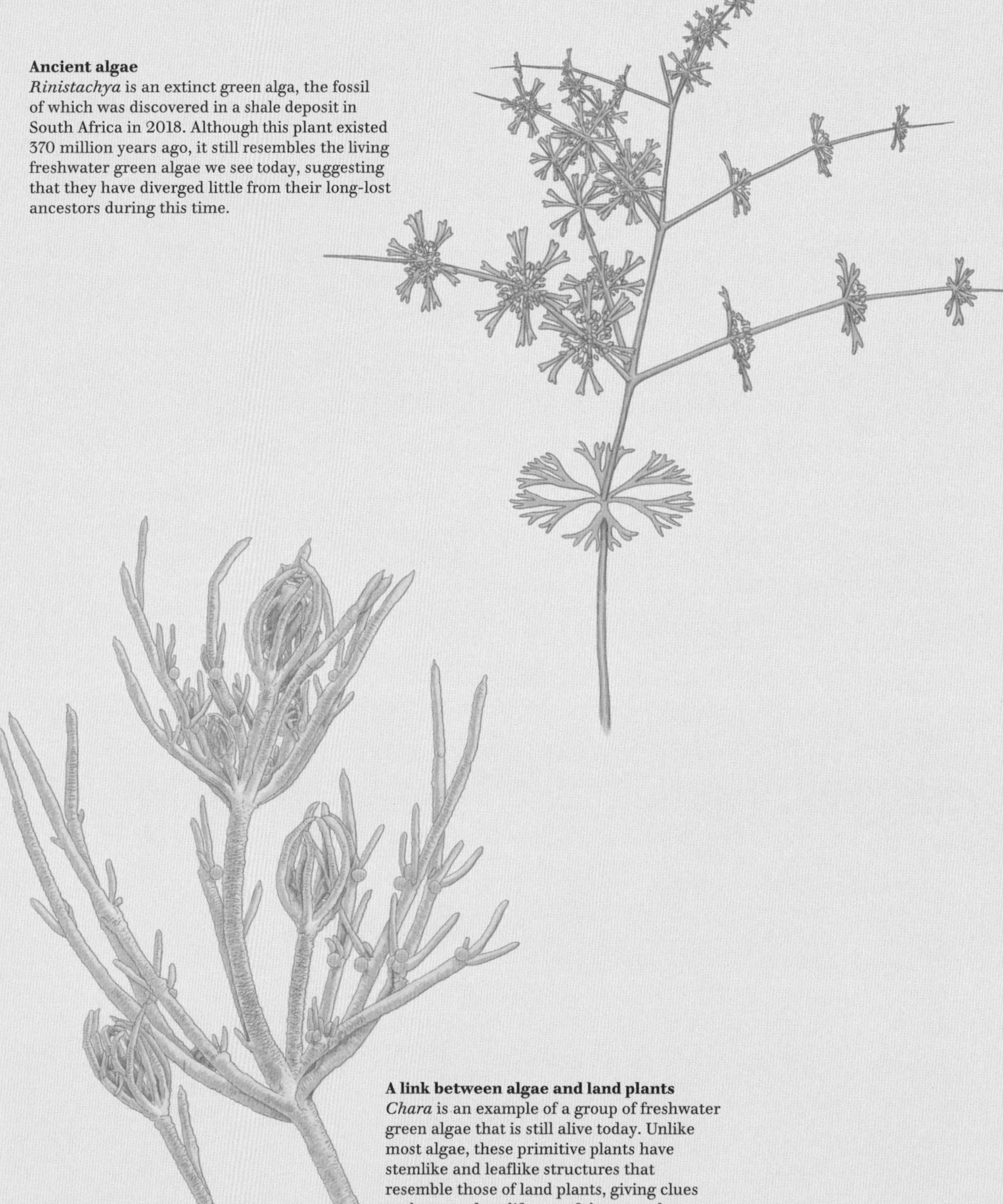

A link between algae and land plants
Chara is an example of a group of freshwater green algae that is still alive today. Unlike most algae, these primitive plants have stemlike and leaflike structures that resemble those of land plants, giving clues to the way plant life out of the water began.

Plants dominate just about every habitat you can think of, including those underwater. Algae were the first plants (in the broadest sense) to evolve, and today they still grow in just about every pond, marsh, lake, and ocean.

WILD WATER WEEDS

"Algae" is a collective term used to describe a diverse range of living organisms, many of which are not closely related, nor considered to be true plants according to the strictest definition. They range from microscopic single cells in puddles, to vast underwater forests of kelp, the largest of which are among the fastest-growing organisms alive today. Although algae do not produce flowers, examining them is important to help scientists understand how all plants, including wildflowers, evolved.

Red algae—or seaweeds—have adaptations that enable them to grow in aquatic environments. Some forms of kelp, for example, possess gas-filled bladders that keep their fronds afloat. Many seaweeds produce rootlike structures called holdfasts that clamp them to the sea floor, anchoring them against the current. Seaweeds form a vital habitat in marine ecosystems all around the world.

Green algae grow in freshwater habitats, such as rivers, ponds, and lakes. These familiar "gloppy" green organisms are often known as pondweed, and you often see them when pond-dipping. They're more important than they perhaps appear. For example, charophytes are a group of green algae that have survived for at least 450 million years. They predated the arrival of dinosaurs by an astonishing 200 million years—and still they soldier on as the world changes around them. While it may seem improbable, all land plants evolved from the ancestor of a plant much like these living pondweeds.

Plants first left the water 470 million years ago and carpeted the land, changing the face of our now green planet. Living ancestors of these land conquerors still exist today: mosses and their relatives, which form forests beneath our feet.

MOSSES AND LIVERWORTS

Mosses, liverworts, and hornworts are living examples of a lineage of plants called the bryophytes. These were the first plants to step out of the prehistoric swamps into terrestrial habitats. Look closely at any tree trunk, stone path, or roof and you are likely to see one of these very ancient plants.

SPORE PLANTS Bryophytes do not produce flowers or seeds, because they belong to a lineage that predates the evolution of these structures. Instead, they reproduce by spores (single-celled units of dispersal that precede the evolution of the seed). The spores are produced in an assortment of peculiar structures. For example, *Marchantia*, a form of liverwort, produces miniature forests of umbrellalike structures from which its spores are dispersed (opposite).

One of the most abundant mosses today is *Sphagnum*, which you can find in just about any bog or freshwater marsh, where it forms extensive green or red blankets. Its spongy tissues have an extraordinary capacity for storing water. As this moss decays it forms layers of peat. Peat bogs formed by *Sphagnum* store vast quantities of carbon, and they are ecologically vital; in fact, these mosses have been described as "ecosystem engineers." Carnivorous plants, such as sundews (p.183), are often found in *Sphagnum* bogs.

Marchantia
A type of liverwort, *Marchantia* spreads along the ground via a leafy thallus. When mature, the thallus sends up tiny umbrellalike structures that produce either sperm or egg cells, and—following fertilization—spores.

Dawsonia
Besides lacking flowers and seeds, mosses and their relatives have no roots or vascular tissue, a fact that limits the size to which they can grow. The world's tallest moss, which grows in the damp forests of Australasia, is called *Dawsonia* and grows to about 24 in (60 cm) high.

Cyathea
This tree fern belongs to a very ancient plant group that dates back hundreds of millions of years, predating the dinosaurs, seeds, and flowers. Like the mosses and liverworts on the previous page, ferns reproduce by spores.

Ferns first unfurled in the Devonian period, about 400 million years ago, and rose to dominance 100 million years after that. Those that exist today are the survivors of a lost kingdom.

FORESTS OF FERNS

Dinosaurs roamed among fern prairies and swamps long before the flowering plants evolved. Like the bryophytes (see p.22), this ancient lineage of plants reproduces with spores rather than seeds. Ferns were very successful, and even today they are one of the most diverse major plant groups, with about 10,000 species worldwide. Some grow as epiphytes—meaning they cling to the branches of trees—while others form great trees themselves. One, called *Azolla*, could fit on your fingertip, and exists floating on the water's surface. Their adaptability is key to the ferns' success.

The fossil record is replete with fern fronds. *Wattieza* is an example of a lost fern relative from between 400 and 80 million years ago, that rose to 26 ft (8 m) in height, like the tree ferns that are alive today. *Wattieza* was one of many fern ancestors that deposited large quantities of leaf litter that would have been ecologically important for other plants and animals. Another extinct fern with treelike proportions was *Psaronius*, which had a colossal trunk with a span of almost 3 ft (1 m).

Tree ferns called *Cyathea* date back to the Silurian era, some 237 million years ago. Today they grow in wet, mossy forests, just as they did then. They are an example of a living fossil.

The true ferns preceded an extinct group of plants known as seed ferns: fernlike plants that were among the first to produce seeds, the sturdy outer casing of which enabled them to grow in drier habitats. These are the ancestors of the plants that dominate nearly every habitat on Earth today.

Today there are just 20 or so species of horsetail. They are the vestiges of a group of plants that ruled the Earth for more than 100 million years.

FOSSIL FORESTS

Horsetails are common wild plants that you may have noticed on woodland fringes, in meadows, or even in gardens. Those that survive today are typically small, but their ancestors towered above the canopy. Their gargantuan, pole-like trunks sprouted strange, spiraled leaves that dinosaurs grazed on.

Calamites is a Goliath of a horsetail that covered vast areas of swamp from the Devonian to the Carboniferous period (359–315 million years ago). It had a cylindrical trunk rising to 98 ft (30 m) and extensive underground runners, with which it colonized vast tracts of land. Another tree horsetail alive at this time was *Pseudobornia*, which bore numerous protruding, leafy branches. These trees were shooting up out of the swamps as giant amphibians slithered around below.

Eventually conditions on Earth changed and were no longer favorable for horsetails with giant proportions. The forests fell, opening up new habitats that were colonized by flowering plants.

LIVING FOSSILS The field horsetail (*Equisetum arvense*) is common in many parts of the world, especially in the northern hemisphere. You can often find it in damp pastures, and it is even considered a weed in some places. The giant horsetail (*E. telmateia*) is like it but much larger, and is found in similar places. Among the tallest living species of horsetail is *E. myriochaetum*, which grows to more than 3 ft (1 m) tall. It forms large stands (groups) in its native North America.

EXTRAORDINARY STROBILI

Horsetails, like the ferns, reproduce by spores. Most ferns produce spores on the underside of their fronds. Horsetails, on the other hand, produce curious structures called strobili, which contain no chlorophyll and are distinct from the leafy stems, which are often borne separately.

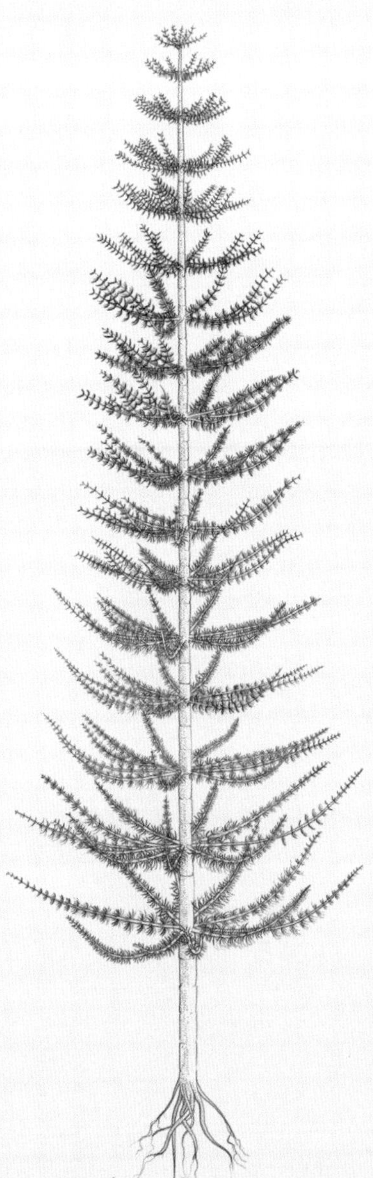

Calamites
This extinct horsetail once covered vast areas of swamps and sandy riverbanks. Unlike its living descendants, this giant grew to heights of at least 65 ft (20 m), and had massive underground runners that allowed it to colonize the land 360–250 million years ago.

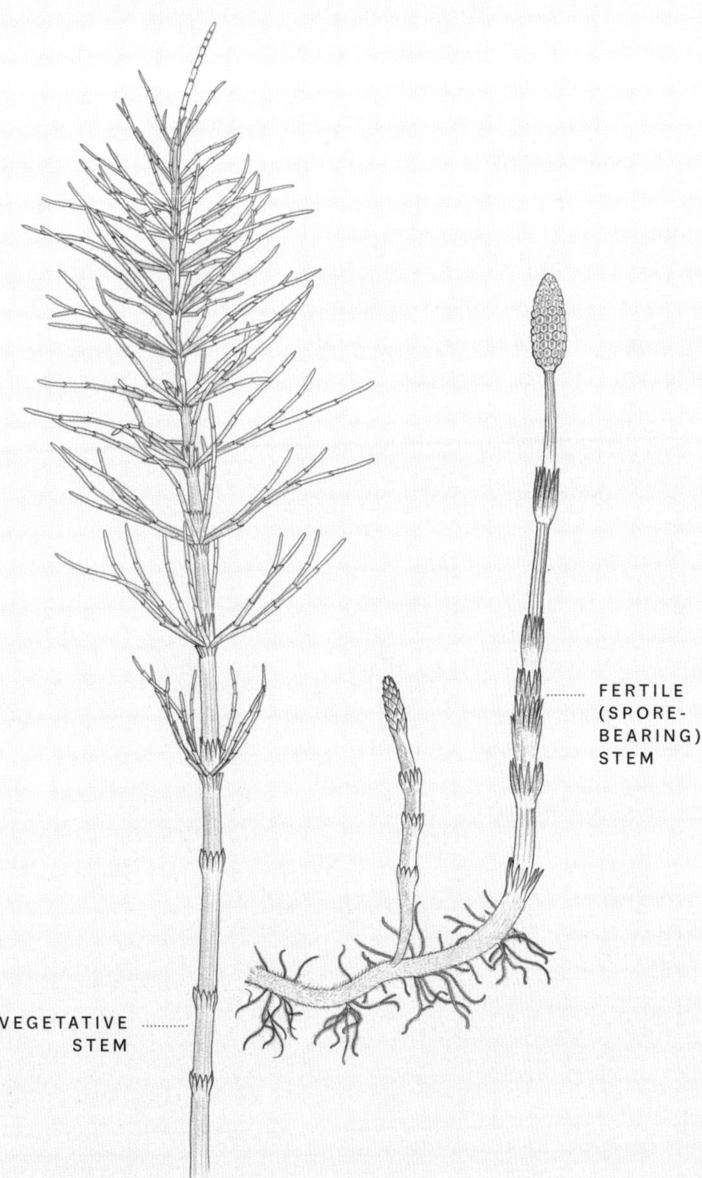

Field horsetail (*Equisetum arvense*)
This plant is abundant in temperate regions across the northern hemisphere. It tends to grow in damp woods, pastures, and fields, and along streams. It also appears in gardens, where it can be difficult to eradicate. The ancient Romans ate its shoots in the same way as asparagus.

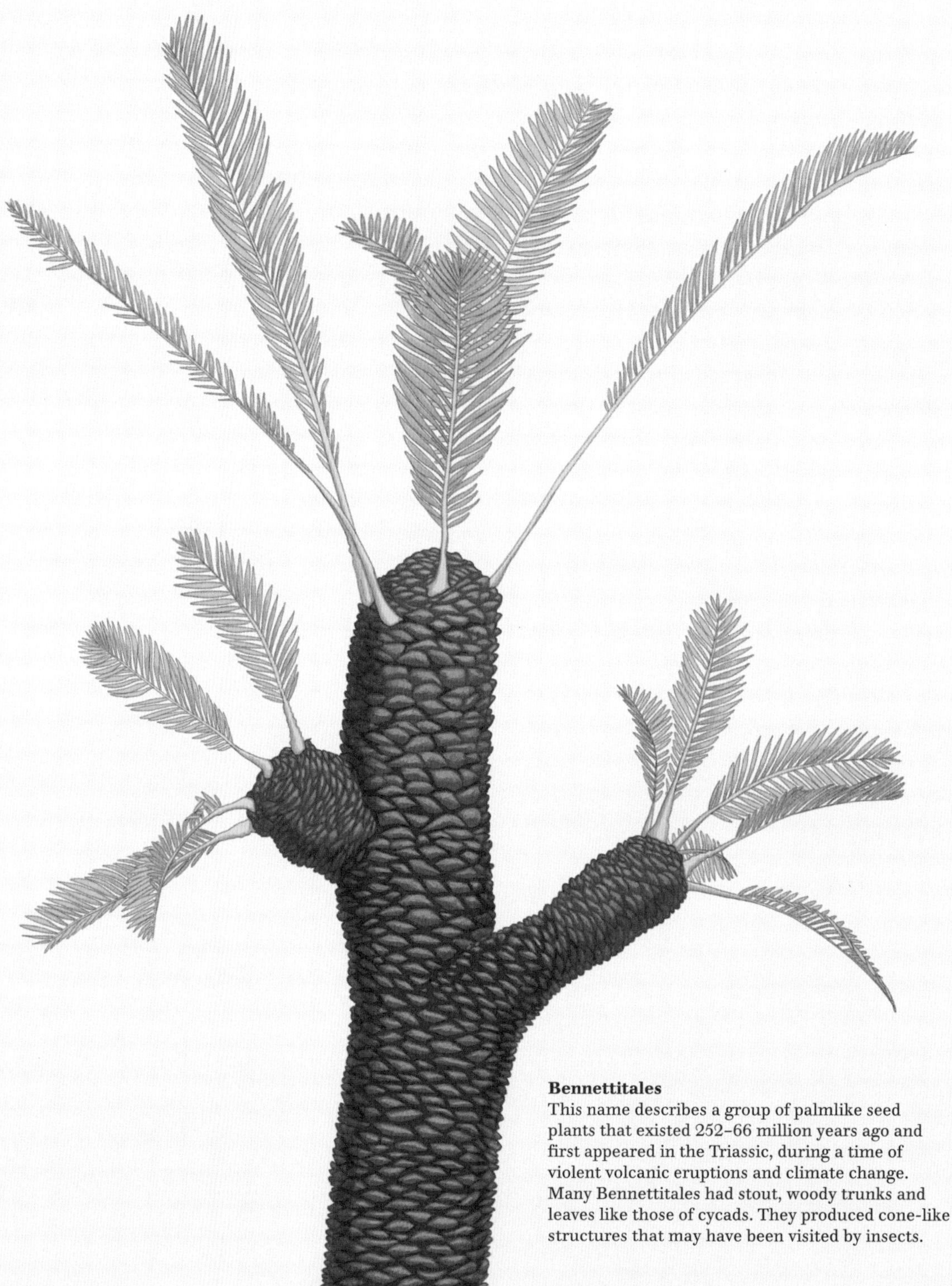

Bennettitales
This name describes a group of palmlike seed plants that existed 252–66 million years ago and first appeared in the Triassic, during a time of violent volcanic eruptions and climate change. Many Bennettitales had stout, woody trunks and leaves like those of cycads. They produced cone-like structures that may have been visited by insects.

Seeds were key to plants conquering the land. These structures enabled plants to remain dormant until conditions became favorable, freeing them from the water and opening up new habitats for colonization.

SPORES TO SEEDS

You can think of a seed as a baby plant enclosed in a tough outer casing. This protective coat enables the seeds to lie dormant, often for long periods or even—in exceptional circumstances—several thousand years. Unlike the spore plants, which required wet habitats to reproduce, seed plants were finally able to conquer the land—just about all of it. They transformed our planet forever.

One of the first seed plants was Bennettitales (opposite), which appeared about 300 million years ago. This small tree would have looked something like a palm tree or cycad. About 100 million years later, at some point in the Jurassic period, another early seed plant evolved, called *Caytonia*, which produced seeds with a fleshy coating. These plants preceded one of the most important plant lineages: the gymnosperms.

CONQUERING CONIFERS Today, gymnosperms are everywhere. These cone-bearing plants include conifers (such as yew trees and pines), cycads, and the familiar ginkgo or maidenhair tree, which is another example of a living fossil that has remained relatively unchanged through deep evolutionary time. Conifers were particularly successful. This lineage of trees survived 300 million years of drifting continents and changing climate, and still they are dominant in some habitats. They also include the tallest living organisms on Earth: "Hyperion" is the name given to a coastal redwood (*Sequoia sempervirens*) in California that is nearly 381ft (116m) tall; meanwhile, the bristlecone pines (*Pinus longaeva*) in the mountains of the western United States can live for thousands of years.

The world changed again 130 million years ago, during the Cretaceous period. The fossil forests fell, surrendering to a new and highly successful lineage: the flowering plants. Life on Earth would never be the same again.

SEEDS OF CHANGE

Charles Darwin described the abrupt appearance of flowering plants (angiosperms) in the fossil record as "an abominable mystery." Today this mystery still hasn't been solved adequately.

Flowers produce pollen, which in most plants must be transferred from one plant to another to bring about cross-fertilization. Plants recruited insects as couriers to take pollen from flower to flower. By the mid-Cretaceous, flowering plants were beginning to dominate just about every habitat on dry land. Perhaps as the dinosaurs grazed, the fast-growing flowering plants were able to recover more quickly than the gymnosperms that preceded them. Whatever the case, they were to become the most successful lineage on Earth: today they make up 90 percent of all plants.

JURASSIC PARK
Flowering plants evolved as dinosaurs were on the prowl. But while most of the early fossils, such as those of *Archaeanthus* and *Lesqueria*, date back to the Cretaceous, some scientists believe that the first flowers in fact appeared even earlier—in the Jurassic. For example, *Nanjinganthus* is a curious plant that is thought to have first unfurled its leaves as far back as 174 million years ago.

FOSSIL FLOWERS Flowering plants developed the first fruit, and these are preserved better than flowers in the fossil record. Among the best-preserved are the fruit of an unusual plant called *Archaeanthus*, which flourished 100 million years ago. It produced fruit in congested, cone-like structures. Another curious fossil flower that grew in the Cretaceous was *Lesqueria*. It too produced tightly packed bunches of fruit. These fossil plants offer a window into what must have been an extraordinary prehistoric landscape.

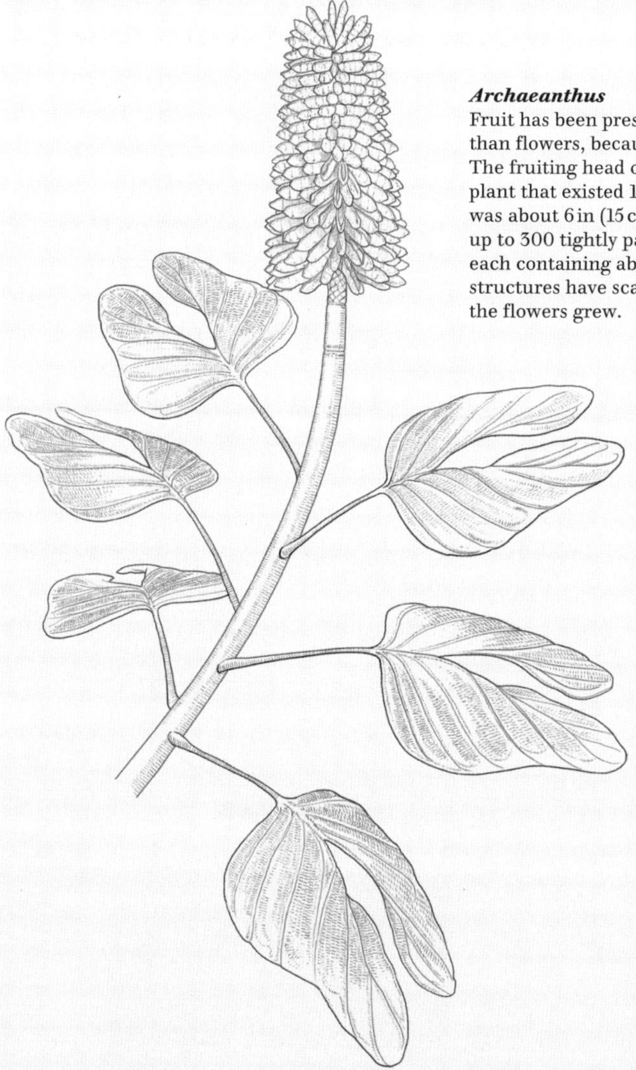

Archaeanthus
Fruit has been preserved as fossils better than flowers, because it was less fragile. The fruiting head of *Archaeanthus*—a plant that existed 100 million years ago—was about 6 in (15 cm) long and contained up to 300 tightly packed structures, each containing about 100 seeds. These structures have scars that mark where the flowers grew.

Lesqueria
Like *Archaeanthus*, the shrub that formed this fossil existed 100 million years ago. It produced flowers similar to those of a magnolia, and fruit about 4 in (10 cm) long, containing hundreds of seeds. Below the fruiting structure were many leafy, diamond-shaped flaps. This peculiar plant grew at a time when dinosaurs called ornithopods darted through the forest.

DNA sequencing technology has revealed that a few hundred ancient living plants were the first to branch off in the flowering plant family tree: the so-called paleoherbs.

WILD PALEO PLANTS

Paleoherbs (known scientifically as "basal angiosperms") are the most ancient living flowering plants, so they may hold clues as to how the flowering plants conquered the vegetation in the fight to dominance. The most ancient of all is a rather unremarkable-looking shrub from New Caledonia called *Amborella*. About 130 million years ago the ancestor of this plant split off from the other flowering plants, making it unique.

Illicium is a more familiar group of paleoherbs, comprising trees and shrubs that grow in the forests of eastern Asia and North America. The genus includes a species popularly known as star anise, which is used in cooking as a flavoring. Another North American paleoherb is *Schisandra*, sometimes known as a "magnolia vine" (although it is not a true magnolia). A particular species of *Schisandra* (*S. chinensis*), native to the forests of northern China, the Russian Far East, and Korea, is known as the "five-flavor-fruit" because its berries possess five basic flavors simultaneously: salty, sweet, sour, spicy, and bitter.

The birthworts (Aristolochiaceae) are another family of about 500 species of paleoherbs with a worldwide distribution. *Aristolochia clematitis* is a rather rare wildflower in Britain and Northern Europe that can be found near ruins and monasteries as a relic of former conservation. Because the tubular flowers were thought to resemble the shape of a uterus, it was believed the plant could speed up childbirth, hence these plants' popular name. Another birthwort, *A. grandiflora* (opposite), is a truly spectacular forest plant with flowers that attract pollinating flies by producing an odor of rotting meat.

Amborella trichopoda
This rainforest shrub grows only on the Pacific island of New Caledonia, where conditions have changed very little for millions of years. *Amborella* is a not especially unusual-looking, but it may hold clues about how flowers first appeared. About 130 million years ago, its ancestor split off from all the other flowering plants in the family tree that are alive today.

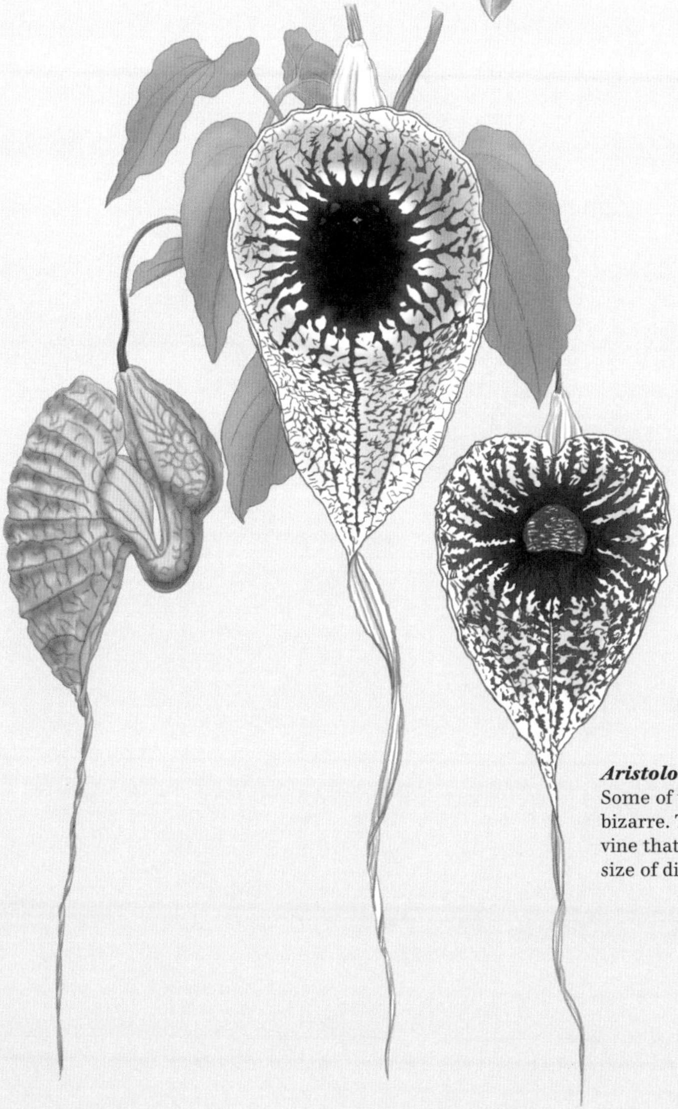

Aristolochia grandiflora
Some of the birthworts are truly bizarre. This one is a tropical vine that produces flowers the size of dinner plates!

Green giant
The largest floating leaf belongs to the giant Amazonian water lily (*Victoria amazonica*), which is native to pools around the Amazon River. Its leaves form enormous disks almost 10 ft (3 m) across, shading out competing plants.

Water lilies have been floating around for almost 100 million years. Not only are they beautiful, they are also among the most ancient flowering plants that exist today.

WATER LILY WILDERNESS

Water lilies are a family of about 70 species that grow in aquatic habitats, such as ponds, lakes, and rivers, around the world—and they have done so for many millions of years. Their roots anchor them to the bed, from where they send up long-stalked leaves that float, and many produce large, showy flowers that are attractive to a variety of insect pollinators including bees, flies, and beetles.

Water lilies have long attracted attention in art and culture owing to their unusual beauty; they are the national flowers of Iran, Bangladesh, and Sri Lanka, and famously featured in the work of the French Impressionist artist Claude Monet. The underneath of a giant water lily leaf inspired Joseph Paxton's design for the Crystal Palace in London in the nineteenth century. More recently, they have attracted the attention of scientists and technologists because their leaves may help to inform the design of floating offshore solar panels (see p.261). What better source of inspiration could there be than nature's own solar panel, tried and tested through millions of years of evolution?

SAILING AWAY *Nuphar* is a yellow-flowered water lily that is common in large ponds and river systems across the northern hemisphere. Its seeds are coated in a layer of slime that traps air bubbles to form a raft. By the time the raft has disintegrated and the seed sinks to the muddy riverbed to germinate, it has reached a new environment far from the parent plant.

The flowering plants took over the planet, flourishing in just about every habitat and outcompeting many of their ancestors. Today there are two major lineages, besides the paleo plants and their close relatives, to which all flowering plants belong: the monocots and the eudicots. Most of the wildflowers you encounter will belong to one of these groups.

MONOCOTS AND EUDICOTS

MONOCOT MEDLEY The monocots evolved early in the flowering plants' evolutionary journey. Some are very familiar, including many food plants, such as ginger, bananas, rice, wheat, and corn, as well as palm trees; other wild monocots are more odd and—as we shall see later in this book—some are downright bizarre. Monocots typically have leaves with parallel veins, and their seeds produce a single seed leaf (monocotyledon) upon germination. Most wildflowers you encounter with long, strap-shaped leaves are monocots; common examples include spring and fall bulbs, irises, and lilies. Orchids are also monocots. The orchid family (Orchidaceae) is the largest of all plant families, containing about 30,000 species.

DOMINANT EUDICOTS Three-quarters of all flowering plants are eudicots. They are the most diverse group of plants alive today, and can be found in every wild environment. Eudicots typically have net-veined leaves, and flowers in multiples of four, five, or seven, and their seeds produce two seed leaves (monocotyledons) upon germination. Familiar edible eudicots include apples, cabbages, soybeans, and sunflowers; common eudicot wildflowers include poppies, foxgloves, daisies, buttercups, primroses, and just about every broadleaf tree you can think of.

CONVERGENT EVOLUTION

The sacred lotus (*Nelumbo nucifera*) may resemble a water lily, but it is actually an eudicot. It belongs to a lineage of plants that includes proteas and plane trees and which branched off early in the evolution of the eudicots. Seeds of the sacred lotus can remain viable for more than 1,000 years. Unrelated lineages evolving similar adaptations occurs by means of a process called convergent evolution (see pp.54–55).

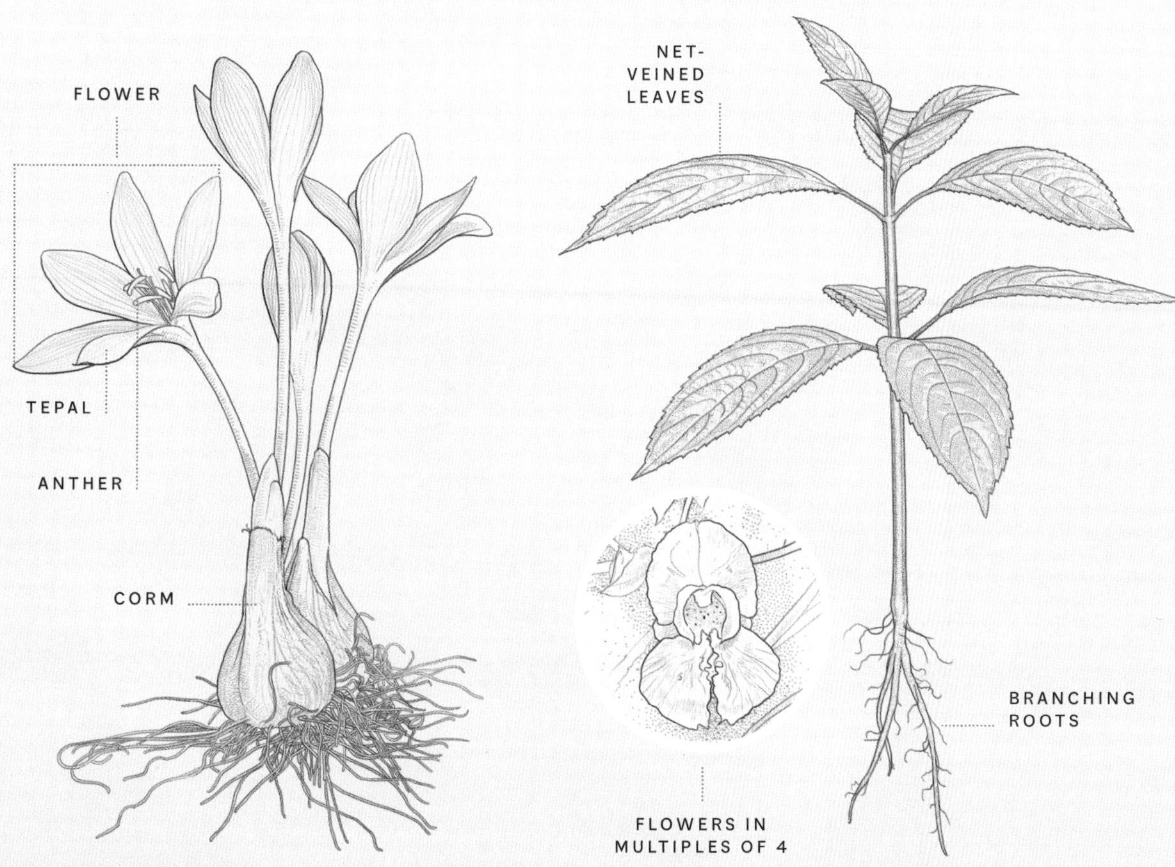

Autumn crocus (*Colchicum*)
This plant has a corm (an underground stem that acts as a storage organ to survive summer drought), which produces strap-shaped leaves with parallel veins in the spring. Typical of monocots, its flowers are in multiples of three (most noticeably the six petallike tepals). Plants with underground storage organs are called geophytes, and they include daffodils, tulips, and lilies as well as crocuses.

Himalayan balsam (*Impatiens glandulifera*)
This plant is a herbaceous (nonwoody) annual (completing its life cycle in a year). It has net-veined leaves, flower parts in multiples of four, and a prominent central root from which lateral branches form; the seedling of a balsam has two seed leaves. All of these features are typical of eudicots. Himalayan balsam, a native of the Himalayas, has naturalized across much of the northern hemisphere and is considered an invasive species in many areas.

Ecballium elaterium

CHAPTER II

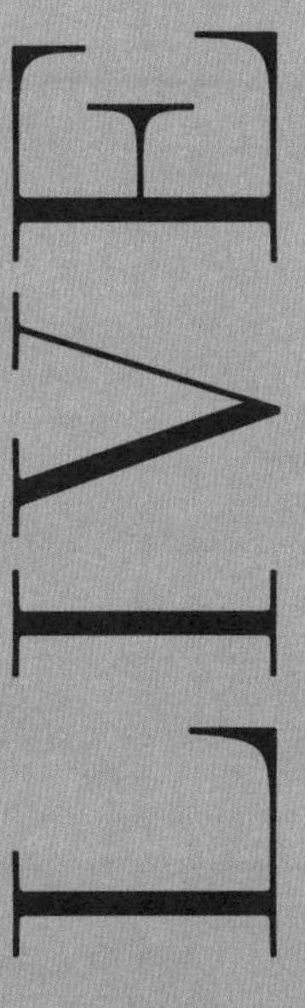

WILDFLOWERS exist in an extraordinary diversity of forms, and live side by side in complex communities that have adapted to face the elements. Plants have evolved astonishing adaptations for surviving in adversity and ensuring cross-pollination for successful reproduction, and they are the bedrock of every ecosystem on land.

The 300,000 species of flowering plant are bewilderingly diverse. From those less than 1⁄32 in (1 mm) wide to the largest measuring more than 3 ft 3 in (1 m) across, flowers come in all shapes and sizes. Despite their diversity, they all possess structures in common.

PARTS OF A FLOWER

Flowers are made up of elements known as whorls—typically four. Each whorl comprises an arrangement of parts: for example, the calyx, made up of sepals (leafy, protective structures); the corolla, made up of petals (which are often showy, to attract pollinators); the androecium, made up of stamens (which produce pollen); and finally the gynoecium, made up of pistils (which, when pollinated, will bear seeds in a fruit).

It is important to recognize the parts of the flower in order to be able to identify a plant. For example, a group of closely related species in a genus might vary subtly in the characteristics of their calyces; another group might vary in the hairiness of the stamens. The parts of a symmetrical, "perfect" flower (one that has both male and female parts) are often easy to identify, whereas the components of other flowers, such as those produced by grasses, can be complex and require experience. Being familiar with floral parts from a range of plant families is essential for the field botanist.

Parts of a flower
The structure of most flowers (shown here in a lily) consists of distinct parts, including: ***Receptacle*** A swollen area of the stalk to which the flower parts are attached. ***Pedicel*** The stalk supporting the flower. ***Petal*** The part of the flower that is often showy, to attract insects for pollination.

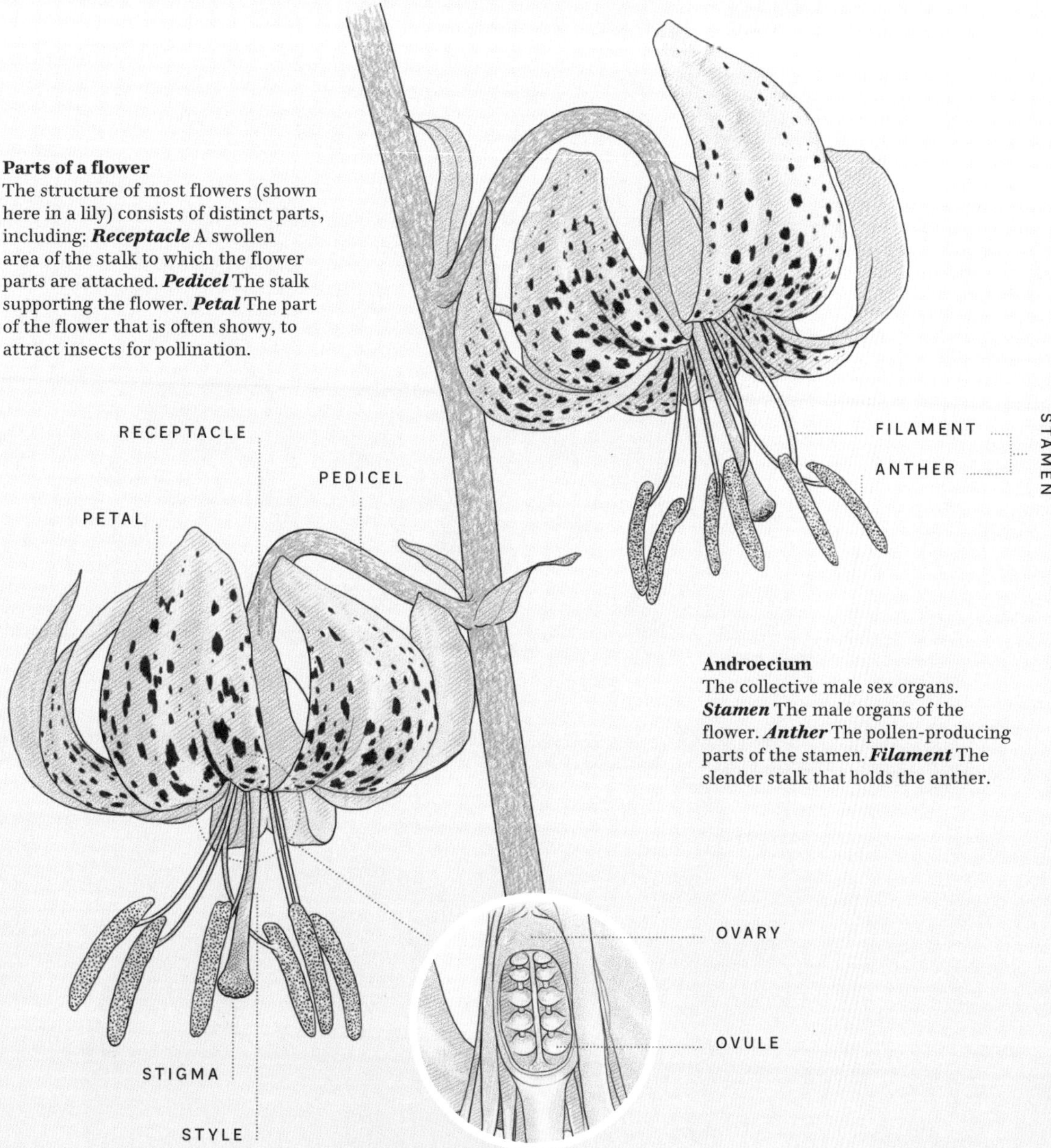

Androecium
The collective male sex organs. ***Stamen*** The male organs of the flower. ***Anther*** The pollen-producing parts of the stamen. ***Filament*** The slender stalk that holds the anther.

Gynoecium
The collective female organs of a flower, in this case, a pistil. ***Stigma*** The sticky part of the pistil, on which pollen grains germinate. ***Style*** The slender stalk that connects the ovary and stigma. ***Ovary*** The part containing the ovules, maturing to become a fruit. ***Ovule*** The part that, when fertilized, becomes a seed.

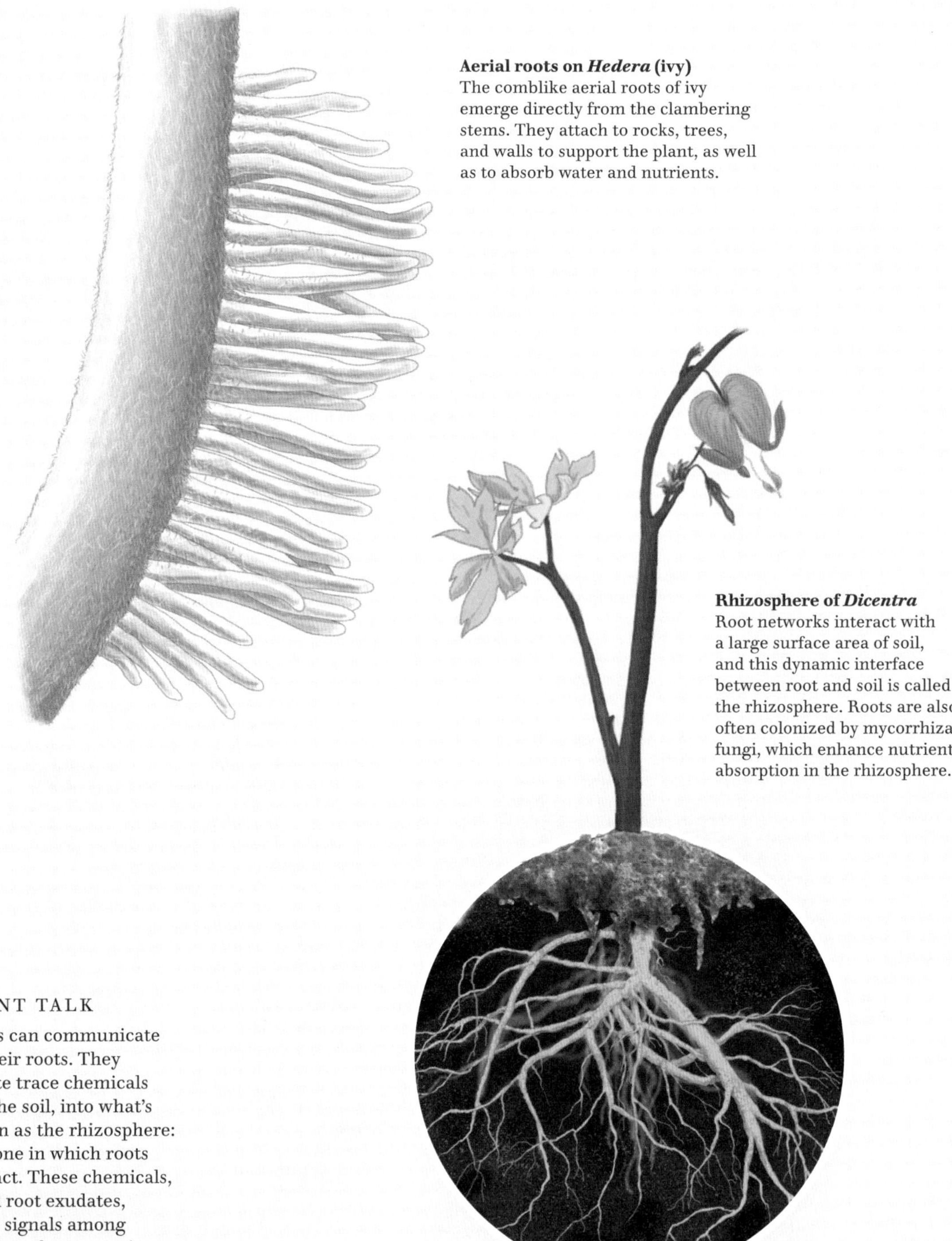

Aerial roots on *Hedera* (ivy)
The comblike aerial roots of ivy emerge directly from the clambering stems. They attach to rocks, trees, and walls to support the plant, as well as to absorb water and nutrients.

Rhizosphere of *Dicentra*
Root networks interact with a large surface area of soil, and this dynamic interface between root and soil is called the rhizosphere. Roots are also often colonized by mycorrhizal fungi, which enhance nutrient absorption in the rhizosphere.

PLANT TALK

Plants can communicate via their roots. They secrete trace chemicals into the soil, into what's known as the rhizosphere: the zone in which roots interact. These chemicals, called root exudates, act as signals among different plants growing in the same habitat.

There's a whole cosmos of life that exists beneath our feet. Roots spread far and wide, burrowing up to 200 ft (60 m) beneath the soil surface and fueling plants' fight to the light. But there's more to roots than meets the eye: they can even communicate!

ROOTS

Roots are typically the least visible parts of a plant, so they are easily forgotten. But they are crucial to most plants' existence. Their main functions are to absorb water and nutrients, and to anchor a plant to the ground. But, despite this common purpose, they come in an extraordinary array of shapes and sizes. Here are some examples that are widespread across the plant kingdom:

TAPROOTS A central, dominant, downward-directed root from which other roots sprout laterally. They are typically long and swollen for storage of food or water. The dandelion is an example of a plant with a taproot.

ADVENTITIOUS ROOTS Roots produced from non-root tissue, such as from stems or tree trunks. The willow is an example of a wild plant with stems that root spontaneously in damp conditions.

AERIAL ROOTS Produced outside the soil, for example in climbing plants. In fact, many aerial roots absorb water and nutrients directly from fog, dew, or humidity in the air. Ivy (see opposite) is an example of a plant that does this.

TUBEROUS ROOTS Fleshy structures, such as those of potatoes and dahlias; they are used to store nutrients. Oxalis is an example of a wild plant that produces tuberous roots.

ROOT NODULES Structures in legumes (peas, beans, and their relatives) that contain nitrogen-fixing bacteria. Clover is a common example.

The curious process of plant growth has intrigued scientists and philosophers for thousands of years—ever since the ancient Greeks, in fact. Plant growth processes can span several orders of magnitude in space: from cell, to plant, to community; and in time: from minutes (a flower unfolding) to centuries (such as tree growth).

HOW A PLANT GROWS

Plant growth begins with the germination of a seed. Seeds remain dormant until conditions are favorable for germination, sometimes for decades, centuries, or even millennia. Seeds require water, oxygen, and an optimal temperature to germinate; in some cases (orchids, for example) they also require specific fungal partners. Once a seedling has germinated, it will put down roots and develop a shoot by tissue growth; this is followed by the production of leaves for photosynthesis, and later (in flowering plants) flowers for cross-fertilization and to make further seeds for reproduction.

Just as in animals, the growth of plant tissue occurs when cells divide and differentiate, becoming specialized to carry out a particular function. This tissue grows from distinct zones, called meristems, in their stems and roots. Those at the tips (the buds) generate shoots for upward or downward growth, increasing the length of stems and roots, while those inside the plant's tissues generate outward growth, increasing the girth of stems and roots. This growth is regulated through plant hormones called auxins, gibberellins, and cytokinins. For example, auxins produced in the uppermost (apical) bud can suppress growth from lateral (axillary) buds farther down the stem, in a process called apical dominance. If this apical bud is removed, the axillary buds will become stronger. That is why gardeners sometimes cut off the tip of a plant to encourage a bushier shape.

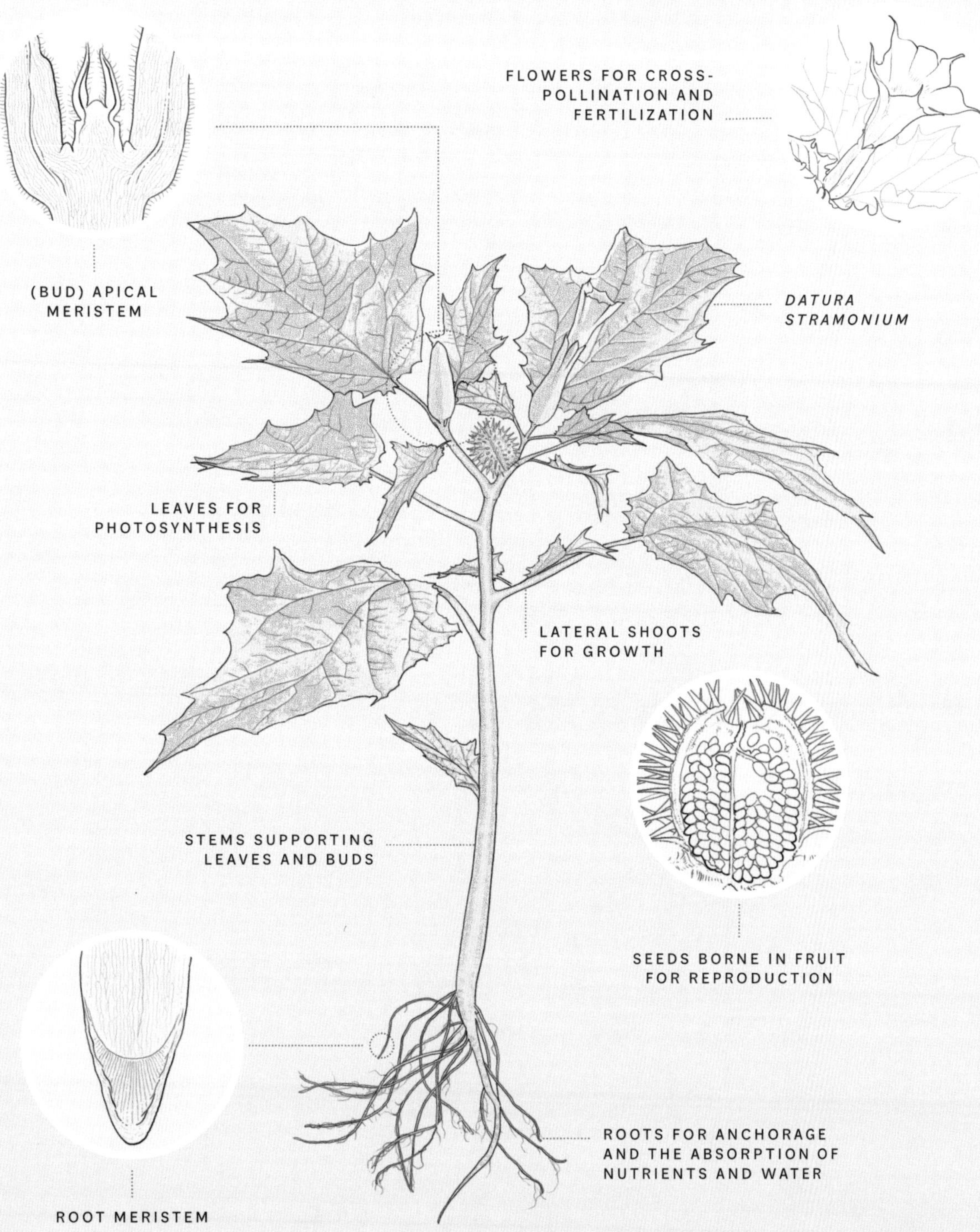
FLOWERS FOR CROSS-
POLLINATION AND
FERTILIZATION
(BUD) APICAL
MERISTEM
DATURA
STRAMONIUM
LEAVES FOR
PHOTOSYNTHESIS
LATERAL SHOOTS
FOR GROWTH
STEMS SUPPORTING
LEAVES AND BUDS
SEEDS BORNE IN FRUIT
FOR REPRODUCTION
ROOTS FOR ANCHORAGE
AND THE ABSORPTION OF
NUTRIENTS AND WATER
ROOT MERISTEM

Leaves come in a bewildering assortment of shapes and sizes—from just 1/32in (1mm) across to the size of a car! Recognizing leaf shape and form is an important part of identifying wildflowers. On these two pages you will find some of the most common forms of leaf, from serrated nettle leaves to palmate horse chestnut leaves.

LEAF SHAPES

SIMPLE (UNDIVIDED) LEAVES: ENTIRE (UNTOOTHED)

Simple leaves are those that have an undivided blade (the flat, expanded part of the leaf—or lamina—where photosynthesis takes place). Leaves that are entire are not toothed, lobed, or compound (see opposite), but rather have simple, smooth edges.

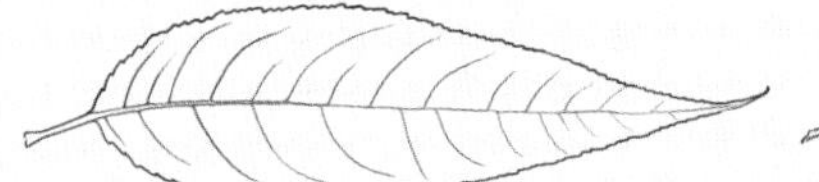

Lanceolate
Wider at the base than at the midpoint.

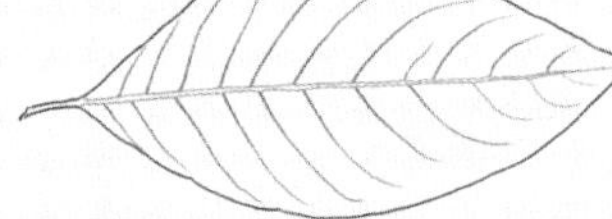

Elliptic
Tapered at both ends from the midpoint.

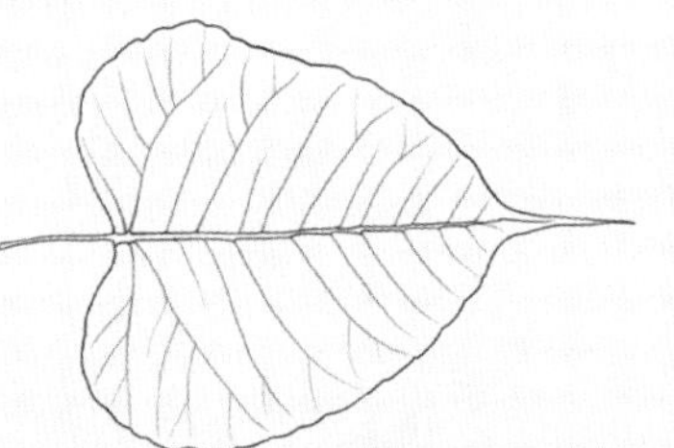

Cordate
Heart-shaped—from the Latin *cor*, meaning "heart."

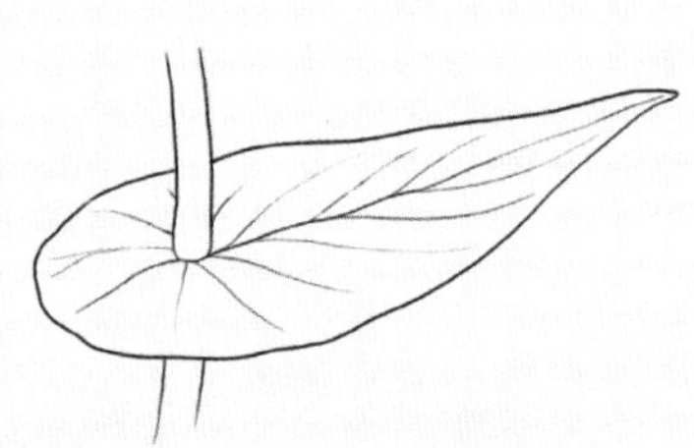

Perfoliate
The base of the leaf united around the stem.

SIMPLE (UNDIVIDED) LEAVES: TOOTHED

Simple leaves, rather than being entire, can possess distinctive edges, for example wavy-edged, toothed, or even double-toothed; some may also be ciliate (with fine hairs), spiny, or a combination of the above.

Sinuate
With wavy edges.

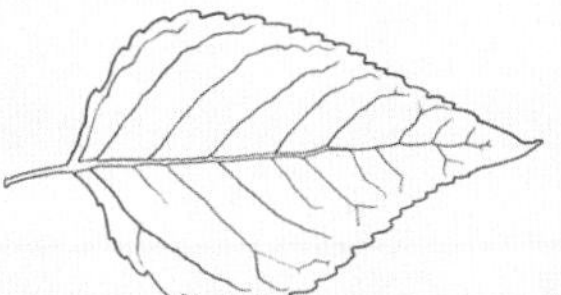

Serrated
With sharply toothed edges.

LOBED LEAVES

Many leaves are lobed, meaning they are indented but not to the middle (midrib) of the leaf. How far into the blade the leaf is lobed and the pattern of lobing—i.e. the shape of the lobes themselves—are both important diagnostic features.

Palmately lobed
Lobes arising from a single, central point.

Pinnately lobed
Lobes arising on either side of the midrib, typically in opposing pairs.

Pinnatisect
Pinnately lobed almost to the midrib, but not into separate leaflets (see below).

COMPOUND (DIVIDED) LEAVES

In a compound leaf, the leaf blade (lamina) is divided into separate parts called leaflets that are attached to the middle vein (midrib), and each has its own stalk. The pattern by which they arise—for example palmately compound leaflets radiating from a central point, or pinnate leaflets in rows along the midrib—is an important identifying feature.

Pinnate
With leaflets arising either side of the midrib, typically in opposing pairs.

Palmate
With leaflets arising from a single, central point.

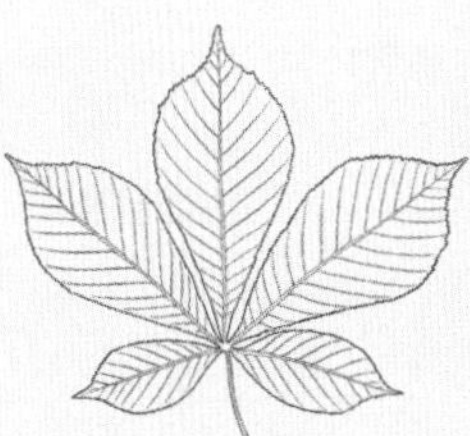

Ternate
Consisting of three leaflets.

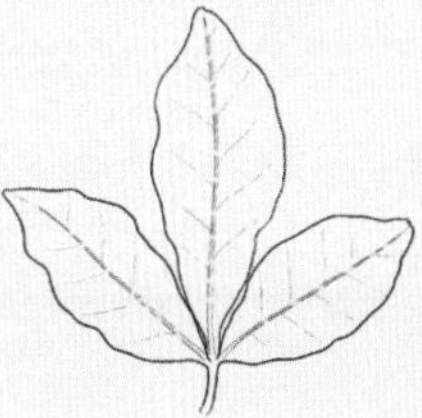

In everyday use, the word "fruit" refers to the edible, fleshy structures of plants that are eaten raw, for example apples, bananas, grapes, and citrus. However, in botany, a fruit is technically any seed-bearing structure of a flowering plant—edible or not—including nuts, bean pods, berries, tomatoes, and even eggplant.

TYPES OF FRUIT

FLESHY

Fleshy fruits have a high moisture content and are typically soft and succulent, although they may harden when dry. They include simple fruits with a fleshy pericarp (fruit wall), such as drupes, and more complex structures, such as aggregate fruits. Some are structures specific to particular plant families, such as hesperidia, which are sectioned.

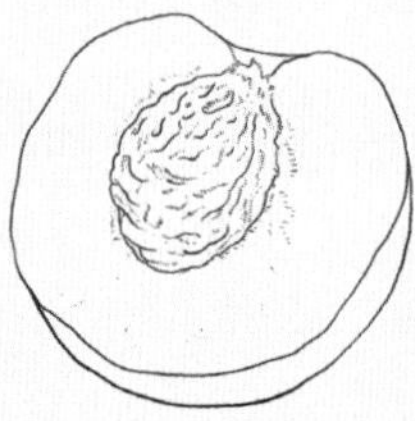

Drupe
Non-splitting, with an outer fleshy part surrounding a single shell with a seed inside. Example: nectarine.

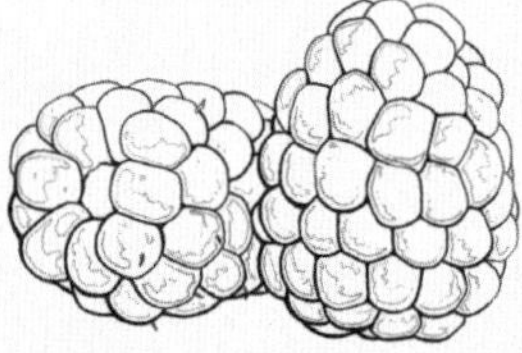

Aggregate
Made up of parts, but derived from a single flower. Example: blackberry.

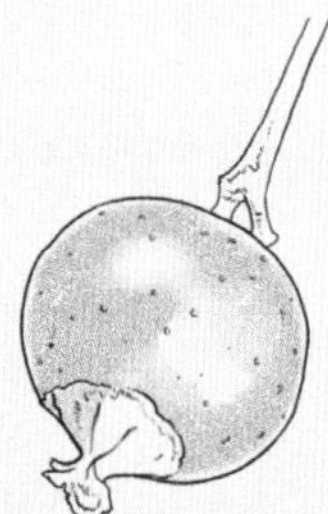

Berry
A single fruit with an outer peel and a fleshy layer containing seeds. Example: blueberry.

Hesperidium
A modified berry with segments containing seeds. Example: grapefruit.

DRY

Dry fruits can be dehiscent (meaning they split open and release their seeds when they mature), such as the pods or legumes produced by plants in the pea family, or indehiscent (meaning they do not split), such as the achenes produced by plants in the daisy family—for example, the seeds of dandelions.

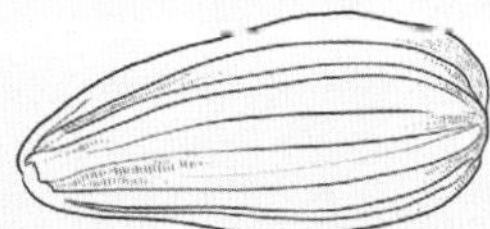

Achene
A dry, single-seeded fruit. Example: sunflower.

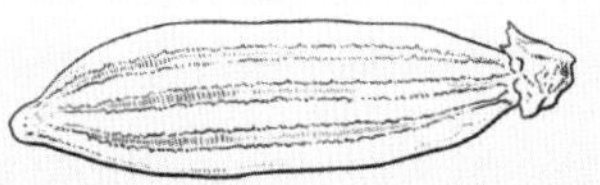

Schizocarp
A dry structure that splits into several (often two) parts, each comprising one seed. Example: fennel.

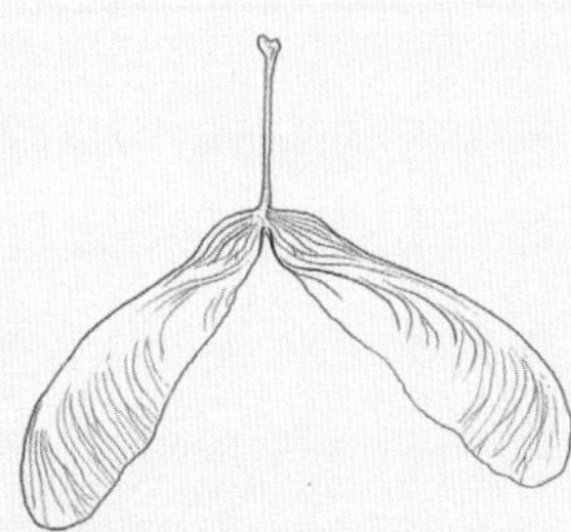

Samara
A winged achene. Example: maple.

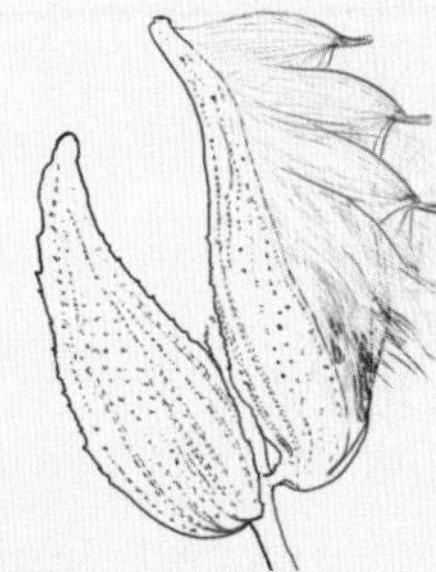

Follicle
A structure that splits to release many seeds. Example: milkweed.

Capsule
A common, simple structure that splits (in various ways) to release seeds. Example: poppy.

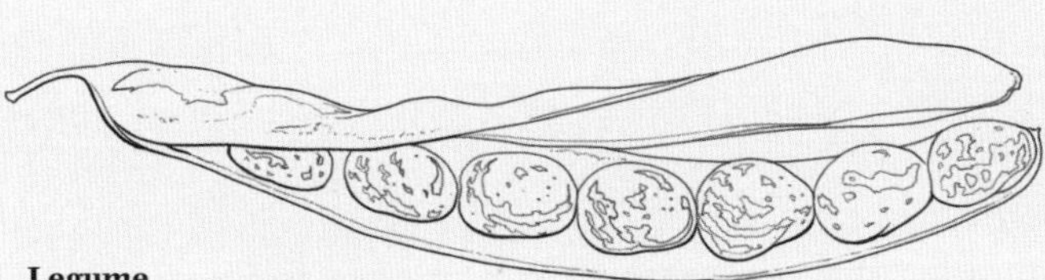

Legume
A structure opening along a seam to release seeds, in the pea and bean family (Fabaceae).

Nut
A non-splitting, dry fruit with a woody protective case (pericarp) containing a single seed. Example: hazelnut.

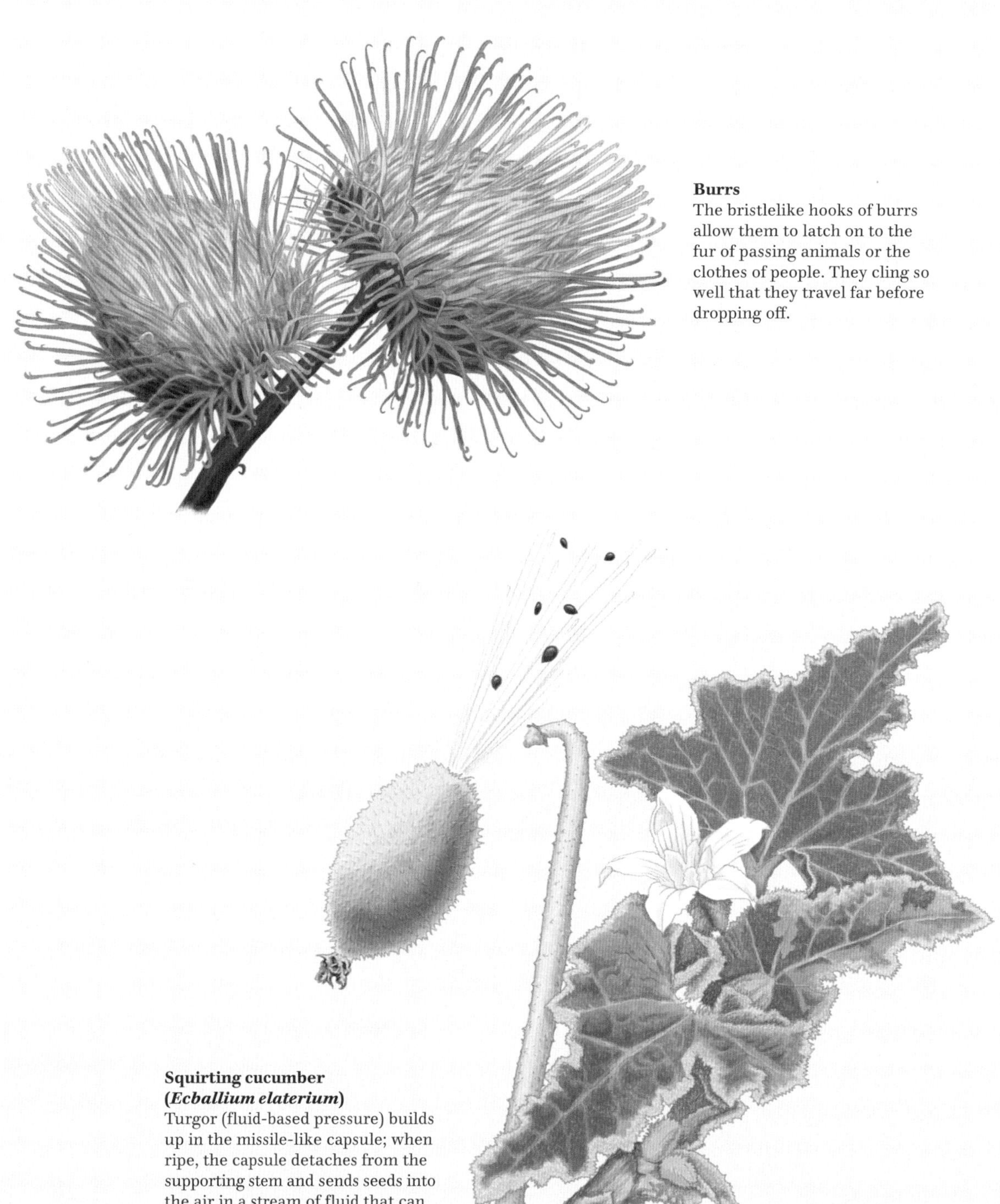

Burrs
The bristlelike hooks of burrs allow them to latch on to the fur of passing animals or the clothes of people. They cling so well that they travel far before dropping off.

Squirting cucumber
(*Ecballium elaterium*)
Turgor (fluid-based pressure) builds up in the missile-like capsule; when ripe, the capsule detaches from the supporting stem and sends seeds into the air in a stream of fluid that can propel the seeds up to 33 ft (10 m).

Plants must travel, just as animals do. Unlike animals, they do this by seeds: units of dispersal that take them from A to B, allowing them to establish in a new environment—in some cases, even across oceans.

GETTING FROM A TO B

Plants colonize new environments by air, by water, or by hitchhiking. Some even launch missiles.

AIR TRAVEL Dandelions send their seeds into the breeze, each bearing a parachute that is carried off on the slightest breath of wind. Rosebay willowherb disperses its seeds similarly, filling the late summer air with its downy cargo.

OVERSEAS TRAVEL Among the farthest-traveling plants are those that take to the seas. The sea bean grows on tropical riverbanks. Its giant pods lean over the water, into which they drop their floating disklike seeds to begin a journey that may take them as far as a beach in Cornwall. Those landing in a suitable place in the tropics may germinate, grow, and colonize a new environment.

ANIMAL COURIERS Plants recruit animals as couriers not only for pollen, but also for seeds. You yourself may have been recruited unwittingly! Burrs are covered in bristlelike hooks that latch on to clothes as well as animal fur. By the time they are brushed off, they are likely to land far from the parent plant.

EXPLOSIONS A few plants disperse their seeds independently of the elements or couriers. Broom's flat seed pods warm up in the sun, but the side facing the sun dries more quickly, causing the pod to split and catapult the seeds out. More extreme is the appropriately named squirting cucumber, an inedible species from the Mediterranean that produces slime-filled missiles under such high pressure that the fruits burst from their stalks, sending the seeds high into the air.

For a flowering plant to reproduce sexually, it must ensure that its pollen reaches the receptive parts of another plant from the same species or genus. Plants have evolved myriad ways of ensuring this cross-pollination, often with the help of insects.

POLLINATION POWER

ON THE WIND Conifers (which lack flowers), grasses, and some broadleaf, flowering trees send their pollen out on the breeze, sometimes in vast quantities. Wind can be an effective means of transportation, carrying pollen over hundreds or even thousands of miles. But it can also be wasteful; the vast majority of pollen grains dispersed in such a way will never reach a plant of the same species.

ANIMAL MESSENGERS, such as insects, provide a more targeted means of transportation. They are recruited by brightly colored, often perfumed flowers, and rewarded with sugary nectar. Plants that advertise successfully are more likely to attract pollinating insects and bear fruit and seeds; for this reason, competition over many millions of years has driven an ever more striking array of flowers.

FLOWER SYMMETRY Form and symmetry influence which pollinators a flower attracts. An open, "actinomorphic" (radially symmetrical) flower, such as a lily, will entice a range of insects. Those that are "zygomorphic" (bilaterally symmetrical, meaning they can be divided along a plane into identical left and right sides), such as salvia or honeysuckle, may be more specialized—excluding certain insects, but driving pollinator behavior by guiding precise contact.

Many zygomorphic flowers also possess nectar spurs, tubular extensions to the petals that hold nectar only an insect with a proboscis of a certain length can reach. Again, this guides pollinator behavior, and excludes non-pollinating insects looking for a free meal.

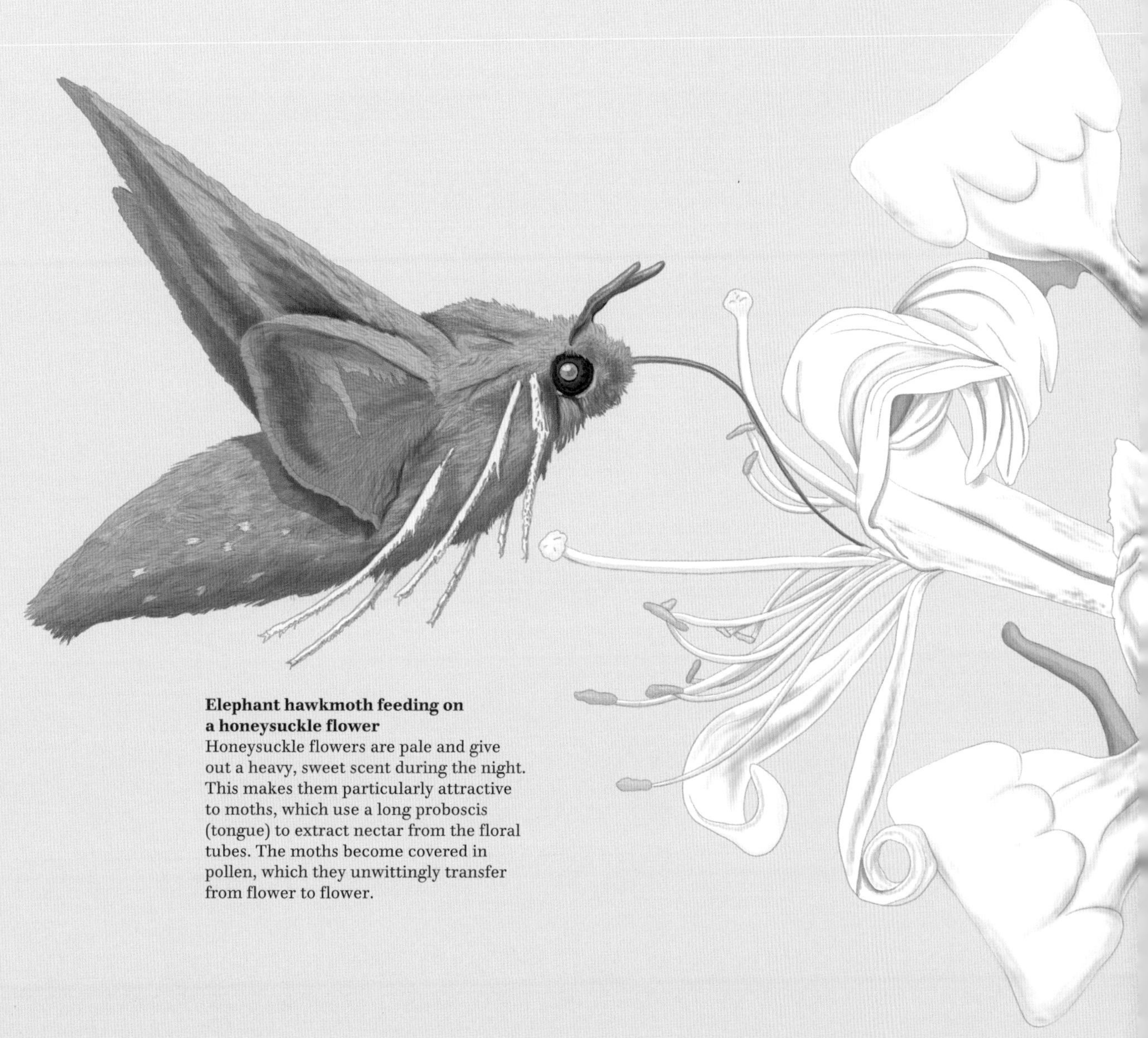

Elephant hawkmoth feeding on a honeysuckle flower
Honeysuckle flowers are pale and give out a heavy, sweet scent during the night. This makes them particularly attractive to moths, which use a long proboscis (tongue) to extract nectar from the floral tubes. The moths become covered in pollen, which they unwittingly transfer from flower to flower.

Plants coexist in complex communities that have adapted to face the elements: from Arctic tundra to the driest deserts, and from fires to floods. They are the bedrock of nearly every ecosystem, and they are strong survivors.

SHOULDER TO SHOULDER

A plant community is a collection of plants that forms a particular type of vegetation. It is influenced by soil, climate, and disturbance, such as fire or flood. Because of shared environmental adaptations and requirements, similar-looking plant forms can often be seen growing side by side, for example a diversity of succulents growing together in a water-stressed habitat, such as the Arizona desert.

Succulents are drought-resistant plants that store water in their stems or leaves. Among the most familiar are the cacti: a diverse family of several hundred species in the rocky deserts and mountains of the Americas. As a result of shared adaptations to water stress, the succulent growth form has sprung up several times across the plant family tree. For example, the cacti of Arizona and Central America look similar to the succulent euphorbias of Africa and the Canary Islands, but when they bloom it is obvious that they are not related. Cactus flowers are often showy, with brightly colored petals and numerous pollen-producing stamens. On the other hand, euphorbia flowers are often greenish and inconspicuous. In the genus *Euphorbia*, for example, the flowers are borne in a complex structure called a cyathium, in which each stamen is solitary (not in dense clusters) and there are no petals at all. The process by which unrelated organisms evolve similar adaptive traits—and therefore look the same—is called convergent evolution.

A. Cacti are curious plants that abandoned leaves long ago, to reduce water loss. Instead, they carry out photosynthesis in their stems, which are swollen and store water. This one is the scarlet hedgehog cactus (*Echinocereus coccineus*).

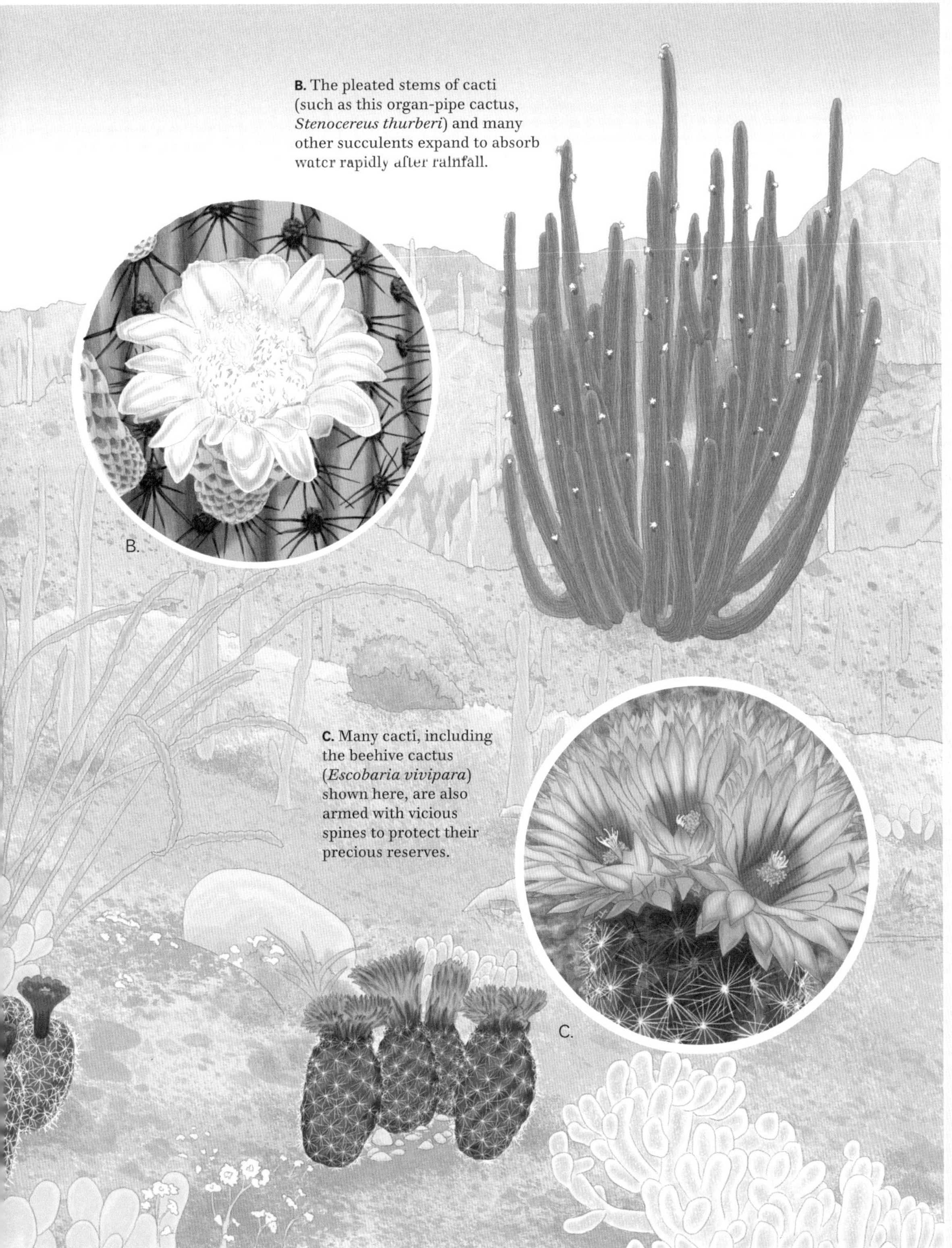

B. The pleated stems of cacti (such as this organ-pipe cactus, *Stenocereus thurberi*) and many other succulents expand to absorb water rapidly after rainfall.

C. Many cacti, including the beehive cactus (*Escobaria vivipara*) shown here, are also armed with vicious spines to protect their precious reserves.

Yellow rattle (*Rhinanthus minor*) is a common ecosystem engineer in grassy habitats. It extracts nutrients from grass roots, suppressing their dominance and allowing other wildflowers to prosper around it.

Marsh lousewort (*Pedicularis palustris*) is an ecosystem engineer of marshes and fens. This plant takes nutrients from the roots of tall sedges, significantly altering the diversity of the vegetation around it.

Organisms that significantly modify those around them relative to their abundance are keystone species, and also known as "ecosystem engineers." Like a keystone in an arch, their removal might cause the collapse of the other species around them.

ECOSYSTEM ENGINEERS

On pages 54–55 we saw how plants stand shoulder to shoulder in complex communities that have adapted to face shared environmental conditions. Some plants have a profound effect on the others with which they coexist: the ecosystem engineers. There are many ecosystem engineers in nature, for example trees in a rainforest, and coral reefs or kelp forests in marine habitats.

VEGETATIVE VAMPIRES Parasitic plants steal their food from other plants. They make up more than 1 percent of all flowering plant species, and some have extraordinary life cycles. Each produces a specialized structure called a haustorium that penetrates the tissues of its host plant, and extracts water and nutrients from them. Hemiparasites possess green leaves and obtain some of their food from other plants; holoparasites, on the other hand, lack chlorophyll and are therefore entirely dependent on their hosts.

Some parasitic plants have a profound effect on the vegetation around them. For example, yellow rattle (*Rhinanthus minor*) is a common hemiparasite of Northern European grasslands. It draws food and water from grasses, suppressing their dominance. This allows other types of wildflower to prosper, significantly influencing the composition of the vegetation. For this reason, yellow rattle is considered an ecosystem engineer of grassland habitats.

A small number of plants not only parasitize other plants, but actually live inside their hosts' tissues. This is called endoparasitism, and it has evolved four times across the plant kingdom.

A PLANT WITHIN A PLANT: ENDOPARASITISM

These plants lack all trace of roots and are reduced to networks of filaments—called endophytes—that creep about the roots and stems of their hosts, cell by cell, unseen. For most of the plants' life cycle, they are externally invisible, emerging only to flower and set seed.

Endoparasites are rare but they can be found worldwide. For example, the genus *Cytinus* comprises eight species with a curiously far-flung distribution that spans the Mediterranean Basin, to southern Africa and Madagascar; all live within the tissues of woody shrubs. *Mitrastemon* is another example of an endoparasite that lives within the tissues of trees in the oak family (Fagaceae) in the forests of Central America and Asia. Finally, *Rafflesia* (see p.174)—the genus possessing the world's largest flowers—is also an endoparasite of a tropical vine, called *Tetrastigma*, in the rainforests of Southeast Asia. Its flowers can measure up to 3 ft 3 in (1 m) across, and smell of rotting meat to attract pollinating flies.

Using DNA sequencing data, scientists have shown that all these plants are unrelated, but evolved the same life cycle. This phenomenon is known as convergent evolution (see pp.54–55).

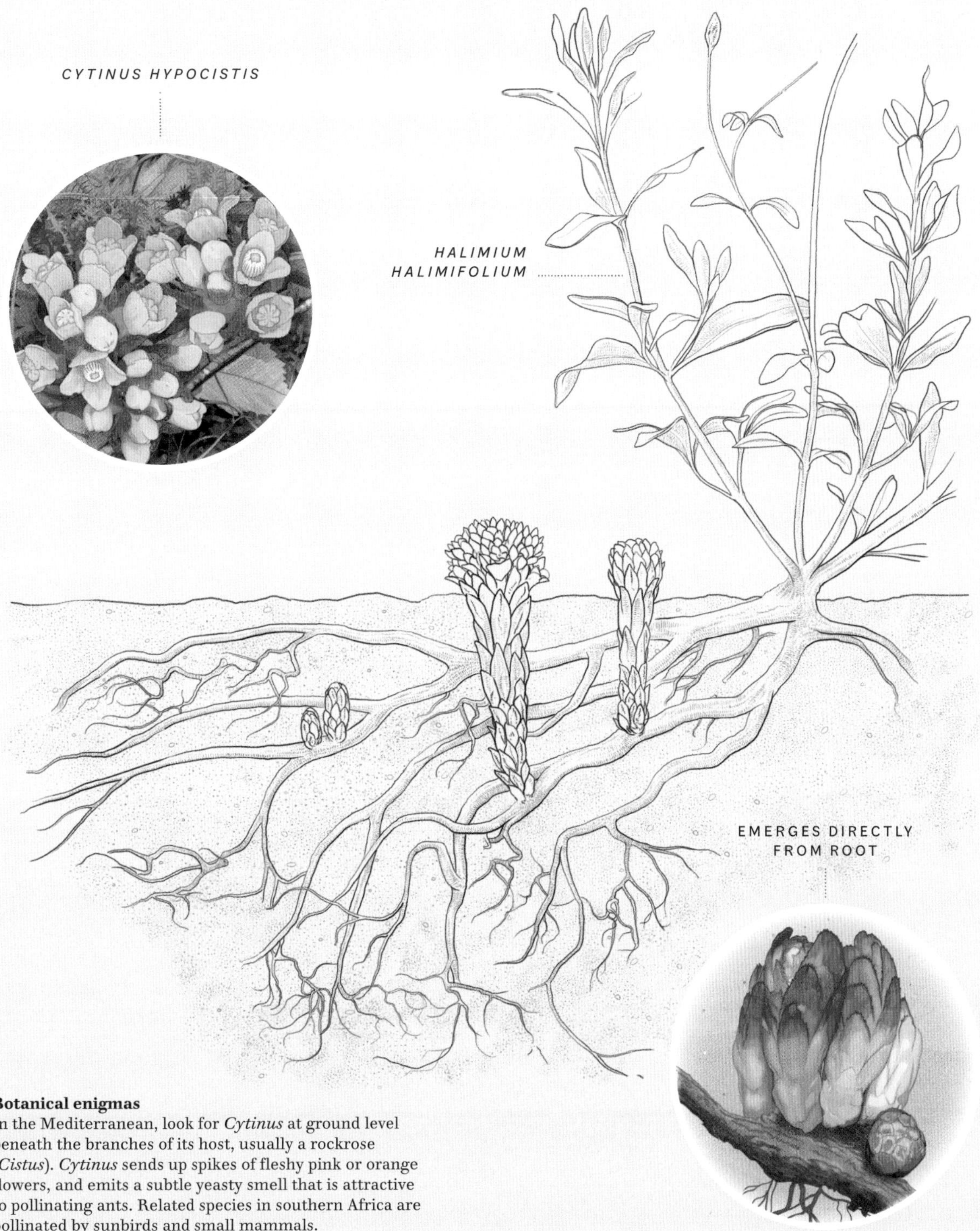

Botanical enigmas
In the Mediterranean, look for *Cytinus* at ground level beneath the branches of its host, usually a rockrose (*Cistus*). *Cytinus* sends up spikes of fleshy pink or orange flowers, and emits a subtle yeasty smell that is attractive to pollinating ants. Related species in southern Africa are pollinated by sunbirds and small mammals.

Sunbird on an aloe

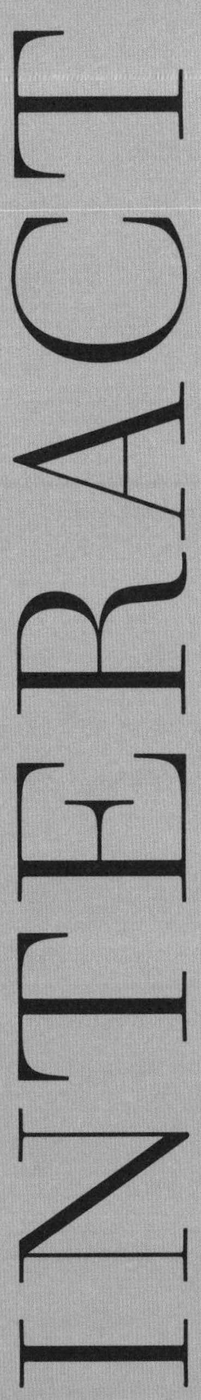

CHAPTER III

WILDFLOWERS ENGAGE in a constant, slow-motion fight with other plants for position. And, since conquering the land, they have developed myriad ways of interacting with animals. Their flowers have taken on an astonishing array of colors and patterns, jostling for attention. From floral fraud to fungal thieving, wildflowers have evolved all sorts of cunning ways to get by.

It's easy to dismiss plants as inanimate because they do not behave like animals, "feel," or move in our time frame. Although it's true to say that plants cannot feel as humans do, they are sensitive to touch, and some can move at breakneck speed.

SENSITIVE PLANTS?

All plants can move, but few do at a speed that we can see. Gradual movements in plants are called tropisms: growth or turning movements that occur in response to an environmental trigger, such as light (phototropism), wind (anemotropism), gravity (geotropism), and touch or contact (thigmotropism; see pp.88–89). Some plants also show rapid movement—in the blink of an eye.

The sensitive plant (*Mimosa pudica*) is a common wildflower in grassy places across the tropics. It holds its splayed, handlike leaves to the sun, and is irresistible to any passing leaf-eating insect, such as a locust. But when such an insect lands on the plant, the leaves seemingly disappear. In just seconds, they fold in on themselves. Should the locust persist, a second movement occurs: the leaf stalks fall, exposing sharp thorns along the main stem. The locust concedes in favor of an easier meal, and a few minutes later the leaves unfold again. This rapid movement is caused by electrical currents that spread from the touched part, along the rest of the leaf.

PLANTS WITH TEETH The Venus flytrap is a notorious "plant predator" that employs rapid movement to ensnare unsuspecting insect prey. It grows in the swamps of the Carolinas, where it catches insects and spiders. Prey that lands within the plant's "jaws" may touch one of the tiny trigger hairs on the surface, activating the trap. If the hair is touched again quickly, the trap is sprung. Further movement then causes the bristlelike "teeth" to lock, imprisoning the prey. Closure can occur in a tenth of a second, and, as with the sensitive plant, this rapid response is caused by electrical currents.

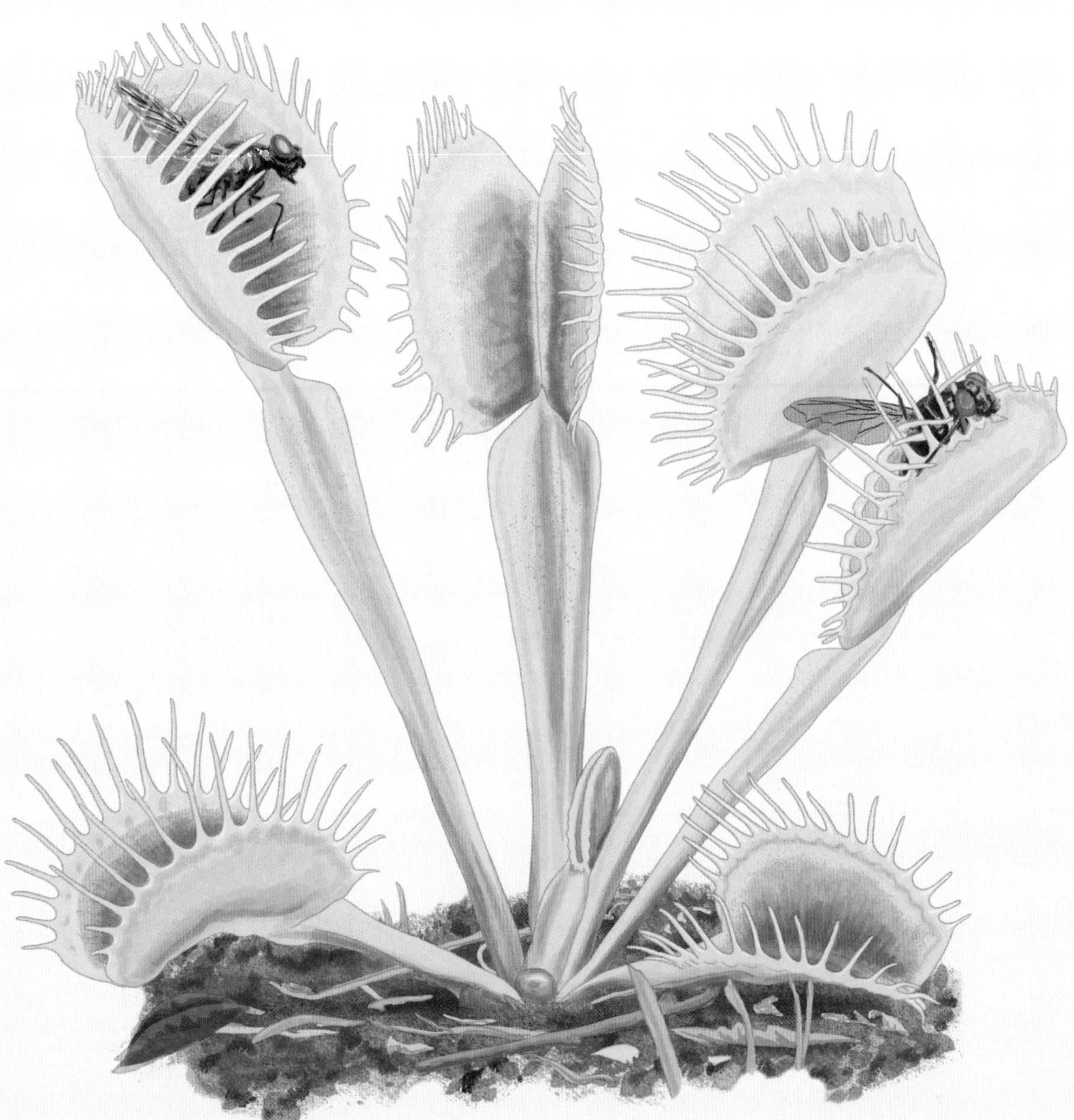

Venus flytrap (*Dionaea muscipula*)
The rapid closure of the plant's formidable-looking trap is caused by an action potential (impulse) rather like that of a human nerve. Further movement of the prey triggers the secretion of digestive enzymes. Once the edges of the trap have compressed together tightly, the sealed cavity forms a veritable "plant stomach."

Insects were plants' first pollen couriers, and they are still the most diverse pollinators today. Many insects have a highly developed sense of smell and vision, which is why flowers are often perfumed and come in an astonishing array of colors and patterns—all jostling for attention.

INSECT POLLINATION

As flowering plants began conquering the land, insects were their vectors for a more targeted and efficient means of pollen transportation, as we saw on pages 52–53. Flowers display a remarkable variety of colorful patterns and forms that evolved cheek by jowl with insects.

Insects do not see the world as we do, nor do they perceive flowers in the same way. The human eye is more sensitive at the red end of the spectrum, but at the blue end, insects can distinguish ultraviolet (UV) colors that we are unable to detect. Many flowers are decorated with markings that act as signposts or "nectar guides" (also known as pollen or floral guides), to direct insects' behavior. They're rather like runway markings in an airport, controlling the direction of visiting insects. Some of these markings are discernible to the human eye; others, to us, are completely invisible.

WIN WIN Observed under UV light, some flowers' nectar guides are complex and transmit multicolored patterns that direct pollinators to their sequestered nectar, for example in the center of the flower, or in nectar spurs (see p.52). Think of this as a "floral map." Nectar guides are mutually beneficial, because they speed up the transportation of pollen and nectar—feeding more insects—and lead to an increased visitation rate, promoting greater pollen transfer among flowers.

Many wild plants produce ***colorful*** *flowers that give off* ***pleasing scents*** *and* ***sweet nectar*** *to entice pollinating* ***insects****.*

Sunbird on an aloe
Bird-pollinated flowers are typically red and tubular, so they can be seen easily by birds, and to accommodate beaks. Sunbirds in South Africa use aloe stems as a perch while feeding on the flowers' nectar.

Birds are important pollinators for plants worldwide, just as insects are. But to entice birds to their flowers, plants require a very different set of characteristics.

BIRD POLLINATION

As with insects, plants have crossed paths with birds for millions of years, leading to fascinating interactions. Birds are effective pollinators, but have different needs from insects. They lack a sense of smell; perfume would be an unnecessary energetic cost to bird-pollinated flowers, so they are odorless. Birds' vision is also very different. As we saw on page 64, insects are unresponsive to the red end of the color spectrum; however, birds detect this color well, so bird-pollinated flowers tend to be red, yellow, or orange. Importantly, most birds are much larger than insects. To accommodate them, a flower must be larger too, and stronger to avoid damage, so many bird-pollinated blooms have leafy perches.

FORM FOLLOWS FUNCTION We have seen that the shapes of insect-pollinated flowers influence which pollinators they attract. Bird-pollinated flowers are often tubular (such as the red angel's trumpet), to accommodate a beak, and produce copious dilute, sweet nectar that is deeply hidden. Their stamens are positioned to dust the forehead or breast of their foraging visitor.

Among the most remarkable nectar-feeding birds are the American hummingbirds. They beat their wings so rapidly that they can hover directly in front of a flower. The little birds zoom from flower to flower, fueled by sugary nectar, picking up and delivering pollen all the while.

Bird pollination is especially prominent in certain plant families, such as the gesneriads (Gesneriaceae) and bromeliads (Bromeliaceae), possibly linked to the parallel lives these groups have led with birds since early in their evolutionary histories. Sunbirds in Africa cannot hover as hummingbirds do, and the plants they visit—aloes, for example—tend to have bracts that act as perches. Bird pollination has appeared several times in the family tree of flowering plants—another example of convergent evolution (see pp.54–55).

Bat-pollinated flowers are arguably among the most beautiful of all: typically large, white blossoms that glance at the moon for just one night, then perish at dawn.

BAT POLLINATION

Many bats are small and chase insects, but there are larger species, with big eyes, that are attracted to night-flowering plants. For example, some cacti in the American deserts bloom at night, rather than in the punishing heat of the day, when most animals are inactive. Their flowers are typically large, and cream or white so that they are visible at dusk. They appear at just the time when bats are migrating north and will benefit from a nectar hit on the way.

The African baobab is another bat-pollinated plant. It sends out enormous cream flowers on long, pendulous stalks, that dangle forth, awaiting their nocturnal visitors. Like the flowers of bat-pollinated cacti, they produce copious pollen that clings to the bats' fur.

GOING BANANAS Wild banana plants are also pollinated by bats. Bananas produce complex blossoms that hang heavily on robust, downward-arching stems. Each row of flowers is protected by a large, leathery, reddish bract (modified leaf). Each night a bract opens to reveal a new row of flowers. Initially the flowers are female, and receive pollen from visiting bats; later in the plant's development, the male flowers open, producing pollen that the bats then collect. If enough banana plants are in bloom at the same time, the bats will cross-pollinate the flowers, bringing about the development of fruits.

Bats for bananas
A nectar bat pollinates the flowers of a wild banana (*Musa*) in Southeast Asia. Bananas produce complex flowering structures, revealing consecutive rows of blooms that are visited by fruit bats. The copious pollen adheres to the bats' fur.

Mother of the forest
African baobabs (*Adansonia* spp.) are perhaps best known for their gigantic bottle-shaped tree trunks. Their large white flowers are also impressive, however, and are cross-pollinated by bats.

Wildflowers are not all sweetness and nectar. Some plants have evolved elaborate mimicry to dupe, baffle, and manipulate their pollinators, without giving them any reward whatsoever.

POLLINATION BY SEXUAL DECEPTION

The flowers of many orchids are unusual or even downright bizarre. Bee orchids are no exception. These ground-dwelling orchids are native to the stony pastures, crags, and hillsides of the Mediterranean Basin. When the winter rain has passed, they send up curious spikes of furry, insect-like flowers that glisten under the warm spring sunshine. Not only do the various bee orchids' flowers all look peculiarly like bees, but also each one *smells* like the female of a particular species of bee. The flowers sit and wait. Before long, amorous male bees flock to the flowers and attempt to mate with them in a buzzing frenzy. In so doing, they inadvertently pick up and deposit pollen—which is just what the plant needs them to do. Unlike with the forms of pollination we've seen on the previous pages, bee orchids manipulate their visitors and offer them no reward.

INSECT EXPLOITATION How did the bee orchids' elaborate sexual deception evolve? Each species of bee orchid targets a specific type of insect. This is efficient because each dedicated pollinator achieves maximum pollen transfer, and valuable pollen is not wasted by being taken to flowers of the wrong kind. The orchids produce airborne (volatile) compounds that are virtually identical to the pheromones of female insects, and in the same relative proportions, to enhance the mimicry. This chemical mimicry evolved from cuticular leaf waxes—compounds that are common among plants to protect against desiccation (drying out). Pollination by sexual swindle is therefore both effective and very efficient.

Bee orchid (*Ophrys apifera*)
The peculiar resemblance of bee orchids' flowers to insects is no coincidence; these flowers dupe male insects into attempting to mate with them, bringing about cross-pollination. The species shown here is common in the UK, but has become decoupled from its south European pollinator species, so at the north of its range it self-pollinates.

Among the most astonishing interactions that have evolved between plants and insects are those of orchids. They intrigued the English naturalist Charles Darwin so much that he dedicated a whole book to them.

DARWIN'S ORCHIDS

The orchid family is the most diverse of all the flowering plants, and its members have evolved the most elaborate pollination systems. Darwin was fascinated by these plants, and in 1862 he wrote *The Various Contrivances by Which British and Foreign Orchids Are Fertilized by Insects*, in which he described experiments, and also the observations of his correspondents from around the globe. He examined how complex ecological relationships resulted in the coevolution of orchids and insects that had been living together for many millions of years.

DARWIN'S ORCHID "Coevolution" refers to species living together that reciprocally affect one another's evolution through the process of natural selection. Among the most celebrated example of coevolution in plants is Darwin's orchid (*Angraecum sesquipedale*) and its pollinating moth (*Xanthopan morganii*), which live together in lowland Madagascar. The flower has an extraordinarily long, whiplike spur (a structure we saw on page 52). Darwin surmised that there must be a moth with a proboscis long enough to reach the nectar the spur sequestered. His suggestion was ridiculed at the time; no one had seen such a creature. Only in 1903—more than 20 years after his death—was such an insect discovered, confirming his prediction.

ORCHIS BANK Darwin found orchids growing in the Kent countryside, and his observations there built on his concept of coevolution between plants and insects. A particular favorite was a valley he referred to as "Orchis Bank," where he examined the pollination mechanisms of several British orchids, for example butterflies visiting pyramidal orchids.

MONKEY GOBLETS
The exotic South American orchid known as the monkey goblet (*Catasetum macrocarpum*) particularly intrigued Darwin as he established his network of friends and collaborators around the world. This orchid and its close relatives eject their pollen forcibly upon their pollinating insects.

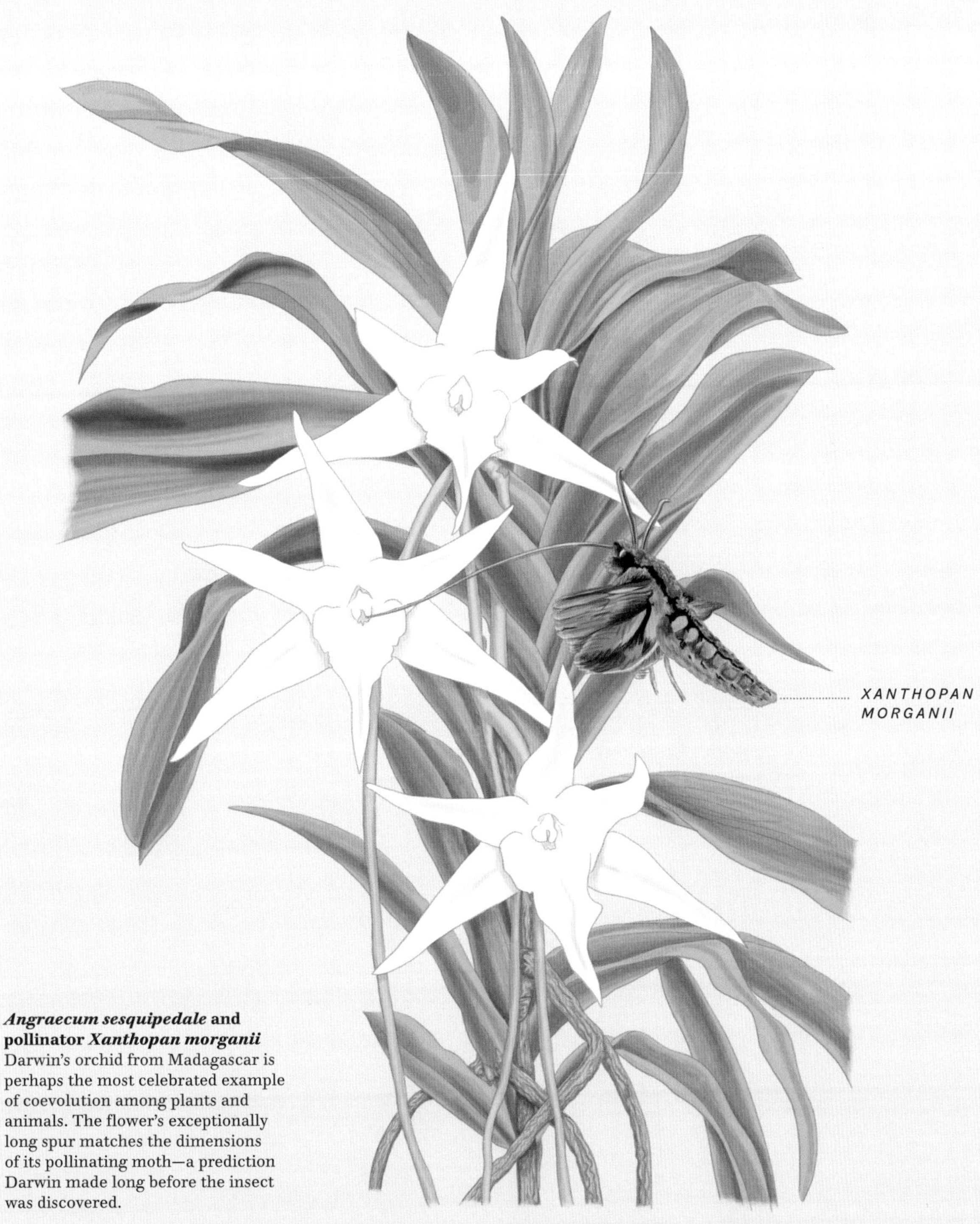

Angraecum sesquipedale* and pollinator *Xanthopan morganii
Darwin's orchid from Madagascar is perhaps the most celebrated example of coevolution among plants and animals. The flower's exceptionally long spur matches the dimensions of its pollinating moth—a prediction Darwin made long before the insect was discovered.

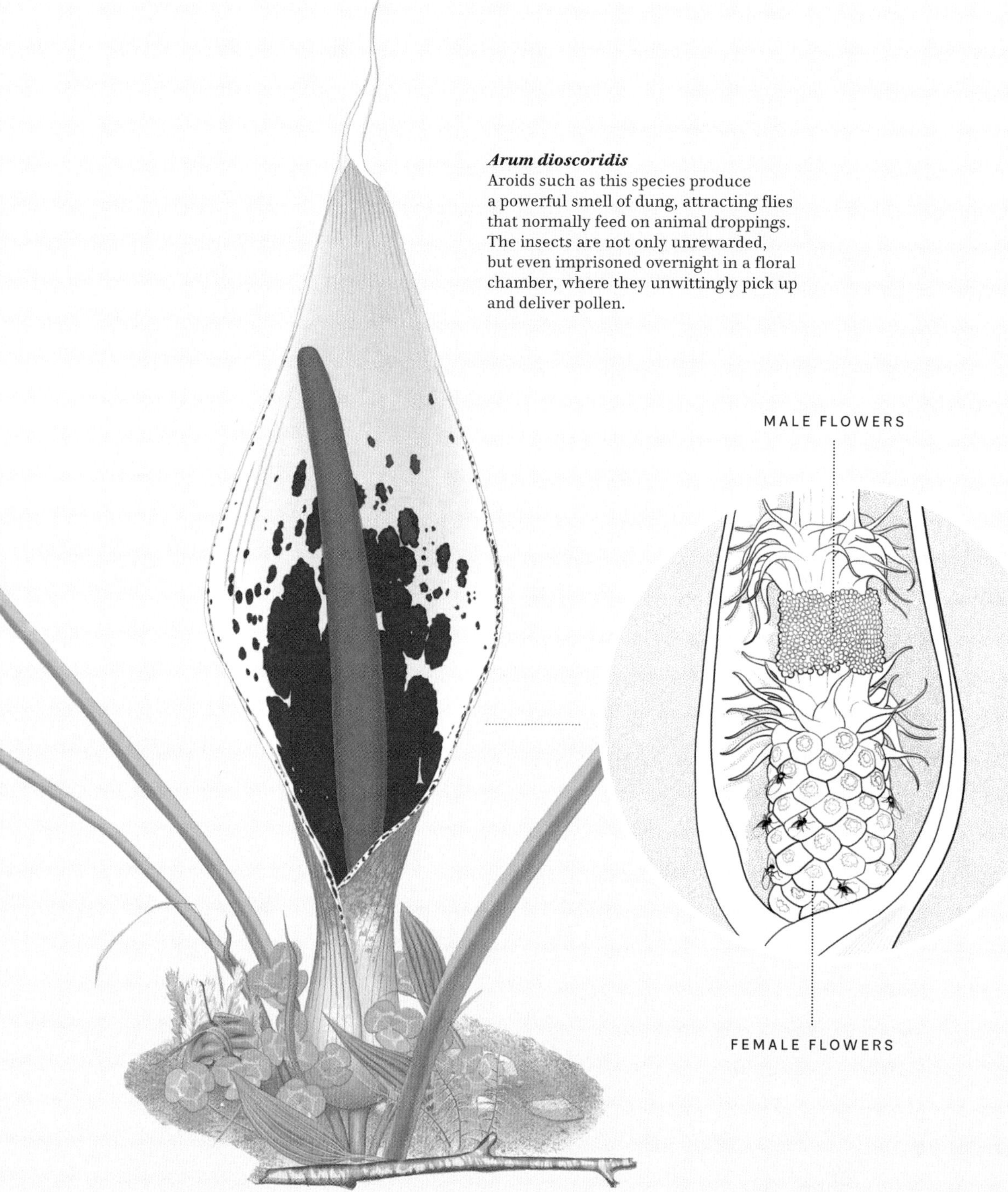

Arum dioscoridis
Aroids such as this species produce a powerful smell of dung, attracting flies that normally feed on animal droppings. The insects are not only unrewarded, but even imprisoned overnight in a floral chamber, where they unwittingly pick up and deliver pollen.

Not all plants and animals live harmoniously side by side. Some plants do not simply exploit their insect pollinators without giving them any reward; they imprison them.

FLY ENTRAPMENT

Some plants evolved prison chambers to incarcerate their pollinating insects. The aroids (family Araceae) comprise about 4,000 species worldwide. They pop up in hedgerows, mountain slopes, and rainforests. The distinguishing feature of aroids is a spikelike structure called a spadix that is shrouded by a bract-like spathe. The true flowers are typically minute and develop around the base of the spadix, with the female flowers at the base and the male flowers immediately above. We'll examine a selection of aroids on pages 105–107.

TEMPORARY INCARCERATION Not only are the male and female flowers of an aroid separated spatially, but also they develop at different times. The female flowers ripen before the male, to prevent self-fertilization. Interestingly, some aroids are also heat-producing (thermogenic), meaning that their blooms become warmer than the surrounding air temperature. This heat, combined with a powerful smell—for example that of animal dung or rotting meat—is highly attractive to flies, which may mistake the plant for carrion. In many aroids, the spathe encloses the tiny flowers in a floral chamber in which insects seeking a place to lay their eggs become trapped overnight by a barricade of downward-pointing spines. These spines shrivel after pollination has taken place the following morning. The insects are incarcerated temporarily—a mechanism that ensures they pick up and deliver pollen.

Up to a third of all orchid species use tricks to deceive their pollinators. One of the most frequent ploys is false advertising: promising nectar with brightly colored, perfumed flowers, but not delivering any.

NECTAR CHEATS

As flowering plants evolved and proliferated, so did the mechanisms—and sometimes shenanigans—they employed to bring about cross-pollination. Up to a third of all orchids (equating to about 10,000 species) rely on deception to attract pollinating insects. One of the most common forms of deception in orchids is "food fraud," which exploits the foraging behavior of nectar-feeding insects. These orchids produce brightly colored, often perfumed flowers and, importantly, they co-occur with unrelated plants that produce similar flowers. But unlike their more virtuous counterparts, these orchids are nectar-less. Recently emerged insects, those foraging from other areas, and those that are just plain forgetful will visit and revisit the empty flowers, bringing about cross-pollination with no reward. We saw on pages 74–75 that flowers mimic food sources, such as dead meat, to attract flies; here the mimicry is subtler: orchids mimicking *other* flowers.

DRUNKEN ENCOUNTER Helleborine orchids (*Epipactis*) do produce nectar, but they are far from innocent. Across Northern Europe, they bloom in late summer, when apples are falling in the orchards and wasps are common. Wasps visiting the helleborines "inoculate" their flowers' droplets of sugary nectar with microorganisms they carry on their feet from decaying apples, so the flowers become veritable Petri dishes. The microorganisms in the nectar produce ethanol (alcohol) that any subsequent wasps that visit will imbibe. Drunk wasps spend longer staggering about the orchids' flowers, and do not manage to rid themselves of the bundles of pollen, so they are more likely to take the pollen to another helleborine, bringing about cross-pollination.

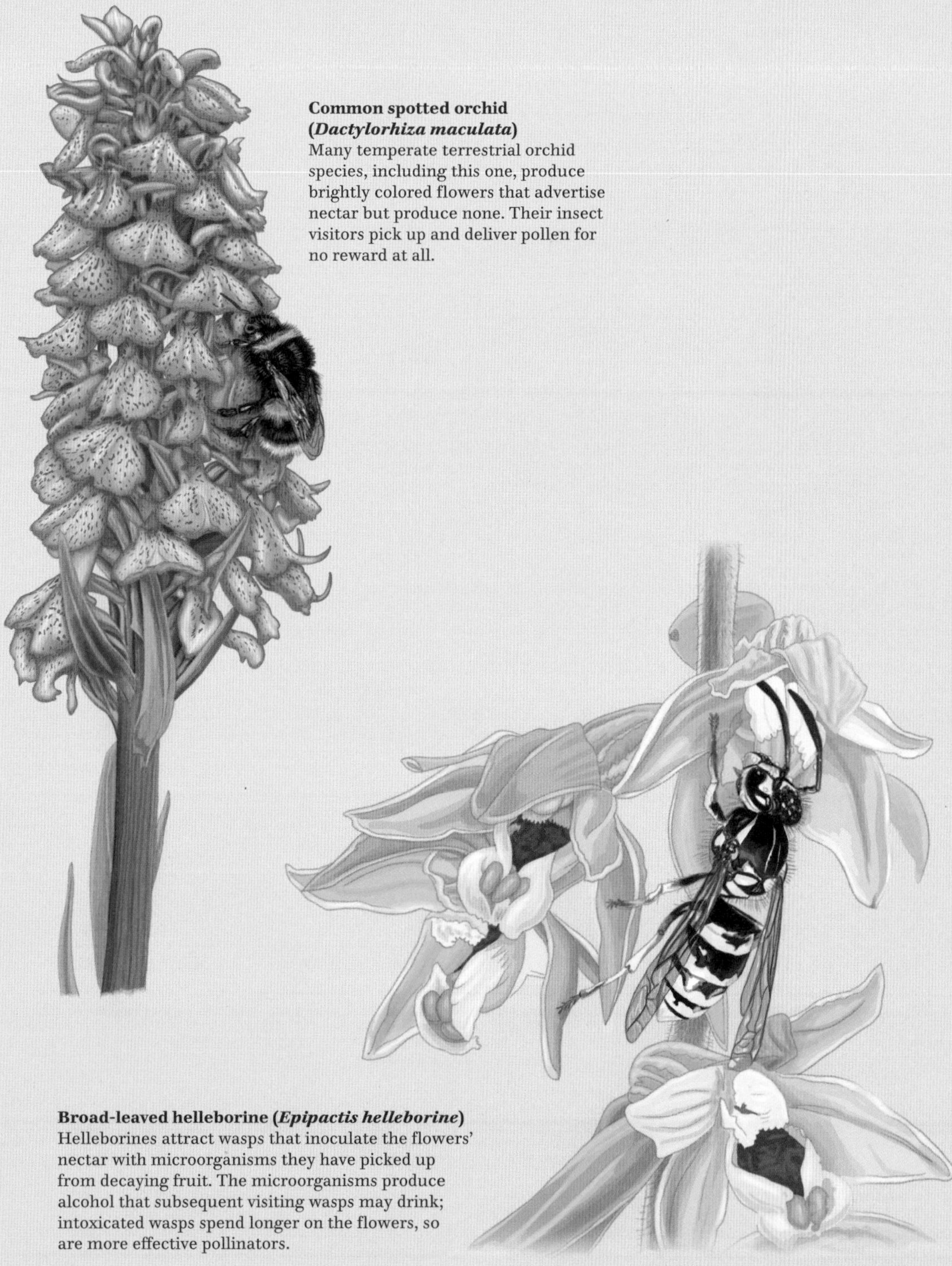

Common spotted orchid (*Dactylorhiza maculata*)
Many temperate terrestrial orchid species, including this one, produce brightly colored flowers that advertise nectar but produce none. Their insect visitors pick up and deliver pollen for no reward at all.

Broad-leaved helleborine (*Epipactis helleborine*)
Helleborines attract wasps that inoculate the flowers' nectar with microorganisms they have picked up from decaying fruit. The microorganisms produce alcohol that subsequent visiting wasps may drink; intoxicated wasps spend longer on the flowers, so are more effective pollinators.

Aristolochia arborea
The little toadstool-like structures in these flowers release a volatile chemical that attracts fungus gnats. Fooled by the flowers' mimicry, the gnats enter, picking up and delivering pollen as they do.

FUNGUS GNAT POLLINATOR

Aristolochia salvadorensis
Known as the "Darth Vader flower," this species attracts tiny fungus gnats in a similar way to the plant shown above. These tiny insects zoom into the "eyes" of the flowers, where they bring about cross-pollination.

Orchids are not the only masters of deception in the plant kingdom. Plants seemingly know no bounds when it comes to fraud.

FRAUDULENT FLOWERS

We've seen many examples of artifice in the plant world: floral fibbers have sprung up all over the last few pages. Dutchman's pipes, also known as birthworts (family Aristolochiaceae) are a diverse group of plants that occur on most continents—as we first examined on pages 32–33. Their flowers are often held suspended on vines or clustered around the base of their stems, and are attractive to a range of small flying insects.

FUNGAL FORAYS *Aristolochia arborea* is a very peculiar species of Dutchman's pipe that grows in the rainforests of Central America. The plant has a shrubby, treelike habit (hence the scientific epithet *arborea*). Its maroon-and-white, mottled blooms sprout directly from the base of the trunk in clusters on the rainforest floor, at a glance resembling a clump of mushrooms. In fact, each bloom has a specialized floral outgrowth in the center that looks exactly like a purplish-brown toadstool. It even emits an earthy, mushroomlike perfume. The structure is very attractive to fungus gnats (Mycetophilidae), small, short-lived, weak-flying insects that are common in moist forest understories and lay their eggs on toadstools, producing larvae that feed on fungal hyphae in decaying plant material. The gnats teem around the plant, so convinced that the blooms are in fact toadstools that they even lay their eggs on them—offspring that will later perish. As they crawl around on the flowers, they pick up and deliver pollen, cross-pollinating the plants.

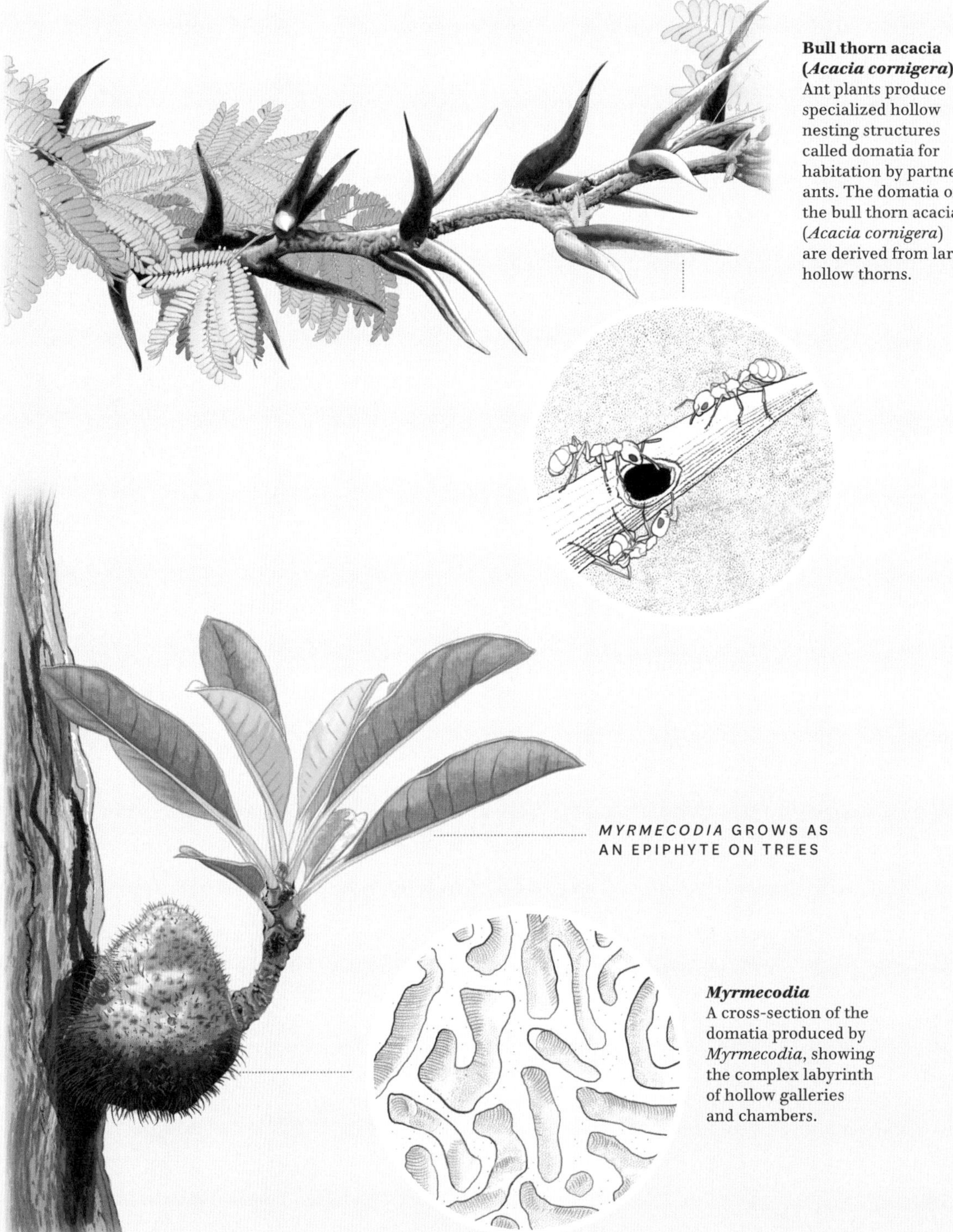

Bull thorn acacia (*Acacia cornigera*)
Ant plants produce specialized hollow nesting structures called domatia for habitation by partner ants. The domatia of the bull thorn acacia (*Acacia cornigera*) are derived from large, hollow thorns.

Myrmecodia
A cross-section of the domatia produced by *Myrmecodia*, showing the complex labyrinth of hollow galleries and chambers.

Plants and insects have crossed paths for hundreds of millions of years, and surprising interactions of all sorts have sprung up along the way. Among the most fascinating and bizarre are those that have evolved among plants and ants.

PLANTS AND ANTS

ANT PLANTS These are species that have developed mutualistic relationships with ant colonies. Some produce highly specialized hollow nesting structures called domatia, which are specifically adapted for habitation by ants. Some species of wild African *Acacia* tree produce domatia derived from large hollow thorns. In exchange for accommodation inside these thorns, the ants patrol the trees' branches and attack would-be predators, protecting their host tree. They even bite through the tendrils of competing climbing plants.

Among the most elaborate domatia are those produced by Southeast Asian ant plants called *Myrmecodia*. These plants produce swollen, spiny domatia at the base of their stems. The domatia, which can reach almost 20 in (50 cm) across, contain a complex labyrinth of hollow galleries and chambers that are connected to the exterior by entrance holes. The smooth-walled cavities are used by the ants for nesting; meanwhile the rough, warty cavities serve as waste chambers in which ants deposit feces, which release nutrients for the plant. *Myrmecodia* are epiphytic, meaning they grow perched high on the branches of trees, so the ants provide them with a valuable source of nutrients that are otherwise scarce.

AGRICULTURAL ANTS Some ant species even tend "gardens" of sap-feeding insects on plants, which yield honeydew on which they feed. Another example of "agriculture" by ants is the encouragement of fungal growth within the domatia. These "fungal farming" ants provide nutrients for the fungi and, in return, use them as a food source for their larvae. It has been suggested that these fungi may also enhance the transfer of nutrients to the plant.

SWEET REWARDS

In addition to purpose-built accommodation, some species of ant plant offer their partner ants food rewards in the form of nectar or specialized nutrient-rich packets. Nectar is typically associated with flowers. But the bull thorn acacia (opposite) produces "extra-floral" nectar—nectar secreted in locations other than in the flowers—which is offered as a reward for the ants.

Figs and fig wasps possess some of the most intimate relationships of all. The life cycles of many figs and wasps are tightly interconnected, and neither could survive without the other.

FIGS AND FIG WASPS

Figs and people have crossed paths since antiquity, but the fig's relationship with wasps goes back much further; they have evolved alongside one another for 60 million years. A fig is not technically a flower, nor is it a fruit; to understand it, it is important to examine the interaction between the reproductive cycles of both fig and wasp.

Dorstenia is a distant relative of the figs. Its flowers are produced in what look like inside-out figs, with a fringe of hornlike projections. This plant may resemble a precursor to the present-day fig and its intimate symbiosis with wasps. Scientists have observed flies laying eggs in *Dorstenia* flowers in the wild, adding weight to this hypothesis.

On the opposite page is a diagram showing the life cycle of the wasps (various members of the superfamily Chalcidoidea) and how it is tied to that of the fig (genus *Ficus*). The tiny wasps drag themselves into the fig through a tight passage called an ostiole, losing their wings along the way. Once inside the fig's cramped central cavity, pollen the wasps have brought from another fig fertilizes some of the flowers, while eggs are deposited in others. The flowers that receive eggs nourish the wasps' developing grubs, and those that receive only pollen go on to develop seeds. A new generation of wasps emerges inside the cavity of the fig, and the wingless males mate with winged females, which pick up pollen as they crawl around. The males bite an exit tunnel through which the insects escape. The males soon die, while the pollen-laden females fly to another fig, where the process is repeated, bringing about cross-pollination.

LIFE CYCLE OF FIG AND WASP

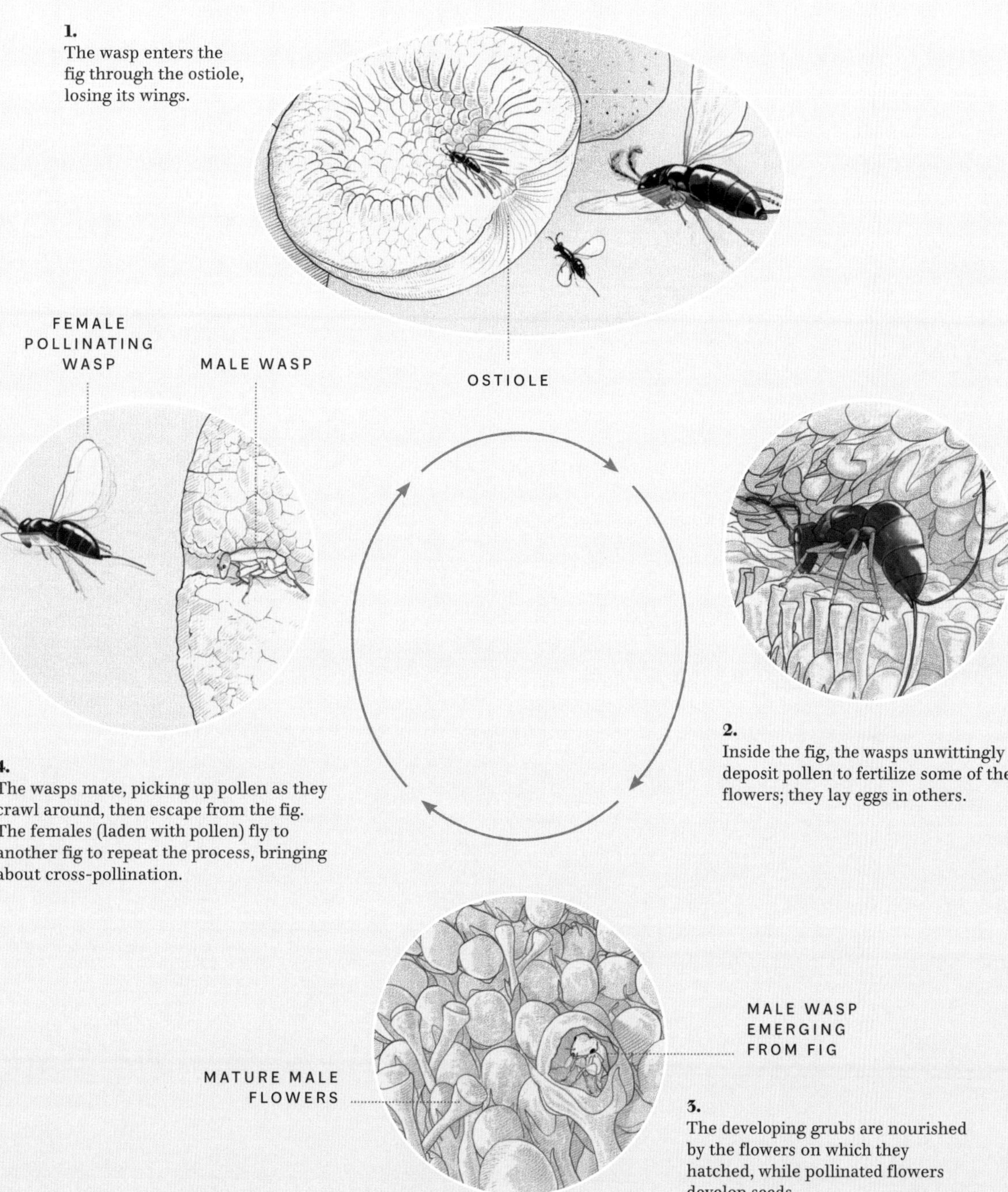

Fruits come in a bewildering variety of colors, shapes, and sizes—and smells—to entice animals. But not all smell pleasant to human noses.

FUNKY FRUIT

SPECIALIZED AGENTS

Wild plants advertise their fruits and seeds when they are ripe for dispersal. Some are very particular about their dispersing agent, however. *Neesia synandra* produces very peculiar-looking bluish fruits that are thought to be dispersed only by hornbills. Perhaps only these birds have bills of the appropriate dimensions to access the seeds in the splitting fruits. The seeds are armed with irritating yellow bristles as a deterrent to animals looking for a free meal. It may be that such specialization is advantageous to the plant because it guarantees the faithfulness and reliability of the agent.

Plants have evolved an astonishing array of forms to facilitate their dispersal. As we saw on pages 50–51, some seeds have parachutes that they employ for wind dispersal, while others float on water to travel vast distances across the world's oceans. Fruits also come in a variety of forms, and some are very unusual.

NOTORIOUSLY STINKY The peculiar durian is often dubbed the "king of fruits." It is highly prized in its native Southeast Asia, and now widely exported. The durian is renowned for its dimensions (each fruit is the size of a rugby ball), spiky appearance, delectable flavor—and, perhaps most of all, for its strong odor.

Many people find the durian's gassy aroma, which has been compared with sewage, overpowering. It is often banned from public spaces. The creamy, custardy flesh, however, is prized for its sweetness. Why does the durian smell so bad? This fruit is an effective hitchhiker. Its distinctive, memorable aroma spreads far and wide and attracts an array of rainforest birds and mammals including orangutans, hornbills, and macaques, which swallow the large brown seeds whole while eating the fruit's flesh. The smell is much more effective than visual appeal over a large area, and these animals make excellent dispersal agents, covering considerable distances across the rainforest.

Durian
This peculiar fruit comes in a range of sizes, colors, and textures. The most commonly grown form is *Durio zibethinus*, pictured here. *D. graveolens* is a wild species that produces fruit with bright red flesh.

Neesia synandra
This tall tree, which tops out at 203 ft (62 m) and emerges from the rainforest canopy in Southeast Asia, produces curious fruit with a blue, snakeskin-like surface. It is an important source of food for orangutans.

Plants can talk. They don't use words as humans do, of course; rather, they deploy chemical and electrical signaling and fungal networks to communicate with one another.

PLANT TALK

It may not seem obvious, but plants can communicate—very effectively and quickly. Plants living together experience environmental and biotic stresses including disease, herbivory (being eaten), and damage. They may seem unarmed and vulnerable in the face of such onslaught, but a key part of their defense is communication: sounding the alarm.

TALKING AND LISTENING Volatile organic compounds (VOCs) are important chemical signals used in plant interaction. They are released into the environment by a plant under attack—for example, one being eaten by a herbivorous insect—as a form of airborne communication, triggering neighboring plants to activate their inbuilt chemical defenses.

Dodder (*Cuscuta*) is a parasitic plant that coils around the stems of other plants and siphons off food from them. It is ubiquitous in many ecosystems; common dodder (*C. epithymum*), for example, is often found growing on heather and gorse in Northern Europe. Scientists have shown that dodder uses VOCs to detect its host plants. All plants release different "chemical signatures" made up of VOCs, so dodder can "choose" the correct host based on the specific signature.

UNDER THE RADAR Plants also communicate below ground via their root networks, using trace chemicals called root exudates, which they release into the rhizosphere. Through fungal threads (mycelia), plants' roots form links that enable the transfer of nutrients. These mycelia can form vast "mycorrhizal networks" that are effective underground systems of information exchange.

Ways of communicating
Plants "talk" above and below ground. Insect attack causes plants to release volatile organic compounds (VOCs) that may deter the pests or attract their predators; they also share defense signals to alert neighboring plants via underground networks. Meanwhile, dodder, a parasitic plant, uses airborne VOCs to detect the presence of its host plants.

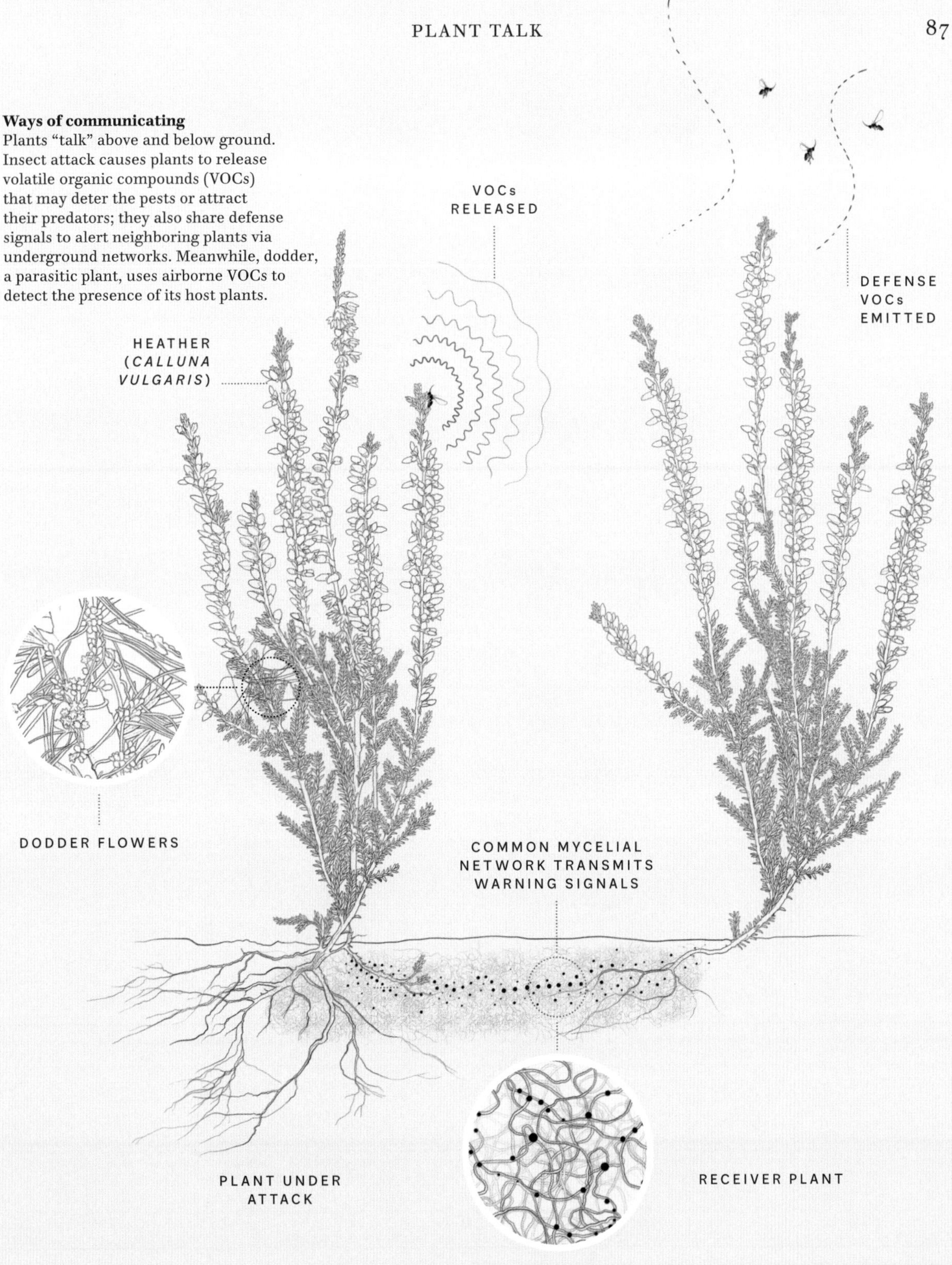

Common vetch (*Vicia sativa*)
Wildflowers coexist in complex communities, where they must compete for space in the sun. Many, including the common vetch, reach the optimal, sunny position using their stems or tendrils for support, grasping other foliage on the way up.

Plants exist in a perpetual, slow-motion fight for dominance. Speed this up, and you would see them climbing, coiling, and lashing their way up to find their place in the sun.

FLIGHT TO THE LIGHT

Plants grow in response to external stimuli, as we saw on pages 62–63—a process referred to as a tropism. Thigmotropism is the response to touch or contact, and it is commonly seen in twining plants and tendrils, where it leads to unilateral growth inhibition. That is to say, the face of the stem being touched grows more slowly than the opposite side, resulting in a coiling response.

Vetches are common wildflowers of woods and meadows in temperate zones. These scrambling and climbing plants have branched tendrils at the ends of their leaves. They grope and flail in circles until they find a nearby stem that can act as a support, hoisting themselves into position.

Bindweed is often considered a nuisance and is dreaded by most gardeners. Unlike vetches and other plants with tendrils, it climbs by dint of coiling stems, to hitch itself along. It can smother surrounding vegetation in the process.

Not all plants grasp their way into position. We have seen that many disperse their seeds via the breeze, but some may never touch the ground. Epiphytes are plants that live perched in the canopy, on the branches of trees. They are not parasites, extracting no food or water from the trees they cling to. Some, such as bromeliads (also known as "tank plants"), collect pools of rainwater in their cupped, leafy rosettes; land crabs, amphibians, and myriad other animals congregate in these strange, suspended microcosms. These reservoirs trap nutrients, enabling the plants to live high in the branches, where soil and permanent water are scarce.

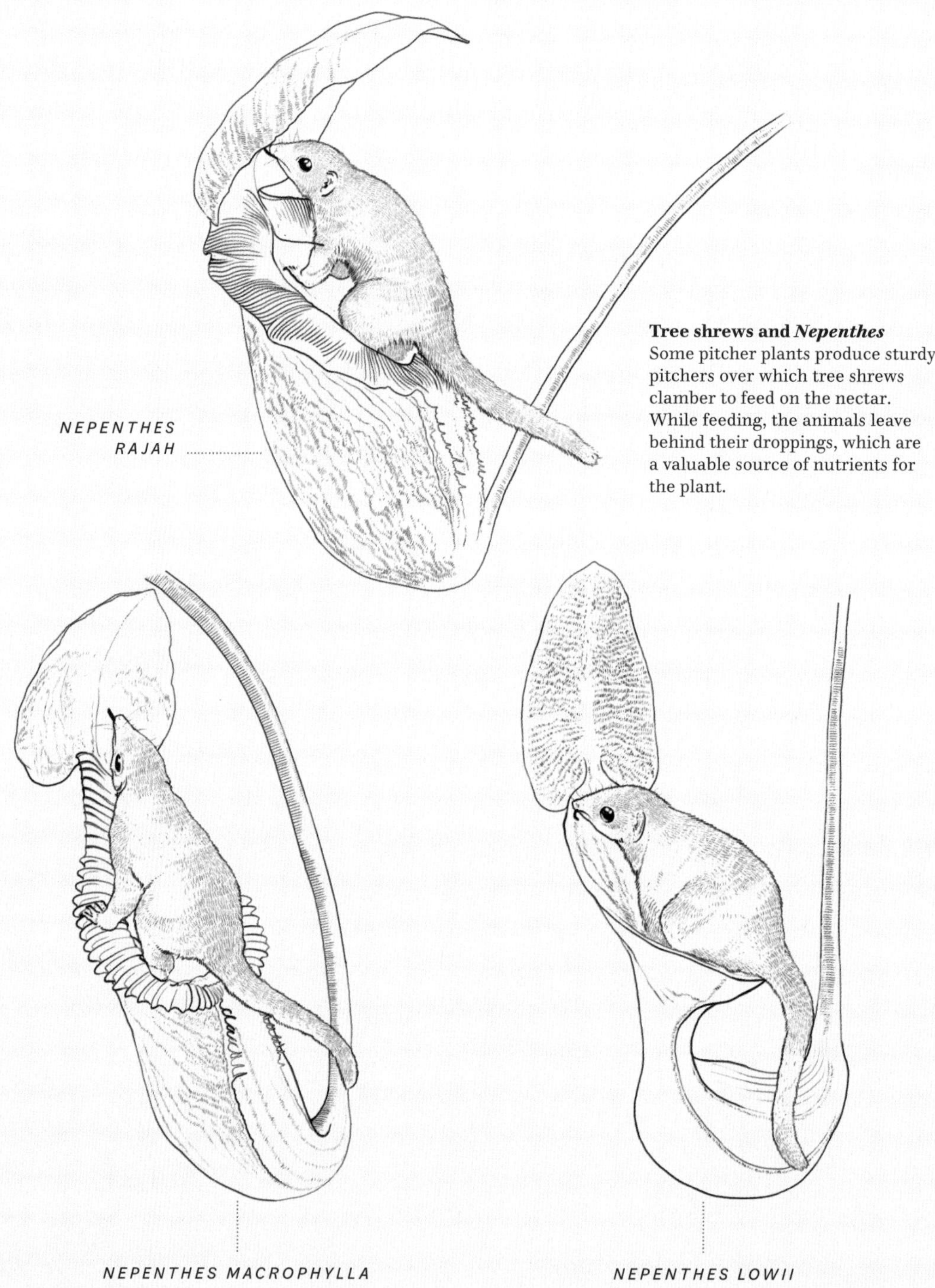

Tree shrews and *Nepenthes*
Some pitcher plants produce sturdy pitchers over which tree shrews clamber to feed on the nectar. While feeding, the animals leave behind their droppings, which are a valuable source of nutrients for the plant.

Plants need sunlight, water, and nutrients, such as nitrogen, to grow. In environments where nitrogen is scarce, some plants have gone to extreme lengths to find it.

TRAPPINGS AND DROPPINGS

Carnivorous plants evolved in environments where nutrients are scarce, for example in waterlogged swamps, on mossy branches, or on rain-leached mountain slopes. They have evolved a striking array of leaf-derived structures to attract, trap, and digest animal prey to supplement their diet in order to compete with neighboring plants. There are nearly 600 species of carnivorous plant, and DNA analysis has revealed that they evolved independently several times. Their traps range from sticky leaves (such as those of sundews; see p.183) to pitfall traps (pitcher plants; see pp.152–155).

Tropical pitcher plants (*Nepenthes*) are widespread across the mountains of Southeast Asia, and there are about 200 species. Their tubular pitchers are often brightly colored and produce sugary nectar to attract insects. While feeding on the nectar, the insects slide from a slippery rim into a pool of digestive fluid, where they die, break down, and release nutrients from which the plant benefits.

EMBRACING VEGETARIANISM A handful of tropical pitcher-plant species have shifted from their carnivorous diet. For example, *Nepenthes lowii*, *N. rajah*, and *N. macrophylla* in Borneo all produce large, woody pitchers with expanded openings. Recently it was discovered that these species acquire nutrients in a way that is quite different from that of most insect-eating pitcher plants. The shape and size of the pitcher mouth match the dimensions of small mammals called tree shrews (*Tupaia montana*). While feeding on the nectar on the inner surface of the spoonlike lid, the animals drop their feces into the pitchers' interiors, and these droppings supply the plants with essential nutrients. Another pitcher-plant species, *N. hemsleyana*, produces slender pitchers in which bats roost. Similarly, the bats' droppings are a source of nutrients for the plant.

Most plants live harmoniously with fungi. In a handful of families, however, plants have evolved means of exploiting fungi, entirely at their expense.

FUNGAL THIEVES

Plants and fungi exist side by side in every habitat on land. Plants are the producers, using the sun's energy to produce sugars from carbon dioxide and water, and locking up carbon. Meanwhile fungi are decomposers, breaking down organic material to obtain nutrients and energy. Together the two groups keep ecosystems functioning.

MYCORRHIZAL CHEATERS Just as we observed on pages 56–59, where plants exist at the expense of other plants, some plants are also parasitic on fungi. These plants are called mycoheterotrophs, and are sometimes referred to as "mycorrhizal cheaters." Mycorrhizal fungi are soil-dwelling fungi that exchange nutrients with plants' roots. They contribute to plant and soil health in the ecosystem, and live mostly in symbiosis, a relationship in which both plants and fungi benefit. But mycoheterotrophs live entirely at the expense of mycorrhizal fungi. They have little or no chlorophyll, or functional photosynthesis, so are dependent on the fungi for their carbon—and give nothing in return. In older texts, mycoheterotrophs are referred to as saprophytes, but this is now known to be incorrect; saprophytes (many fungi, for example) feed by breaking down decaying matter, but plants are unable to exist in this way.

Mycoheterotrophs have evolved in several plant families, especially in the monocots (see pp.36–37), and also in the family Ericaceae, for example sugarstick (*Allotropa virgata*), a particularly colorful species that grows in the forests of the Pacific Northwest, and snow flower (*Sarcodes sanguinea*) in California.

MÉNAGE À TROIS? Because these plants take their food from mycorrhizal fungi, which in turn exist in symbiosis with other (green, or autotrophic) plants—such as trees—mycoheterotrophs can be considered "epiparasites": they exist in a tri-trophic (three-layer) interaction within the ecosystem. In other words, mycoheterotrophs take carbon from trees via a fungal bridge, or symbiont.

Fungal bridges
Mycoheterotrophs, such as the snow plant, do not obtain food via photosynthesis; instead, they extract carbon from neighboring trees via a fungal bridge, or "symbiont": in this case a red fir tree, via a species of false truffle, in the evergreen forests of California.

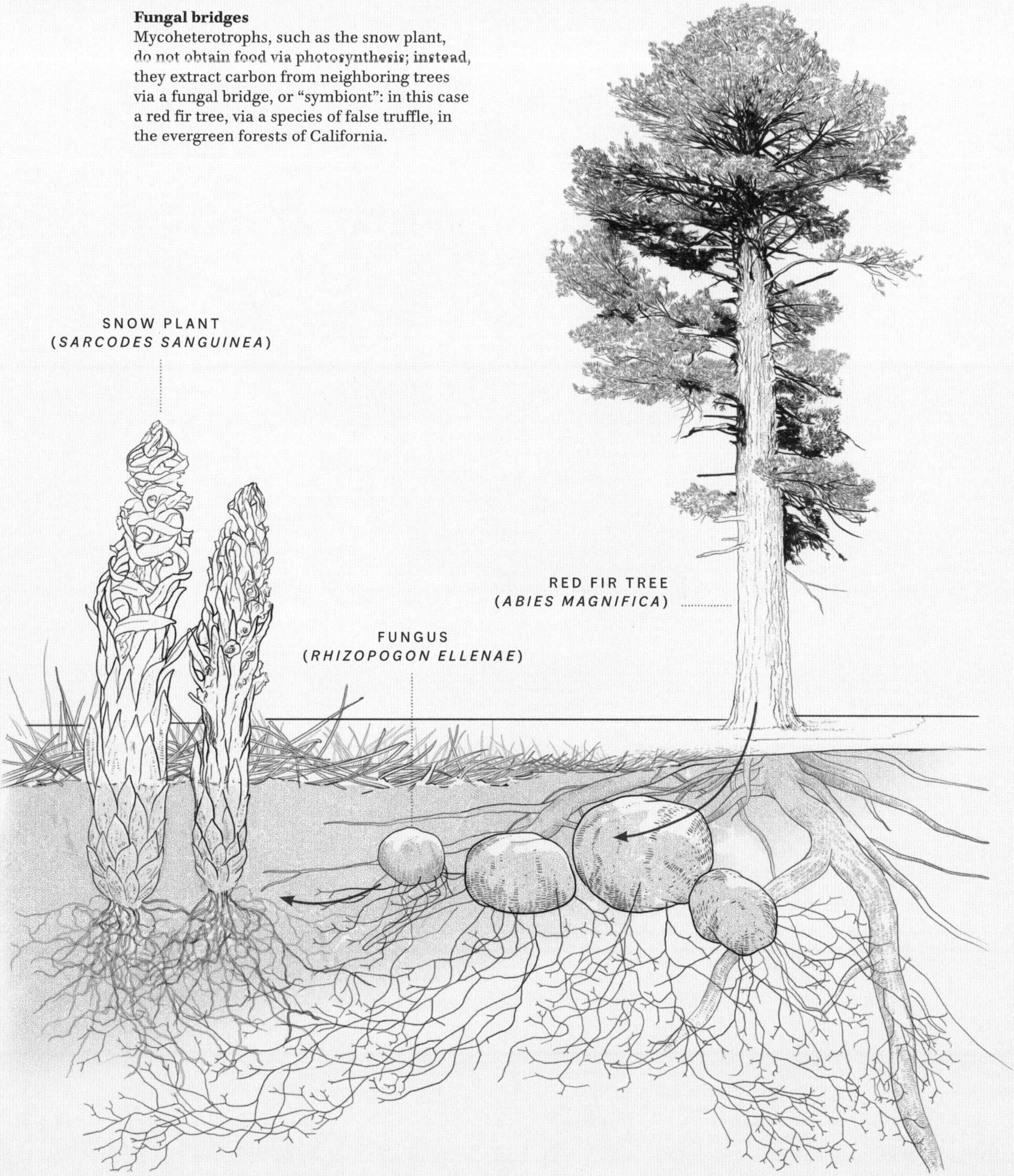

SNOW PLANT
(*SARCODES SANGUINEA*)

RED FIR TREE
(*ABIES MAGNIFICA*)

FUNGUS
(*RHIZOPOGON ELLENAE*)

Cerinthe major

CLASSIFY

CHAPTER IV

SCIENTISTS MAKE SENSE of the seemingly unfathomable diversity of wildflowers by sorting them into families according to their genetic relatedness, based on DNA analysis. There are more than 600 plant families around the world. This chapter introduces 17 of the most important or conspicuous, and highlights some of their key characteristics.

FERULA ASSA-FOETIDA
Asafoetida

SIZE 6 ft 6 in (2 m) high.

HABITAT & ECOLOGY Dry slopes.

DISTRIBUTION Iran (related species occur across West Asia and in China).

This plant is the source of a substance called asafoetida (named after the plant itself), sometimes referred to as stinking gum—a dried, powdered latex extracted from the plant's roots that has a pungent smell, and a leek-like taste when used in cooking. The ingredient is sourced from the species illustrated here; some close relatives are used in Iran, Afghanistan, Central Asia, northern South Asia, and northwestern China.

UMBELLIFERS
APIACEAE

The umbellifers make up a family (formerly known as the Umbelliferae) of aromatic flowering plants. It includes many well-known edible species: root vegetables, such as carrots and parsnips; culinary herbs, such as dill, celery, parsley, chervil, and cilantro; spices, such as anise and cumin; and many more besides. The umbellifers also include many poisonous species, such as giant hogweed and hemlock. This is one of the larger families of flowering plants, containing some 3,800 species in more than 400 genera.

Most umbellifers are annual or perennial herbs, often with leaves clustered around the stems, or in basal rosettes—often dissected into leaflets—and inflorescences (groups of flowers) borne on long, branched stems. The leaves and stems, when crushed, are often aromatic, sometimes unpleasantly scented. A key characteristic of the family is the formation of umbels: small flowers crowded into disk- or dome-shaped, parasol-like inflorescences; the individual flowers are usually co-sexual (containing both male and female parts) with five petals, and actinomorphic (radially symmetrical), although zygomorphic (bilaterally symmetrical) flowers are sometimes produced at the perimeter of the umbels. The flowers are often white or yellow, but exist in a range of colors. The fruit is a structure called a schizocarp, consisting of two fused carpels that separate at maturity into mericarps, each containing a single seed (see pp.48–49).

FERULA COMMUNIS

Giant fennel

SIZE To 6 ft 6 in (2 m) high.

HABITAT & ECOLOGY Dry hills and roadsides; maquis (scrub) vegetation.

DISTRIBUTION Mediterranean Basin; naturalized elsewhere across Europe north to the UK.

Giant fennel is much larger than its distant culinary relative, garden fennel (*Foeniculum vulgare*). It has a deep taproot from which it sends forth tufted, dissected leaves, and, when the plant is mature, gigantic treelike stems of yellow blossom in the spring; these remain long after the plant dies. Giant fennel has a long history of use in herbal medicine and can be toxic to livestock, which avoid it as a result, so it is frequent in heavily grazed areas.

THAPSIA VILLOSA

Deadly carrot

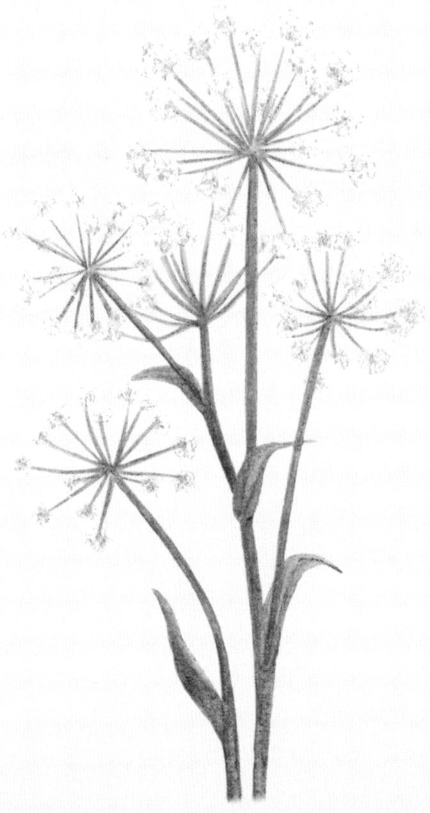

SIZE To 3 ft 3 in (1 m) high.

HABITAT & ECOLOGY Dry hills and stony pastures; maquis (scrub) vegetation.

DISTRIBUTION Atlantic coasts and the western Mediterranean.

Thapsias are a group of plants that somewhat resemble the giant fennels (*Ferula* spp.). They are perennials with rosettes of dissected leaves and sturdy stems carrying ball-like umbels of yellow blossom. Although toxic in large quantities, like *Ferula communis*, thapsias have a long history of use in herbal medicine, and are the source of thapsigargin—a compound examined for use in modern medicine, including against COVID-19.

HERACLEUM MANTEGAZZIANUM

Giant hogweed

SIZE To 10 ft (3 m) high.

HABITAT & ECOLOGY Damp habitats.

DISTRIBUTION Native to the western Caucasus; widely naturalized across Western Europe, the US, and Canada.

This plant was introduced to the UK in the nineteenth century as an ornamental garden curiosity, but it escaped cultivation and spread to suitable habitats across the northern hemisphere. It is phototoxic, meaning that the sap can cause serious burns, blisters, and scars to the skin; it is therefore considered a noxious weed.

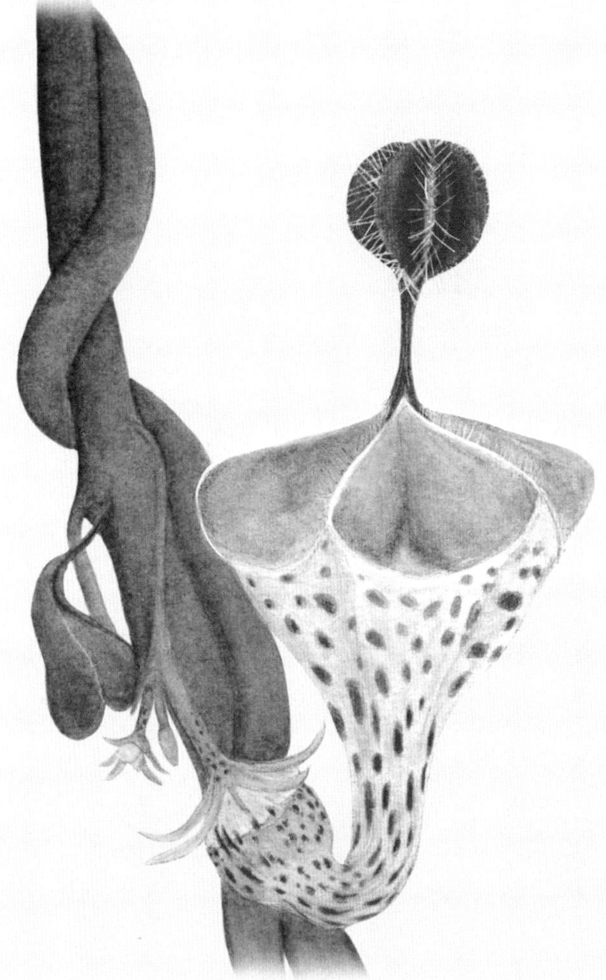

CEROPEGIA DISTINCTA

Parachute flower

SUBFAMILY Asclepiadoideae

SIZE Trailing stems to 10 ft (3 m); flowers 1½ in (4 cm) long.

HABITAT & ECOLOGY Seasonally dry tropical scrub.

DISTRIBUTION Southern Africa: Angola, Mozambique, and South Africa.

The parachute flower belongs to a group of plants (genus *Ceropegia*) with blooms that come in various lanterns, pipes, tubes, and umbrellas. The five petals are fused at the tips to form a parasol-like canopy or cage, sometimes with projections. In the species shown here, this conspicuous structure is geometrically unusual and covered in bristles. Parachute flowers are pollinated by flies.

ASCLEPIADS
APOCYNACEAE

Asclepiads are also known popularly as milkweeds (although this refers to a particular genus of asclepiads; see below), and there are about 2,400 species of them. They comprise a subfamily, the Asclepiadoideae, that belongs to an even larger group called the dogbane family (Apocynaceae), which is distributed worldwide. Formerly the asclepiads were treated by taxonomic botanists as a separate family in their own right (called the Asclepiadaceae), and this is reflected in older texts. Asclepiads are perennial herbs, twining shrubs and vines, and occasionally small trees; many of those that occur in arid or semi-arid regions are leafless succulents.

Many asclepiads possess unusual, five-parted flowers that often employ strange pollination mechanisms, sometimes involving flies. Members of this group produce pollen in bundles called pollinia, similar to those of orchids; like the orchids, many have evolved means of pollination by deceit (see pp.76–77). Asclepiads produce seeds in twinned, hornlike pods—a characteristic feature.

The milkweeds (genus *Asclepias*) are a group of asclepiads that occur throughout North and South America. The larvae of many butterflies, such as monarchs, feed on milkweed plants, the milky sap of which may make the larvae and adult butterflies distasteful to predators.

APTERANTHES EUROPAEA

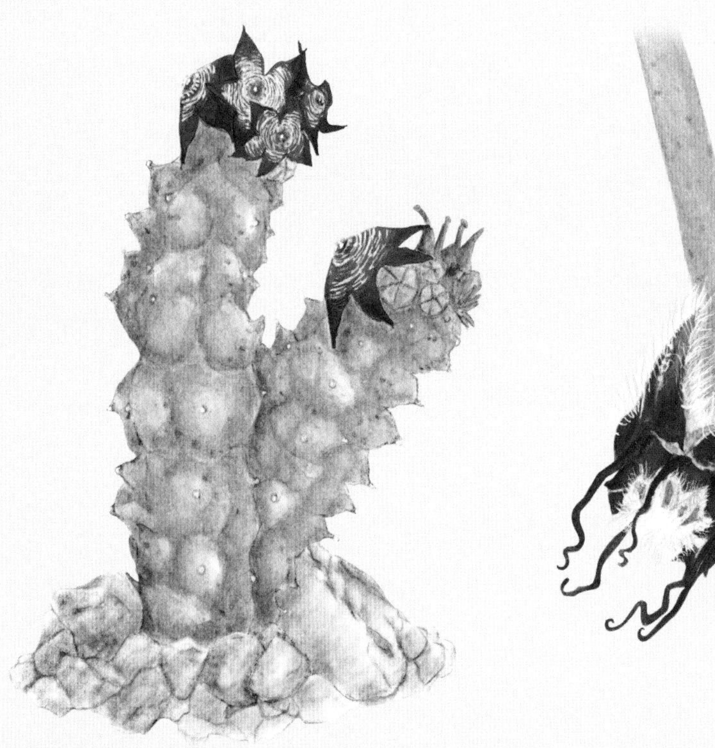

SUBFAMILY Asclepiadoideae

SIZE Stems to 6 in (15 cm); flowers ¾ in (2 cm) across.

HABITAT & ECOLOGY Dry, sun-baked cliffs, rocky slopes, and ledges; rather rare and local.

DISTRIBUTION Mediterranean and West Asia: southeastern Spain, southern Italy, Morocco, Tunisia, Libya, Egypt, Israel and Palestine, and Jordan.

This characterful little succulent grows in the driest rocky habitats of southern Europe, and in West Asia. It has finger-thick, gray, angular stems that, after rainfall, send out clusters of striped, starfish-shaped flowers that are pollinated by flies. After cross-fertilization, these are followed by hornlike fruit that release wind-dispersed seeds.

PERIPLOCA APHYLLA

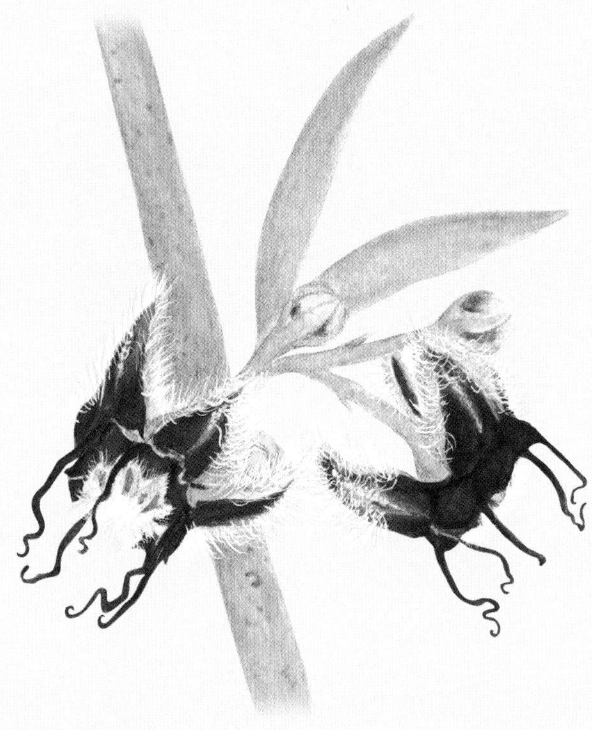

SUBFAMILY Asclepiadoideae

SIZE To 6 ft 6 in (2 m) high; flowers ⅕ in (1 cm) across.

HABITAT & ECOLOGY Sun-baked, rocky slopes.

DISTRIBUTION West Asia: Israel and Palestine, Sudan, and Sinai to Arabian Peninsula and northwestern India.

Periploca is a genus of succulent, often scrambling shrubs that thrive under harsh, arid conditions. The species shown here is a xerophytic (drought-tolerant) one with leafless, gray, pencil-thick stems. The spiderlike flowers are borne in clusters; each is blackish-purple with tufts of white hairs and curved, thornlike projections.

ASCLEPIAS SYRIACA

Common milkweed

SUBFAMILY Asclepiadoideae

SIZE To 5 ft (1.5 m) high.

HABITAT & ECOLOGY Grassland, verges, pasture.

DISTRIBUTION Common across much of North America; widely naturalized and locally invasive elsewhere, for example in Eastern Europe.

Also known as butterfly flower, silkweed, silky swallow-wort, and Virginia silkweed, this perennial is attractive to monarch butterflies, which lay their eggs on it. It has succulent stems that yield a milky juice when broken. The dull purple flowers are borne in globes, and are attractive to many nectar-feeding insects.

AMORPHOPHALLUS PAEONIIFOLIUS

Elephant-foot yam

SIZE To about 60 in (150 cm) high; tuber about 16 in (40 cm) across.

HABITAT & ECOLOGY Understory of tropical forest ecosystems; also commonly grown in gardens and smallholder farms.

DISTRIBUTION Probably originated in Southeast Asia but now cultivated across much of the tropics; commonly cultivated in India.

An extraordinary-looking plant that produces large, parasol-like leaves that arise from an underground tuber. After the leaf dies, a flowering shoot is produced, often during the rainy season. The bizarre, wrinkled spadix releases an unpleasant smell to attract pollinating flies. The fruits are borne in long spikes of berries.

AROIDS
ARACEAE

Aroids (popularly called arums and arum lilies) belong to a monocot family of about 140 genera. They are especially diverse in the tropics, but they occur in most major terrestrial ecosystems. As we saw on pages 74–75, aroids are distinguished by their minute flowers crowded around the base of a spikelike spadix enclosed in a bract-like spathe, and many trap their pollinators overnight in a floral chamber. Most aroids possess separate male and female flowers in the same structure (a group of flowers together is referred to as an inflorescence); in these species, the female flowers shut off their receptivity once the male flowers ripen—a mechanism that prevents self-fertilization. Some species are dioecious, meaning that the male and female flowers are borne on separate plants.

Some tropical aroids have enormous leaves more than 3 ft 3 in (1 m) wide, and the family includes the largest unbranched inflorescence of all: that of the titan arum (*Amorphophallus titanum*). Edible aroids include the tropical elephant-foot yam (opposite), taro (*Colocasia esculenta*), and Mexican breadfruit (*Monstera deliciosa*)—the last of which is also popularly known as the Swiss cheese plant, and grown as an indoor plant. Many members of the family are poisonous, among them the Northern European cuckoo pint (*Arum maculatum*) and its relatives.

ARUM MACULATUM

Cuckoo pint, lords and ladies

SIZE To 16 in (40 cm) high.

HABITAT & ECOLOGY Woods, hedgerows, and thickets, sometimes in gardens. In hot regions, it is restricted to montane forests.

DISTRIBUTION Occurs across most of Europe, as well as eastern Türkiye and the Caucasus; farther south, it grows at high altitude.

A familiar woodland and hedgerow wildflower that blooms in the spring. The leathery, glossy, arrow-shaped leaves appear in late winter, and sometimes bear dark spots. The spadix is typically chocolate-brown, and the spathe light green. In Britain, the plant reputedly has more common names than any other plant.

ARISAEMA TRIPHYLLUM

Jack-in-the-pulpit

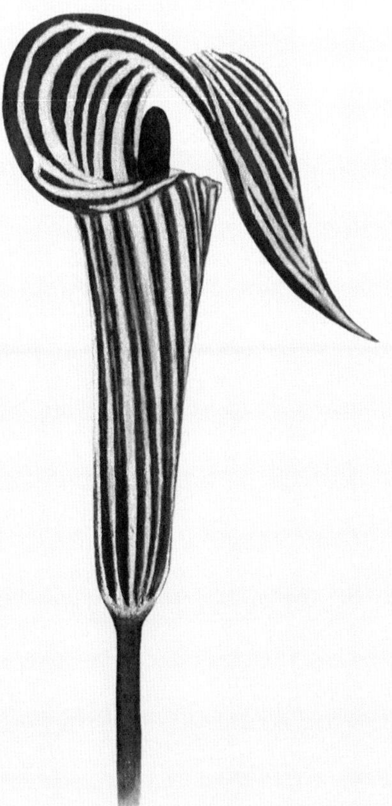

SIZE To 16 in (40 cm) high.

HABITAT & ECOLOGY Various shady habitats, including damp deciduous woods, bogs, swamps, and wetlands.

DISTRIBUTION Widespread across eastern North America.

This plant has myriad common names, including Indian turnip, bog onion, and brown dragon. The scientific epithet *triphyllum*, "three-leaved," refers to the distinctive three-parted leaves (not shown). The spathe-hood is conspicuously striped. The plant contains organic acids known as oxalates and can be poisonous if ingested, although the oxalates are reduced by boiling and it has traditionally been eaten as a root vegetable.

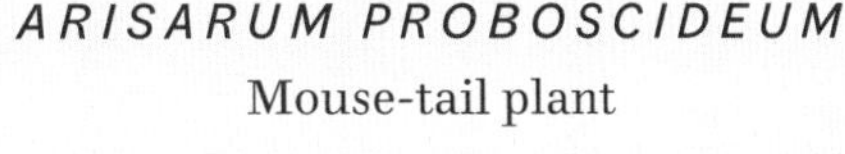

ARISARUM PROBOSCIDEUM

Mouse-tail plant

SIZE To 6 in (15 cm) high.

HABITAT & ECOLOGY Shady habitats, such as temperate woods and thickets.

DISTRIBUTION Southern Europe, in Spain and Italy.

A peculiar-looking aroid with a hooded, chocolate-colored spathe that extends at the apex into a long, threadlike appendage like a mouse's tail—hence the common name. As in many aroids, this structure temporarily traps small pollinating insects (in this case, fungus gnats). The plant can be grown in temperate gardens under cold frames in frost-prone areas; it is sometimes cultivated as a curiosity in the UK, New Zealand, and North America.

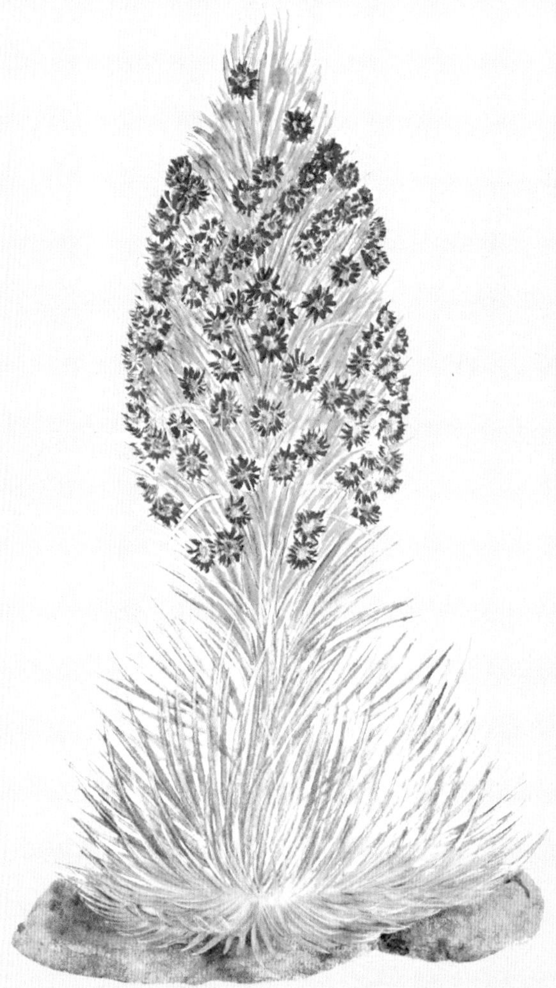

ARGYROXIPHIUM SANDWICENSE
Hawaii silversword

SIZE To 6 ft 6 in (2 m) high.

HABITAT & ECOLOGY Rocky volcanic slopes at elevations above 6,890 ft (2,100 m); rare and endangered; much declined owing to grazing.

DISTRIBUTION Hawaii.

The Hawaii silversword is arguably the most spectacular of all the tens of thousands of species in the daisy family. It produces a rosette of leaves covered in silvery hairs, and, at maturity, a towering spike of flower heads; the plant lives for several decades and blooms only once, after which it dies. The silvery hairs protect the plant from the environmental extremes of its exposed habitat.

DAISIES
ASTERACEAE

The daisies belong to what is arguably the second-largest family of flowering plants (the Asteraceae; formerly called the Compositae), rivaled only by the orchid family (Orchidaceae). The daisy family contains an estimated 33,000 species from nearly 2,000 genera, and is split into 13 subfamilies. The family includes such popular garden plants and crops as asters, calendulas, sunflowers, and lettuces.

Most daisies and their relatives are annual, biennial, or perennial herbaceous plants, but some are shrubs, vines, and trees. Many produce long taproots (see p.43) and exude a latex when cut (members of the subfamily Cichorioideae). The family is cosmopolitan, occurring from subpolar to tropical regions, in a wide variety of habitats from deserts and steppe grasslands to mountains and rainforests; its members are found on every continent but Antarctica. The uniting characteristic of plants in this family is the production of minute flowers (called florets) in flower heads called capitula, enclosed by a whorl of protective involucral bracts (see p.235). The florets in the central disk are called disk florets, while those that look like petals at the perimeter are known as ray florets. Therefore, technically a sunflower is not a flower but rather an inflorescence (specifically a capitulum): a group of many tiny flowers united in a single structure.

PALLENIS HIEROCHUNTICA

Resurrection plant

SIZE 4 in (10 cm) across.

HABITAT & ECOLOGY Desert slopes.

DISTRIBUTION Macaronesia, North Africa, and West Asia.

Also known as the rose of Jericho and the dinosaur plant, this species is adapted to growing in xeric (extremely arid) environments. “Resurrection plant” is the name given to several unrelated plants that grow in deserts and respond to rainfall after long, dry periods of dormancy. In this species, the closed, dry flowering receptacle (see pp.40–41) reopens when it is dampened. The plant produces a small rosette of silkily hairy leaves and a central yellow, daisylike flower head.

PETASITES HYBRIDUS

Butterbur

SIZE Leaves to 4 ft (1.2 m) across; flower stalks to 8 in (20 cm).

HABITAT & ECOLOGY Damp habitats, such as riverbanks and flooded meadows.

DISTRIBUTION Native to central Europe, from British Isles to Caucasus, and southern Italy to southern Scandinavia; similar species distributed in temperate regions worldwide.

Butterburs form swathes in damp, shady areas. The large leaves (which mature after blooming; not shown) were used to wrap butter, hence the common name. The plant is dioecious (meaning its male and female flowers occur on separate plants), producing flower spikes that emerge with or shortly before the leaves, in early spring.

BELLIS PERENNIS

Lawn daisy

SIZE To 8 in (20 cm) high; flower heads ¾ in (2 cm) across.

HABITAT & ECOLOGY Common in fields; lawns; other grassy, disturbed habitats; and waste places.

DISTRIBUTION Native to western, central, and Northern Europe; naturalized in temperate regions worldwide.

This familiar plant produces capitula (groups of flowers in a single structure) consisting of yellow disk florets, framed by white ray florets, sometimes red-tipped. The fruit (achenes; see p.49) lack a "parachute" (or pappus). The plant has been used as a traditional herbal medicine, a salad plant, and a potted herb for millennia.

ECHIUM WILDPRETII
Tower of jewels

SIZE To 10 ft (3 m) high.

HABITAT & ECOLOGY Seasonally dry, loose volcanic slopes.

DISTRIBUTION Endemic to the Canary Islands (mainly in the national park around Mount Teide, Tenerife); widely planted in gardens elsewhere.

This imposing plant is a spectacle in its native Canary Islands, and has become popular with gardeners in tender climates elsewhere. It is a biennial that produces a rosette of silvery leaves in its first year; the following year, it sends up a spire of red blossom that is very attractive to bees. The plant is monocarpic, meaning that it dies after flowering.

BORAGES
BORAGINACEAE

The borages, forget-me-nots, and their relatives belong to a family of about 2,000 species of herbs, perennials, shrubs, and trees that are distributed worldwide. Most species produce co-sexual flowers (those that contain male and female parts), often with copious nectar, and they are very attractive to pollinating bees.

Common characteristics of the borages and their relatives include inflorescences (groups of flowers; called cymes in this family) that develop in a coiled formation; five-part flowers in a range of colors; small, dry fruit (nutlets) in a persistent calyx, often splitting into four; and leaves and stems that are covered in hairs and bristles. These bristles are often coarse, being high in silicon dioxide and calcium carbonate, and can bring about an unpleasant skin reaction when touched. Another common feature among these plants is a color change in the developing flowers over time; they often turn from pink or red upon opening, to blue or white as they mature. This is a signal to pollinators that the flowers have already been visited.

Forget-me-nots (*Myosotis*), also known as scorpion grasses, are a well-known genus of borage relatives that are native to temperate regions around the globe, especially western Eurasia, often in damp habitats. They produce copious sky-blue blossoms, and have become popular garden plants.

BORAGO OFFICINALIS

Borage, starflower

SIZE To 24 in (60 cm) high.

HABITAT & ECOLOGY Disturbed ground.

DISTRIBUTION Native to the Mediterranean Basin, but widely planted in gardens and naturalized elsewhere.

Borage has a long history of use. Ancient Greek herbalists believed the plant was a remedy for forgetfulness when mixed with wine, and it has been used for a variety of purposes since—including, more recently, as a garnish and ingredient in Pimm's and gin, respectively. It has distinctive starry flowers that are blue (sometimes pink or white), with a black-and-white central cone.

CERINTHE MAJOR

Honeywort

SIZE To 8 in (20 cm) high.

HABITAT & ECOLOGY Disturbed, sandy, and grassy habitats.

DISTRIBUTION Native to the Mediterranean Basin, but sometimes planted in gardens and naturalized elsewhere.

Honeywort in bloom is often teeming with bees and other insects, its bell-shaped flowers borne in nodding formation. When ripe, the fruit splits into two, unlike that of most other members of the family, which split into four. Like borage, honeywort has been celebrated since ancient times, and features in early herbals. Easily grown from seed, it is a popular garden plant for attracting bees.

ONOSMA ERECTUM

Golden drops

SIZE Plant to about 12 in (30 cm) high; flowers to 1 in (2.5 cm) long.

HABITAT & ECOLOGY Cliffs, crags, and dry, rocky slopes in pine forests.

DISTRIBUTION Restricted to southern Greece and Crete.

Despite the epithet *erectum*, the flowers of golden drops nod gracefully; the name refers to the stems. Like many members of the family, it is covered in white bristles. The rather beautiful, elongated, bell-shaped flowers are butter-yellow. Several species of *Onosma* are cultivated as rockery garden plants or in alpine plant collections as novelties, for their unusual blossoms.

MAMMILLARIA HERRERAE

Golf-ball cactus

SIZE 3 in (8 cm) high.

HABITAT & ECOLOGY Dry, open shrubland among rocks and boulders.

DISTRIBUTION Mexico (Guanajuato to Hidalgo); threatened by illegal collection.

This miniature cactus produces little globose (spherical) stems covered in close-set rings of white spines arranged in starlike formations. These small, white globes have a bizarre resemblance to a golf ball, hence the common name. Mature plants produce flowers in shades from pink to violet in a ringlike formation around the circumference of the stem.

CACTI
CACTACEAE

Cacti (or cactuses) are all members of the cactus family, which contains about 130 genera and close to 2,000 species. All members are succulents (succulent is a word to describe a plant with fleshy, water-storing stems or leaves). As we saw on pages 54–55, thanks to convergent evolution, the cacti of Arizona and Central America look remarkably similar to the succulent euphorbias of Africa and the Canary Islands. Therefore, it is true to say that all cacti are succulents, but not all succulents are cacti.

Cacti come in all shapes and sizes, from barrels, bottles, and even golf balls to towering trees. They are native to the Americas and usually occur in arid environments—even in some of the driest habitats on Earth—where their water-storing capacity gives them a strong selective advantage. Most cacti have lost their true leaves during the course of evolution; this reduces water loss. To compensate, the plants carry out photosynthesis in their enlarged stems. Many cacti possess a tough armor of spines to protect them from thirsty animals seeking to bite a way into the plants' precious water reserves.

CARNEGIEA GIGANTEA
Saguaro

SIZE 39 ft (12 m) high.

HABITAT & ECOLOGY Deserts; the saguaro is considered a keystone species, supporting many other flora and fauna in its habitat.

DISTRIBUTION The Sonoran Desert in Arizona, the Mexican state of Sonora, and locally in California.

This enormous cactus with its colossal stems can live for up to a century. It absorbs water quickly after rare rainfall, and its pleated stems expand in hours to increase their storage capacity. The plant's blossom is the state wildflower of Arizona, and the Saguaro National Park was established in this state to protect the plant and its habitat.

FEROCACTUS WISLIZENI

Barrel cactus

SIZE 3ft 3in–6ft 6in (1–2m) high.

HABITAT & ECOLOGY Deserts; often facing south, earning it the name "compass barrel cactus."

DISTRIBUTION Northern Mexico and the southern US.

Barrel cactus is a generic name given to various members of two genera: *Echinocactus* and *Ferocactus*; the species shown here is also known as fishhook barrel cactus, owing to its vicious, hooked spines. Its robust, columnar stems can be nearly 3ft 3in (1m) wide and it lives for more than a century. The attractive yellow to orange-red flowers are borne in summer and pollinated by cactus bees (*Lithurgus*); deer, birds, and ground squirrels eat the fruit.

CORYPHANTHA ELEPHANTIDENS

Elephant's tooth

SIZE To 5½in (14cm) high.

HABITAT & ECOLOGY Rocky desert slopes; stems often partially buried.

DISTRIBUTION Beehive cacti are widespread in Central America and Mexico through Arizona, New Mexico, and western Texas, north to Montana. The species shown is native to Mexico.

The elephant's tooth belongs to a wider group known as the beehive cacti, a genus of about 60 species characterized by stems with tubercles (lumpy outgrowths) rather than ribs, commonly terminating in a ring of bristlelike spines. The stems are often clustered and bear beautiful rose-pink, whitish, or yellow flowers.

LOBELIA DECKENII

Giant lobelia

SIZE To 16ft 6in (5m) high.

HABITAT & ECOLOGY Mountain pastures at altitudes of 12,500–14,000ft (3,800–4,300m).

DISTRIBUTION Tanzania.

This extraordinary member of the family produces enormous spikes of flowers from robust leafy rosettes. Each rosette grows for several decades, produces a single large inflorescence (group of flowers) and hundreds of thousands of seeds, then dies (a trait known as monocarpy). *L. telekii* is another, rather similar species that is found in the alpine zone of Mount Kenya, Mount Elgon, and the Aberdare Mountains of East Africa. Both species are bird-pollinated.

CAMPANULAS
CAMPANULACEAE

Also known as the bellflowers, the campanulas comprise about 90 genera and 2,000 species of herbs, shrubs, and occasionally small trees, sometimes yielding a milky sap. They occur on all continents except Antarctica, in a variety of habitats, from rainforest to desert. Some have evolved curious forms to cope with environmental stress, for example cushion plants growing at high altitude, or the imposing giant lobelias of Mount Kilimanjaro, which tolerate exposed locations and nightly frost. Other campanulas have attractive flowers and have become popular as ornamental garden plants in northern temperate regions, especially in rock gardens and on old walls. Canterbury bells (*Campanula medium*), for example, is a commonly cultivated ornamental.

Campanulas typically have alternate leaves, often with toothed margins; opposite or whorled leaf formations are rare in the family. The form of the inflorescence is diverse in the family; in some genera the flowers are borne in a formation that looks superficially like that of the daisy family (Asteraceae; pp.108–111). The flowers are typically co-sexual (with male and female parts in the same flower), with petals fused into a corolla tube with between three and eight lobes, often in a star- or bell-shaped form—hence the name of the genus, which is derived from the Latin for bell, *campana*.

CANARINA CANARIENSIS
Canary Island bellflower

SIZE Stems to 10 ft (3 m); flowers to 2½ in (6 cm) long.

HABITAT & ECOLOGY Laurel forests.

DISTRIBUTION Western Canary Islands.

This rare wildflower belongs to a genus of three species distributed from the Canary Islands to eastern Africa. It is a scrambling perennial with smooth, opposite leaves with toothed margins. The flowers are bell-shaped, orange with darker veins, and borne on annual scrambling stems in the winter and spring. These are bird-pollinated (by chiffchaffs, for example) and followed by large, fleshy, edible berries in the summer. In cooler regions, the plant is cultivated in conservatories.

CAMPANULA ROTUNDIFOLIA
Harebell

SIZE 12 in (30 cm) high.

HABITAT & ECOLOGY Dry, undisturbed ground, especially grassland.

DISTRIBUTION Common in northern temperate Europe and North America.

The harebell's graceful, nodding violet flowers are familiar to walkers on grasslands, hillsides, sand dunes, and cliffs in cool regions. The blooms are an important source of fall nectar for bumblebees and honeybees. This creeping perennial has club-shaped leaves at the base and elongated stem leaves. Confusingly, in Scotland it is known as bluebell (the name of an unrelated woodland plant, *Hyacinthoides non-scripta* and its relatives).

ARENARIA POLYTRICHOIDES

Hummock sandwort

SIZE Leaves ⅛ in (2–3 mm) long; flowers 1/32 in (1 mm) across.

HABITAT & ECOLOGY Stony slopes and among rocks at an altitude of about 16,500 ft (5,000 m).

DISTRIBUTION The Himalayas: Kashmir to southeastern Tibet (China).

Hummock sandwort is a remarkable plant that is well adapted to the cold, dry, mountain slopes of the Himalayas to which it is restricted. It forms dense, mosslike hummocks of tiny, congested leaves. In late summer, clouds of minute white flowers, each with five petals, are borne on the surface of the hummocks.

CITRULLUS COLOCYNTHIS

Colocynth

SIZE Stems to 20 in (50 cm).

HABITAT & ECOLOGY Seasonally wet desert flats; damp habitats in otherwise arid places.

DISTRIBUTION Canary Islands eastward to North Africa and West Asia.

Colocynth is a desert wildflower and fruit, and is also grown across West Asia and northern Africa for its medicinal properties. The fruit is extremely bitter and a powerful laxative; the seeds are edible. Unlike other members of the family that have been bred intensively and scarcely resemble their wild ancestors, cultivated forms of this species are little different from the wild forms. The bristly vines produce ball-like fruit that is green and mottled, and ripens to orange in the sun.

CUCURBITS
CUCURBITACEAE

The cucurbits, or gourd family, comprise nearly 1,000 species in 100 genera. As wild plants, they are common in a range of habitats worldwide. Many have also been cultivated since antiquity for food and medicine, most commonly members of the genera *Cucurbita* (squashes, pumpkins, zucchini, and edible gourds), *Cucumis* (cucumbers), and *Citrullus*, which includes the watermelon. Other important cucurbits are the bitter melon (*Momordica*), calabash (*Lagenaria*), and luffa (p.127). The wild relatives and ancestors of these multipurpose plants are diverse, especially in the morphology (form) of their fruit. The characteristic gourd-like form of fruit is in fact a modified berry, called a pepo. An extreme example is the squirting cucumber (see pp.50–51), which fires its seeds into the air in a jet of liquid.

Many cucurbits are annual or perennial vines, such as white bryony (*Bryonia dioica*), a familiar hedgerow wildflower in the UK—but this species happens to be highly toxic, unlike its culinary relatives. Other growth forms in the family include tropical woody lianas (vines), as well as thorny shrubs and trees. Many possess showy yellow or white flowers, and tendrils for support. The flowers are unisexual, meaning that they are either male or female, and borne either on the same plant (in a monoecious plant) or on different individuals (dioecious).

Because cucurbits have such a long history of human use and cultivation, it is difficult to be sure of the wild origins of some species.

HODGSONIA MACROCARPA

Lard seed

SIZE Vines to 98 ft (30 m) long.

HABITAT & ECOLOGY Tropical forests; widely cultivated.

DISTRIBUTION South and Southeast Asia: Mainland Southeast Asia to West Malesia.

Lard seed is a vigorous, fast-growing, woody evergreen climber that supports itself by means of coiled tendrils. The unusual flowers have long, filament-like appendages, and the squash-like, whitish to yellowish fruit contains large, edible seeds that are rich in oil. The plant is commonly used for food across its native range, as well as for traditional herbal medicine.

TRICHOSANTHES CUCUMERINA

Snake gourd

SIZE Fruit to 3ft 3in (1m) long.

HABITAT & ECOLOGY Tropical forests; widely cultivated.

DISTRIBUTION Cultivated as a vegetable and for traditional medicine throughout much of the tropics, including southern Asia, tropical Africa, and Madagascar.

This tropical cucurbit produces bizarre, snakelike fruit that is remarkably long, whitish, often streaked with green, and turns reddish when mature. Smallholder farmers sometimes tie rocks to the end of the developing fruit to straighten out the peculiar coils. Like the lard seed (opposite), this plant has intricately beautiful white flowers.

LUFFA ACUTANGULA

Luffa gourd

SIZE Fruit to 12in (30cm) long.

HABITAT & ECOLOGY Tropical forests, plains, and kitchen gardens.

DISTRIBUTION Across Asia; grown widely in the tropics (the form shown here originated in India).

Two of the nine luffa species are widely grown: *L. aegyptiaca* and *L. acutangula* (shown here). Both are cultivated for their fruit, which is eaten as a vegetable and is a source of the loofah sponge used for cosmetic purposes or as a pan-scourer, owing to its tough fibers. Over the long history of cultivation, many types have been developed by artificial selection, and the form shown is not strictly "wild."

COLUTEA ARBORESCENS

Bladder senna

SIZE To 10 ft (3 m) high.

HABITAT & ECOLOGY Dry banks, roadsides, and scrub.

DISTRIBUTION Native to the Mediterranean Basin; grown widely elsewhere and naturalized across Northern Europe.

Bladder senna is an upright shrub with pinnate leaves composed of ovate leaflets, and yellow flowers with reddish markings. The most remarkable feature of this plant is the fruit: a pinkish, inflated, bladderlike pod (legume) that ripens with a papery texture. The leaves are a diuretic and purgative, and have been used in the past as a substitute for senna (hence the common name), as a laxative.

LEGUMES
FABACEAE

The legumes, peas, and beans belong to a large and economically important family of plants (also known as the Leguminosae). Legumes have been a staple food for people for millennia, besides grains, rice, and some fruit. Today, agriculturally important legumes include soy (*Glycine max*), peas and beans (*Pisum sativum* and *Vicia faba*), fenugreek (*Trigonella foenum-graecum*), chickpeas (*Cicer arietinum*), licorice (*Glycyrrhiza glabra*), and lentils (*Vicia lens*). Commonly encountered wildflowers in northern temperate regions include clovers (*Trifolium*), bur clovers (*Medicago*), and milk vetches (*Astragalus*). Some legumes are also cultivated as garden ornamentals, for example lupins (*Lupinus*).

Around the world there are more than 750 genera of legumes containing some 20,000 species that range from annual herbs to great trees. This is the largest plant family after the orchids and daisies; in fact, up to 7 percent of all flowering plants are legumes. Most legumes are easily recognized by their compound (often pinnate) leaves, stipules (leafy outgrowths at the base of the leaf stalks), zygomorphic (bilaterally symmetrical) flowers made up of three types of petal—banner, wings, and keel—and podlike fruit, themselves known as legumes. Leguminous plants have a distinct ecology: they host bacteria in underground structures called root nodules that fix nitrogen (see p.43). Some species of *Acacia*, the so-called ant plants (see pp.80–81), have also evolved fascinating symbioses with ants.

ASTRAGALUS CRASSICARPUS

Buffalo plum, ground-plum milk vetch

SIZE To 24 in (60 cm) high.

HABITAT & ECOLOGY Grassy plains.

DISTRIBUTION The Great Plains of Canada and the US, from British Columbia east to Ontario and south to Texas; similar, related species are found around the world in a range of habitats, from mountains to deserts.

Astragalus is one of the largest genera in the legume family. Most milk vetches have pinnately compound leaves (see p.47), and flowers borne in clusters in a raceme (see p.235), followed by legumes in various shapes and sizes, from sickles to inflated pods and balls. The fruit of the species shown here was once used by Indigenous peoples of North America as food and horse medicine.

MUCUNA NIGRICANS

Black jade vine

SIZE Vine to 35 ft (10 m); leaflets 6 in (15 cm) long.

HABITAT & ECOLOGY Subtropical forests.

DISTRIBUTION *Mucuna* is widespread across tropical and subtropical forests in the Americas, sub-Saharan Africa, Asia, New Guinea, Australia, and the Pacific Islands; the species shown is native to India.

The plant shown here, with its striking blackish-purple flowers, belongs to a genus of woody climbers that, together, are popularly known as velvet beans, deer-eye beans, donkey-eye beans, ox-eye beans, hamburger seeds—and many more besides. The sea bean (see p.51) also belongs to this genus.

SWAINSONA FORMOSA

Sturt's pea

SIZE Flowers to 3½in (9 cm) long.

HABITAT & ECOLOGY Deserts.

DISTRIBUTION Central and northwestern Australia.

This is one of Australia's most iconic desert-dwelling plants, growing in the arid central and northwestern regions of the country, where rainfall is very scarce. The seeds of this legume remain viable in the dry sand for many years until the rain returns and conditions are conducive to germination. After rainfall, the seedlings establish long roots and the plant matures quickly, producing blood-red-and-black flowers and setting seed in advance of the return of unfavorable hot, dry weather.

IRIS ATROFUSCA

Judean iris

SIZE 20 in (50 cm) high.

HABITAT & ECOLOGY Seasonally arid hillsides and deserts.

DISTRIBUTION West Asia.

The Judean iris belongs to a group called the Oncocyclus irises—bearded irises with rhizomes. In common with those of other irises, its flowers have two stacked pairs of petals: three large outer sepals, known as falls, and three inner, smaller tepals, known as standards. The flowers are an unusual shade of blackish-maroon, and have a black area (known as a signal) and a thick, brown tuft of hairs (the beard).

IRISES
IRIDACEAE

The iris family contains several well-known plants besides irises, including crocuses, freesias, and gladiolus—all popular garden plants. This is a monocot family (see pp.36–37), its representatives being perennials that grow from bulbs, corms, and rhizomes. Most have an erect form and strap-shaped or grasslike leaves, often with a sharp folded keel. Originally the irises and their relatives were grouped with the lilies (see pp.140–143), but DNA sequence data support their distinction, showing a stronger relatedness to the asparagoid lilies (Asparagales), a diverse order of plants that includes the orchids.

The iris family is so large and diverse that, in common with some other plant families (daisies and legumes, for example; see pp.108–111 and 128–131), it has been divided into subfamilies. These plants occupy a range of habitats around the world. Because of their root storage organs, many are capable of surviving environmental extremes, such as cold or drought, by entering a period of seasonal dormancy. They are thus adapted to life in deserts, marshes, forests—and just about every terrestrial habitat in between. Many irises and related plants have highly zygomorphic flowers that have evolved close relationships with a limited number of pollinators, or even a single species. These range from solitary bees, moths, and sunbirds to butterflies.

IRIS RETICULATA

Netted iris, golden netted iris

SIZE 6 in (15 cm) high.

HABITAT & ECOLOGY Mountain slopes.

DISTRIBUTION Türkiye to northern Iran; widely grown in gardens.

The netted iris is probably better known as a popular garden plant than as a wildflower. Easily grown from a bulb as a garden plant in northern temperate regions, it belongs to a group of irises characterized by their fibrous, netted bulb tunics (coverings), small size, and early flowers. The flowers are typically blue or purple with a conspicuous spotted yellow patch on the falls (the large outer sepals).

IRIS PSEUDACORUS

Yellow flag

SIZE 3 ft 3 in–5 ft (1–1.5 m) high.

HABITAT & ECOLOGY Riverbanks, ditches, and lakesides.

DISTRIBUTION Widespread across Europe, western Asia, and northwestern Africa; invasive in the US.

This perennial forms swathes of erect, sword-shaped leaves by standing or slow-moving water, often alongside cattails (*Typha* spp.). The flowers are bright yellow with brown filigree veins and markings; these are followed by fruiting capsules containing brown seeds. The plant's roots and leaves are poisonous.

CROCUS SATIVUS

Saffron crocus

SIZE 4 in (10 cm) high.

HABITAT & ECOLOGY Dry hillsides; widely naturalized in a range of habitats.

DISTRIBUTION Probably native to the eastern Mediterranean, but now throughout Eurasia and grown across the northern hemisphere.

This crocus is the source of the spice saffron, which is harvested from the vivid red styles and stigmas that identify this species. Saffron crocus has such a long history of domestication that it is unknown in the wild. It may descend from the similar species *C. cartwrightianus*, which is known as "wild saffron." Both species are fall-flowering.

UTRICULARIA VULGARIS
Greater bladderwort

SIZE To 16 in (40 cm) high; underwater stems to 3 ft 3 in (1 m) long.

HABITAT & ECOLOGY Ponds, wet ditches, peat bogs, and fens.

DISTRIBUTION Suitable habitats throughout Asia and Europe.

A rootless, free-floating plant that has distinctive yolk-yellow, snapdragon-like flowers carried on slender, erect purple stalks emerging from the dense mat of floating underwater stems. These stems bear finely divided leafy structures, and numerous bladderlike traps that capture small, underwater prey.

BUTTERWORTS AND BLADDERWORTS
LENTIBULARIACEAE

This family contains three distinct and unusual genera: the corkscrew plants (*Genlisea*), the butterworts (*Pinguicula*), and the bladderworts (*Utricularia*). These plants are all carnivorous, as are the pitcher plants (pp.90–91 and 152–155); they are unrelated to these plants but, like them, evolved in nutrient-poor environments, such as bogs, swamps, and acidic heaths. Early in the evolution of the butterworts and their relatives, nutrient-absorbing glands probably provided the plants with additional nutrients from trapped insects, giving them a selective advantage and fueling their competition with the surrounding species.

Butterworts are a genus of about 120 species in Europe, North America, northern Asia, and especially South and Central America. They produce overlapping rosettes of convex, fleshy leaves that glisten with dewy secretions, or mucilage, which are produced by minute glands. Small insects in search of water are attracted to the plant; they alight on the leaves, triggering the production of more mucilage, which ensnares them. Enzymes are released that break down the digestible parts of the insects; the fluids are then absorbed through minute holes, feeding the plant. They are a veritable living flypaper!

Bladderworts are a genus of nearly 300 species with a worldwide distribution (except for high mountains and deserts). They capture small organisms, such as water fleas, by means of bladderlike traps that grow in the soil or underwater.

UTRICULARIA INFLATA

Swollen bladderwort

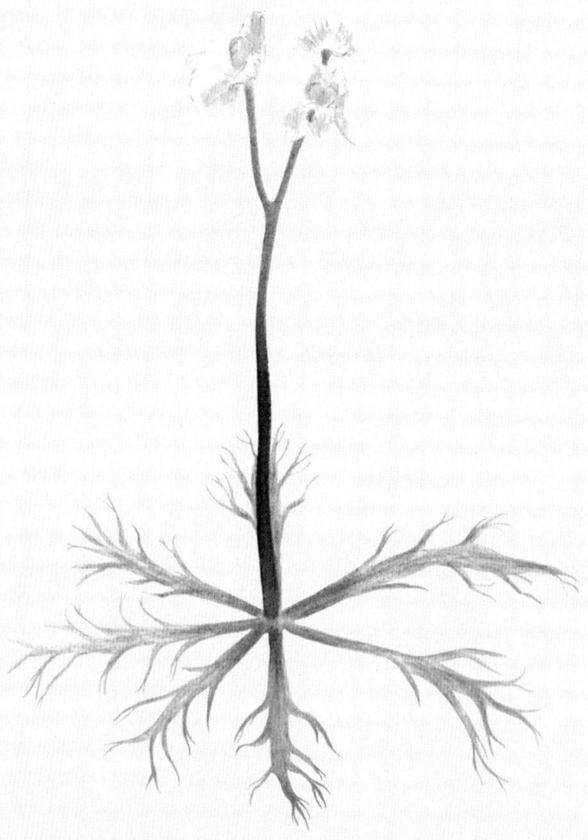

SIZE To 3 in (8 cm) high; underwater stems to 3 ft 3 in (1 m) long.

HABITAT & ECOLOGY Low-altitude lakes, ditches, and swamps at various depths.

DISTRIBUTION Native to the southeastern US.

Like the greater bladderwort, this rootless plant exists suspended in water and produces a tangle of underwater stems with bladderlike traps. When small prey touch the trigger hairs around the mouth of one of these, a trapdoor-like flap swings open and the bladder sucks the organism in, where it is trapped and digested. Swollen bladderwort produces a distinctive ring of inflated stalks for buoyancy.

PINGUICULA VULGARIS

Common butterwort

SIZE To 6 in (16 cm) high.

HABITAT & ECOLOGY Bogs, marshes, seeps, and mossy rocks near streams.

DISTRIBUTION Widespread across Europe, Russia, Canada, and the US.

This widespread carnivore produces little starry rosettes of apple-flesh-colored leaves that sit stalkless upon the ground; they are easily missed. In common with other butterworts, it depends on capturing insects for its supply of nitrogen. In the summer, erect stems emerge carrying purple (sometimes white) funnel-shaped flowers with a fringe of soft hairs inside.

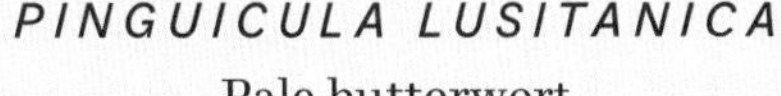

PINGUICULA LUSITANICA

Pale butterwort

SIZE Leaves to 1¼ in (3 cm) long; stems to 6 in (16 cm).

HABITAT & ECOLOGY Beds of *Sphagnum* moss in waterlogged bogs and fens; wet rocks and seasonally flooded seeps and marshes.

DISTRIBUTION The Atlantic seaboard from western Britain and Ireland, France, and Portugal, south to northwestern Africa.

This delightful miniature butterwort has small, folded, ground-hugging rosettes of leaves that are conspicuously curled along the edges. The flowers are smaller than a fingernail, white, flushed rose-pink, and carried on delicate stems. Easily propagated from seed, pale butterwort is popular as a potted plant among carnivorous-plant enthusiasts.

LILIUM CANADENSE

Canada lily

SIZE To 5 ft (1.5 m) high.

HABITAT & ECOLOGY Wet meadows and woodland fringe habitats.

DISTRIBUTION Eastern North America; cultivated elsewhere.

The Canada lily—also known as the wild yellow lily or meadow lily—is common in New England and the Appalachian Mountains, and widely grown elsewhere in the northern hemisphere. Its flowers are typically lily-shaped and hang downward; they are produced in early summer and range in color from yellow to reddish-orange, often with darker markings. The roots were reputedly gathered and eaten by some Indigenous peoples of North America.

LILIES
LILIACEAE

The lilies are an iconic monocot family (see pp.36–37) of 15 genera and more than 600 species. Most are herbaceous perennial geophytes, meaning they produce underground bulbs. As in many monocots, their actinomorphic (radially symmetrical) flowers are arranged in parts of three, and possess six tepals (petals and sepals, all similar), six stamens, and an ovary—which is superior, meaning that it is attached above the other flower parts—that develops into a fruit capsule. The leaves are typically linear, with parallel veins.

Because of their showy flowers and ease of cultivation, many lilies and related plants are grown in gardens or for the cut-flower trade. The best-known are the "true lilies" (genus *Lilium*), which are prominent in culture and literature, and occur across the northern hemisphere and into the subtropics. It's important to note that many plants referred to as lilies (water lilies, for example) do not belong to the same family. Many of the true lilies and their relatives are poisonous to people and animals.

The lily family was described in the eighteenth century and grew uncontrollably as taxonomists assigned ever more species to it. With the advent of DNA sequencing, it was revealed that many unrelated plant groups had been assigned to this family (it was what phylogeneticists call paraphyletic); they have since been redistributed. Older wildflower guides therefore refer to the Liliaceae in its traditional, broad sense, while in recent (scientifically accurate) texts, the family contains far fewer species, reflecting the plants' genetic relatedness.

FRITILLARIA MELEAGRIS

Snake's-head fritillary

SIZE To 16 in (40 cm) high.

HABITAT & ECOLOGY Wet meadows and floodplains.

DISTRIBUTION Europe to western Asia.

Also known as the chess flower—and numerous names besides—this is a familiar wildflower of floodplains in Northern Europe, where it often grows in great abundance. The nodding flowers are borne on slender stems in the spring, and usually have a checkered pattern in various shades of purple; sometimes the flowers are pure white. In some meadows the plant has been established for centuries but may have originated as a garden escape.

CARDIOCRINUM GIGANTEUM

Himalayan lily

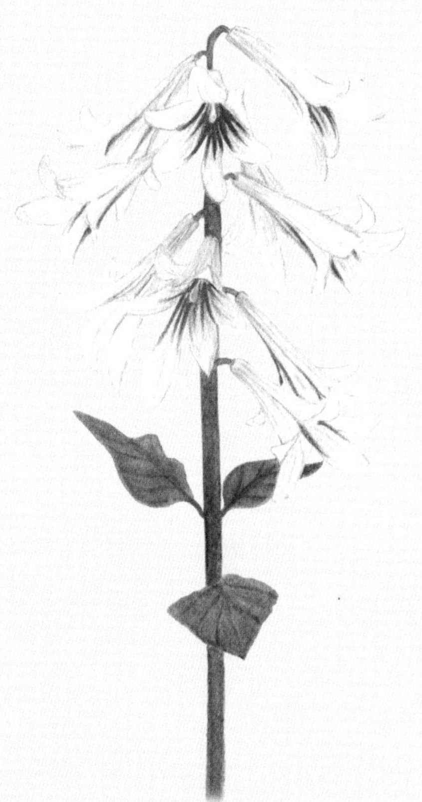

SIZE To 12 ft (3.5 m) high; flowers 8 in (20 cm) long.

HABITAT & ECOLOGY Woodland clearings.

DISTRIBUTION The Himalayas, China, and Myanmar.

This is the largest of all the lilies, and colossal in stature (hence the name *giganteum*); it is sometimes grown as a curiosity in woodland gardens. The large bulbs send forth robust stems that carry white, green-tinted, fragrant, trumpet-shaped flowers with purple markings. It is monocarpic, meaning that it flowers only once, after which the main plant dies.

TRICYRTIS HIRTA

Japanese toad lily

SIZE To 24 in (60 cm) high.

HABITAT & ECOLOGY Shady forest cliffs and stream banks.

DISTRIBUTION Japan; widely planted elsewhere.

This is an unusual member of the lily family; its white flowers, which are produced in late summer and early fall, are splashed and spotted all over with purple—thought to resemble the markings of a toad, hence its common name. The flowers are pollinated by bumblebees, and have become popular in gardens across the northern hemisphere because of their unusual form.

CYPRIPEDIUM MONTANUM
Mountain lady's slipper, white lady's slipper

SIZE To 28 in (70 cm) high.

HABITAT & ECOLOGY Mountain woods.

DISTRIBUTION Northwestern US and western Canada.

This very beautiful orchid belongs to a genus known as the slipper orchids. In the species shown here, the sepals and petals are maroon-brown and the pouch is white. Similar species include *C. parviflorum* (also in North America), and *C. calceolus* (in Northern Europe), both of which produce yellow pouches. In some places these striking orchids are threatened by poaching, and must be protected by cages of wire mesh.

ORCHIDS
ORCHIDACEAE

The orchid family is the most diverse of all the flowering plants, and they have evolved the most elaborate pollination systems, as we saw on pages 70–71 and 76–77. This family has conquered every terrestrial habitat on Earth, except glaciers. There are about 30,000 species of orchid, potentially making up about 10 percent of all seed plants, and horticulturists have created many tens of thousands more exotic hybrid cultivars.

Characteristic traits include zygomorphic (bilaterally symmetrical) flowers, often with a highly modified lower petal called a labellum (see, for example, the bee orchids on pp.70–71), fused stamens and carpels, and pollen bundled into masses called pollinia. All species produce tiny, dustlike seeds that depend on symbiosis with fungi for their early development. Orchids are monocots (see pp.36–37), typically having linear leaves with parallel veins, and they lack woody structures. Terrestrial orchids, for example in north temperate regions, may be rhizomatous or form corms or tubers. Some sympodial orchids (those that produce a lead branch plus lateral branches)—especially epiphytes that cling to tree branches—produce pseudobulbs. These are typically swollen structures, derived from the thickening of the stem between the leaf nodes. These epiphytic orchids also produce long aerial roots that absorb moisture from the atmosphere.

EPIPOGIUM APHYLLUM

Ghost orchid

SIZE To 12 in (30 cm) high.

HABITAT & ECOLOGY Deciduous and coniferous woods, often in remote, mountainous areas.

DISTRIBUTION Europe and northern Asia, south to the Himalayas. A similar, pinkish species (*E. roseum*) occurs in Africa, Australia, and South, Southeast, and East Asia.

Not to be confused with the American ghost orchid (*Dendrophylax lindenii*), this species is a mycoheterotroph, meaning it lacks green leaves (see pp.92–93). It is famously erratic and unpredictable; in the UK it has been repeatedly declared extinct, only to reappear years or decades later, each time creating a national sensation.

ORCHIS SIMIA
Monkey orchid

SIZE To 12 in (30 cm) high.

HABITAT & ECOLOGY Grassland, open limestone woods, and mountain scrub. In many places (such as the UK), the plant is rare and protected.

DISTRIBUTION Europe, south to the Mediterranean Basin; Russia and Asia Minor; east to Iraq, Iran, and Turkmenistan.

This curious plant is celebrated for its flower's lower lip (labellum), which bizarrely resembles the outline of a little monkey. Several related species have striking labella that are said to resemble a man (*O. anthropophora*), a naked man (*O. italica*), a woman (*O. purpurea*), and a soldier (*O. militaris*).

RHIZANTHELLA GARDNERI
Underground orchid

SIZE Underground stems to 24 in (60 cm) long.

HABITAT & ECOLOGY Bush and scrub. Native fossorial (underground-dwelling) marsupial mammals are likely dispersal agents for the seeds.

DISTRIBUTION Australia.

The species illustrated here belongs to a small genus of orchids, all of which flower underground. The plant was discovered by accident in the 1920s as a result of farming, and all subsequent discoveries were made in a similarly unexpected way. Like the ghost orchid (opposite), *Rhizanthella* is mycoheterotrophic (parasitic on fungi), and lacks functional leaves and chlorophyll.

KOPSIOPSIS STROBILACEA

California groundcone

SIZE To 8 in (20 cm) high.

HABITAT & ECOLOGY Parasitic on the roots of Pacific madrone (*Arbutus menziesii*) and manzanita (*Arctostaphylos* spp.) in dry, open, mixed conifer woods and scrub.

DISTRIBUTION Southern US and Mexico.

This species superficially resembles a pine cone in its form and stature, hence its common name. It has spoon-like, cupped, blackish-purple bracts between which the flowers protrude. The corolla (petal structure) is pinkish to maroon, with paler margins, and the yellow anthers are prominent. Underground, the plant possesses a thick, fleshy stem that is attached at the base to the roots of its host plant.

BROOMRAPES
OROBANCHACEAE

The broomrape family comprises about 90 genera and 1,600 species of annual and perennial herbs and shrubs, and they occur on every continent except for Antarctica. The name is derived from "turnip of broom," a reference to the plant's swollen stem base, which attaches to the roots of its host (a host that is typically broom in the species that was first documented). Broomrapes, toothworts, and their relatives in this family are all parasitic plants. Also in the family are the desert hyacinths (*Cistanche*), a genus used in herbal medicine that we will examine on pages 242–243, and distantly related to yellow rattle, the ecosystem engineer discussed on pages 56–57. There are hundreds of species of broomrape, and they are most diverse across the Mediterranean Basin and West Asia.

Each species of broomrape has a preferred range of host plants, and some grow exclusively on a single species. Broomrapes produce many thousands of dustlike seeds, which are dispersed on the wind to increase the likelihood that some will fall within reach of the roots of a suitable host plant. Some broomrapes have shifted from their natural host to cultivated crops, upon which they can inflict significant damage. Others are rare or poorly known to science; indeed, new species of broomrape are described every year.

Broomrapes are renowned for being taxonomically challenging. Plants that seem distinctive in the field can become brown and featureless when pressed to make herbarium specimens, rendering them almost unrecognizable.

OROBANCHE RAPUM-GENISTAE

Greater broomrape

SIZE To 35 in (90 cm) high.

HABITAT & ECOLOGY Parasitic on broom, gorse, and other shrubby legumes in rough grassland and scrub.

DISTRIBUTION Widespread across northwestern Europe and the Mediterranean Basin.

Greater broomrape is a brownish, yellowish, or reddish perennial, often clumped beneath the branches of its host shrub. The stem is glandular-hairy, strongly swollen at the base, and usually a dull brownish, sometimes reddish or pinkish. The yellow stigmas have well-spaced lobes—a feature that distinguishes greater broomrape from its close relatives. The flowers are visited by bees.

LATHRAEA SQUAMARIA

Common toothwort

SIZE To 8 in (20 cm) high.

HABITAT & ECOLOGY Deciduous woods.

DISTRIBUTION Throughout Europe to northern Iran and the Himalayas.

The toothworts are a small genus of parasitic plants native to temperate Europe and Asia, and close relatives of the broomrapes. They were formerly placed in a different family (the Scrophulariaceae), but DNA sequence analysis revealed them to be allied with the broomrapes. The species shown here is locally frequent in Northern European woods; a carpet-forming relative with purple flowers (*L. clandestina*) is also planted as a curiosity in gardens, under willow trees.

AEGINETIA INDICA

Indian broomrape

SIZE To 10 in (25 cm) high.

HABITAT & ECOLOGY Moist deciduous and semievergreen forests of tropical/subtropical areas.

DISTRIBUTION Widespread across tropical and subtropical Asia, west to the Himalayas.

Also known as the Indian pipe or the forest ghost flower, this curious plant sends up slender, leafless stems in clumps. Each carries a distinctive, nodding flower, the corolla (petal structure) typically pink or purple, half enclosed by a pale, leafy bract often streaked maroon or blackish-purple. The plant is a root parasite of various tropical grasses, such as sugarcane, and is used in traditional herbal medicine, rituals, and festivals.

SARRACENIA PURPUREA

Purple pitcher plant, northern pitcher plant

SIZE Pitchers to 8 in (20 cm) high.

HABITAT & ECOLOGY Swamps and marshes, especially in *Sphagnum* moss.

DISTRIBUTION Eastern Canada and US; locally naturalized in heather and peat bogs in Northern Europe.

The purple pitcher plant produces squat, red-veined pitchers that recline on the ground in rings. These pitchers quickly fill with rainwater and contain bacteria that help break down insect prey. In the spring, curious purple flowers are borne on long slender stalks. This is the most cold-hardy and widespread of the North American pitcher plants.

NORTH AMERICAN PITCHER PLANTS

SARRACENIACEAE

"Pitcher plant" is the name given to several unrelated groups of plants that evolved pitfall traps (another example of convergent evolution; see pp.54–55). Those in the family Sarraceniaceae are unrelated to the tropical pitcher plants (*Nepenthes*) we examined on pages 90–91. However, like them, these pitcher plants lure insects with bright colors and sugary nectar; the insects tumble into a leafy vessel, break down in a pool of digestive fluid, and release nutrients, which are absorbed by the plant. Some North American pitcher plants contain bacteria in their pitcher fluids to help break down their insect prey; downward-pointing hairs are also employed that act as a chute, guiding insects down into the pitcher.

In common with the other carnivorous plants we have seen, North American pitcher plants occur in nutrient-poor, acidic conditions, such as pine-forest swamps and *Sphagnum* bogs. The insects they catch are a nitrogen supplement in an environment where this nutrient is scarce. Unlike the tropical *Nepenthes* pitcher plants, the traps of which are suspended from a vine, the North American pitcher plants' traps spring from a rhizome, and die back during the winter.

North American pitcher plants are popular houseplants, being easy to grow with plenty of sunlight and rainwater, if kept wet in the summer and slightly damp in the winter. Some (*Sarracenia purpurea* and *Darlingtonia californica* in particular) are quite cold-hardy in northern temperate regions, if given a little protection from the hardest winter frosts.

SARRACENIA FLAVA

Trumpet pitcher, yellow pitcher plant

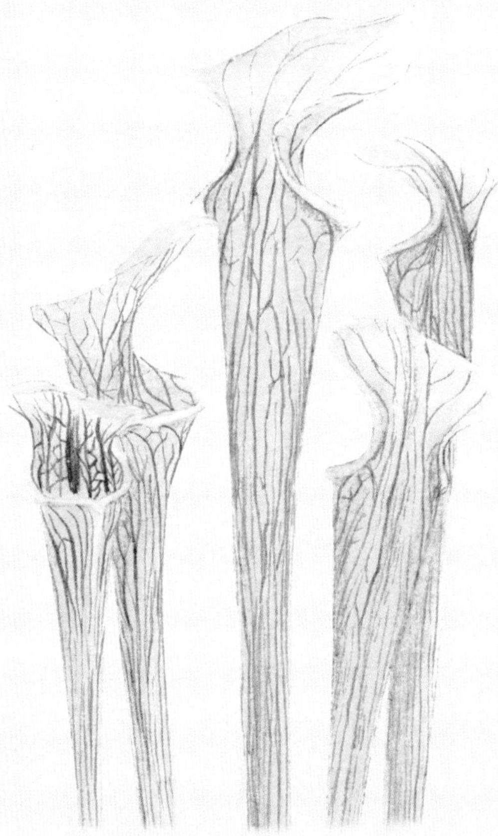

SIZE To 35 in (90 cm) high.

HABITAT & ECOLOGY Pine-forest swamps.

DISTRIBUTION Southeastern US.

This species produces a paralyzing narcotic in its nectar, which may intoxicate its insect prey, leading them to lose their footing on the slippery rim. After falling into the pitchers, the drowsy insects are barricaded in by a series of downward-pointing hairs that prevent them from escaping. The plant produces dense stands of pitchers from spreading underground rhizomes, and has umbrellalike yellow flowers in late spring.

SARRACENIA PSITTACINA

Parrot pitcher plant

SIZE Pitchers about 6 in (15 cm) long.

HABITAT & ECOLOGY Pool margins in pine-forest swamps.

DISTRIBUTION Southeastern US.

The pitchers of this species have a small, tunnellike entrance concealed under an inflated hood. Insects that enter cannot find an escape route—a mechanism known as a lobster-pot trap, and particularly effective at catching ground-dwelling insects. Inside, insects are probably disorientated by sun shining through translucent spots on the opposite side of the pitcher, and these false exits lead them farther in. Eventually they crawl into the narrow tube at the base and die, exhausted, in a pool of digestive juices.

DARLINGTONIA CALIFORNICA

Cobra lily

SIZE To about 12 in (30 cm) high.

HABITAT & ECOLOGY Wet rocks, slopes, and cold-water seeps.

DISTRIBUTION West Coast US (northern California and Oregon).

The name "cobra lily" derives from the plant's resemblance to a rearing cobra, with a protruding leafy structure that resembles a forked tongue. The pitchers secrete digestive enzymes to break down insect prey and release nutrients that are then absorbed by the plant. In common with the parrot pitcher plant, the cobra lily has light-conducting translucent spots that may disorientate trapped insects, or perhaps play a role in attracting prey.

ATROPA BELLADONNA
Deadly nightshade

SIZE 5 ft (1.5 m) high.

HABITAT & ECOLOGY Woodland fringe habitats on chalk soils; sometimes in gardens or waste places in warmer regions.

DISTRIBUTION Europe, east to Iran; widely planted elsewhere.

This plant has a long and rich history of use as a medicine, cosmetic, and poison. It is a source of atropine, and women are reputed to have used eye drops derived from the plant to dilate their pupils and make their appearance more seductive. Commonly mistaken for woody nightshade (which has red berries), deadly nightshade is easily identified by its liver-colored, bell-shaped flowers and glossy black berries framed by a five-parted calyx.

NIGHTSHADES
SOLANACEAE

Nightshades and their relatives belong to a diverse family that includes agriculturally important culinary foods, such as tomatoes, eggplants, potatoes (all *Solanum*), and peppers (*Capsicum*), as well as tobacco (*Nicotiana tabacum*). The family also includes medicinal plants and spices, and is replete with poisonous species too—deadly nightshade being a well-known example. Many species are rich in compounds called tropane alkaloids, including atropine, scopolamine, and hyoscyamine; these are particularly potent in mandrake (pp.250–252), and nicotine is, of course, derived from tobacco.

There are close to 3,000 species of nightshade and their relatives—half of which belong to the genus *Solanum*. They are found on all continents except Antarctica, and they are especially prevalent in Central and South America. Some species, among them thornapple (*Datura stramonium*), have become cosmopolitan ruderal weeds (occurring on wasteland). Most members of the family have co-sexual (containing both male and female parts), insect-pollinated flowers, sometimes with the anthers touching, in a prominent cone or ring.

Besides the culinary importance or toxicity of many species, some have become economically important and widespread ornamentals—such as petunias, which are popular bedding plants. Meanwhile, South American cultivars of *Brugmansia* (known as angel's trumpets) are popular tender conservatory shrubs, grown for their large, pendulous, fragrant, trumpet-shaped flowers.

HYOSCYAMUS NIGER

Henbane

SIZE 5 ft (1.5 m) high.

HABITAT & ECOLOGY Disturbed alkaline habitats and wasteland near the sea.

DISTRIBUTION Native to temperate Europe; widely naturalized elsewhere.

Like its relatives deadly nightshade and mandrake, henbane has long been used in potions and poisons, and for its psychoactive properties (ingesting it can lead to visual hallucinations). The species shown here is common in Northern Europe; the similar white henbane (*H. albus*) is frequent in the Mediterranean, and many similar yellow- and purple-flowered species occur in arid regions of West Asia.

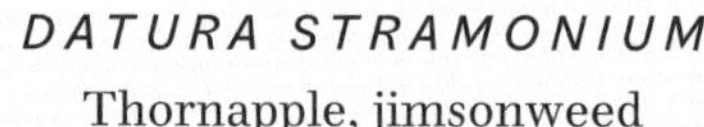

DATURA STRAMONIUM

Thornapple, jimsonweed

SIZE 5 ft (1.5 m) high.

HABITAT & ECOLOGY Disturbed wasteland.

DISTRIBUTION Probably originated in Central America; now naturalized worldwide.

This extremely poisonous plant, like henbane, has psychoactive effects that can lead to profound and long-lasting disorientation, and has a long documented history of use, despite its potency. It is a fast-growing annual with irregularly lobed leaves and large white to mauve trumpet-shaped flowers. The fruit is spiny and splits when ripe to release copious brown seeds.

PHYSALIS CRASSIFOLIA

Yellow nightshade ground cherry, thick-leaf ground cherry

SIZE Stems to 32 in (80 cm) long.

HABITAT & ECOLOGY Rocky mountain deserts.

DISTRIBUTION Southwestern US and northern Mexico.

Yellow nightshade ground cherry belongs to the genus *Physalis*, characterized by plants with a large, papery husk derived from the calyx, which partly or fully encloses the fruit; in some species (cape gooseberries and tomatillos, for example), this fruit is edible. In the species shown here, the flowers are yellow, and are followed by an inflated, lantern-like structure that points to the ground.

THISMIA SITIMERIAMIAE

SIZE ¾in (2 cm) high

HABITAT & ECOLOGY Tropical rainforest floors.

DISTRIBUTION Peninsular Malaysia.

Scientists at Oxford University and in Malaysia described this species of fairy lantern in 2020. It had been discovered the previous year by a local rainforest explorer, Dome Nikong, who found it growing along a popular tourist track on Gunung Sarut, a mountain within the Hulu Nerus Forest Reserve in the state of Terengganu. The plant's unique and remarkable "miter" (the umbrellalike structure at the top of the plant), color, and surface texture make this one of the most eye-catching wildflowers to be described from Peninsular Malaysia in recent years.

FAIRY LANTERNS
THISMIACEAE

Plants and fungi coexist in all terrestrial ecosystems. But, as we saw on pages 92–93, some plants are parasitic on fungi—the mycoheterotrophs (also known as mycorrhizal cheaters). Fairy lanterns belong to a family of mycoheterotrophs that occur mainly in the tropical and subtropical forests of the Americas and Asia, and in a few places in temperate parts of the US, Japan, New Zealand, and Australia. The largest and most widespread genus in the family is *Thismia*, which contains 100 species, and new forms are found and described every year; indeed, most have become known to science only since about 2000. Their obscurity is linked to their furtive ecology: most fairy lanterns grow in remote tracts of forest and flower very sporadically and unpredictably, and in some cases the flowers remain hidden under leaf litter on the forest floor. Put simply, we rarely see them.

Fairy lanterns possess remarkable floral morphologies (forms), quite unlike those we have examined elsewhere in this book. They come in an assortment of shapes, sizes, and colors, including oranges, yellows, and even sea-blues and greens. The flower structure is made up of a tube called a hypanthium that has six lobes (tepals). The stamens hang down from within the hypanthium and can be examined only by dissecting the flowers. Most species appear to be pollinated by fungus gnats (see pp.78–79).

THISMIA RODWAYI

SIZE Less than ¾in (2 cm) high.

HABITAT & ECOLOGY Forest floors.

DISTRIBUTION Australia (Tasmania, Victoria, and New South Wales) and New Zealand.

Here is another small and obscure fairy lantern that illuminates the dark forest floor. As with most fairy lanterns, its biology and life cycle remain a mystery, and it has never been propagated. This species is characterized by its orange-red floral tube with six perianth lobes, the inner three curving forward and the outer three reflexed (curving backward); the flowers are borne on slender, colorless underground stems.

THISMIA NEPTUNIS

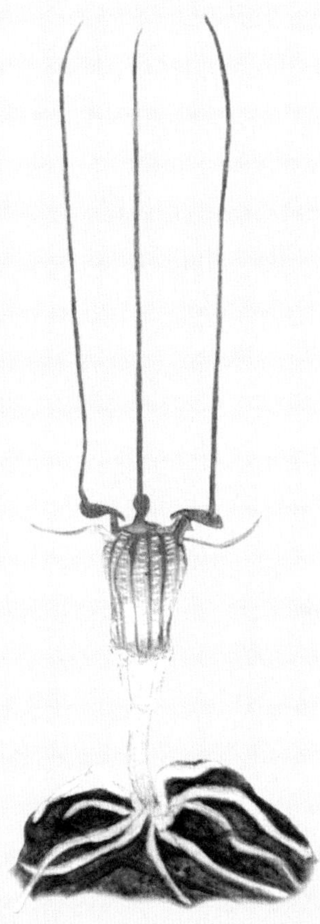

SIZE Less than ¾in (2 cm) high.

HABITAT & ECOLOGY Montane rainforest.

DISTRIBUTION Malaysian Borneo.

This fairy lantern is endemic to Malaysian Borneo. It was first documented officially by an Italian botanist in 1866, and described in 1878. However, the plant was lost to science and not observed again until 2017, when it was first photographed by a team of biologists from the Czech Republic, in the Gunung Matang massif in western Sarawak. The long, threadlike appendages probably attract pollinating insects, although their precise function remains unknown so far.

OXYGYNE SHINZATOI

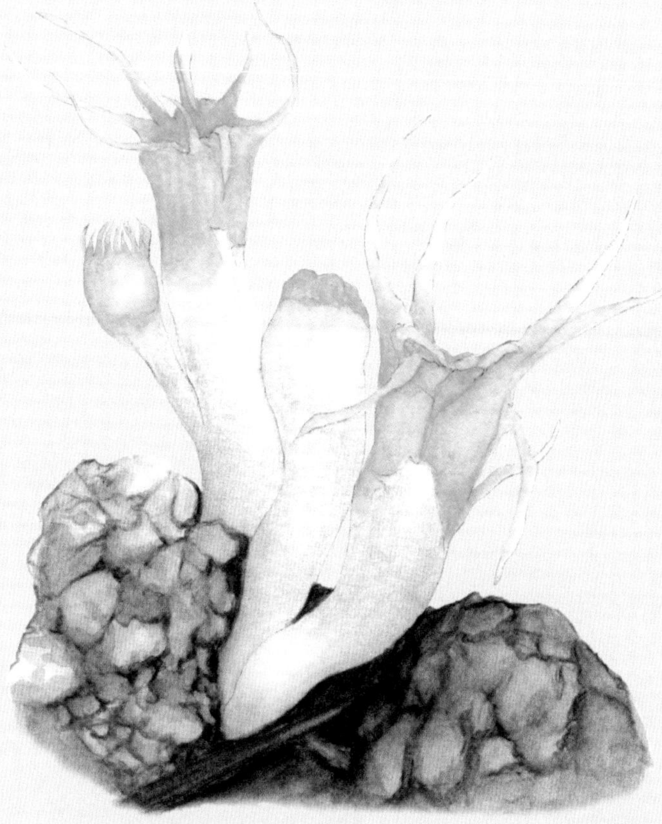

SIZE Less than ¾in (2 cm) high.

HABITAT & ECOLOGY Subtropical rainforest.

DISTRIBUTION Japan (the species shown), and west-central Africa.

Fairy lanterns belonging to the genus *Oxygyne* are exceptionally rare, and the known species have a highly disjunct distribution, occurring in just a few places in Japan and Africa (yet nowhere in between). Those in Africa are orange, while the plants in subtropical Japan are an unearthly luminous blue. Little is known about the ecology of these plants; they have never been propagated and are difficult to study in nature because of their erratic appearance.

Lychnis flos-cuculi

CHAPTER V

WALK

WHEREVER YOU ARE IN THE WORLD, you're never far from wildflowers. Plants have evolved extraordinary adaptations to survive in just about every environment imaginable, from mountaintops to deserts and shallow seas. Search for wildflowers in your nearest forest or grassland, and discover them closer to home—in your backyard or even on the roof!

Pines and related conifers are evergreen, so they block out sunlight all year round from the plants growing beneath them. They also deposit a thick carpet of needles on the forest floor. Many of the wildflowers that can survive in this unique type of habitat are highly specialized.

PINE FORESTS

Pine, spruce, and fir woods are examples of coniferous forests. Open, rocky pine forests, for example in the Mediterranean maquis, and mixed woodland on mountain slopes tend to support a richer, more varied vegetation than the dense coniferous forests that are planted in close stands for commercial timber production.

Great white trillium (*Trillium grandiflorum*) is an example of a wildflower that can survive in both broadleaf (deciduous) and coniferous woodland, or in mixed woodland. This North American wildflower occurs from Quebec to Georgia on wooded slopes, sometimes in vast swathes.

Wild ginger, western wild ginger, or long-tailed wild ginger (*Asarum caudatum*) is another North American woodland wildflower that grows in the moist understory of coniferous forests. It has heart-shaped leaves and distinctive three-lobed flowers, and is a relative of the birthworts (family Aristolochiaceae; see pp.32–33).

Among the most curious wildflowers of the North American coniferous woodlands is the ghost pipe (*Monotropa uniflora*; opposite). This plant is a mycoheterotroph (see pp.92–93) that lacks leaves and chlorophyll and forms strange, ghostly white stands of blossoms on the shady forest floor.

YELLOW BIRD'S-NEST (*MONOTROPA HYPOPITYS*)

This yellow mycoheterotroph is related to the ghost pipe, and appears sporadically in Northern European coastal pine forests; it is also a rare wildflower of beech woods on chalk. Look for it in areas of deep shade in early summer.

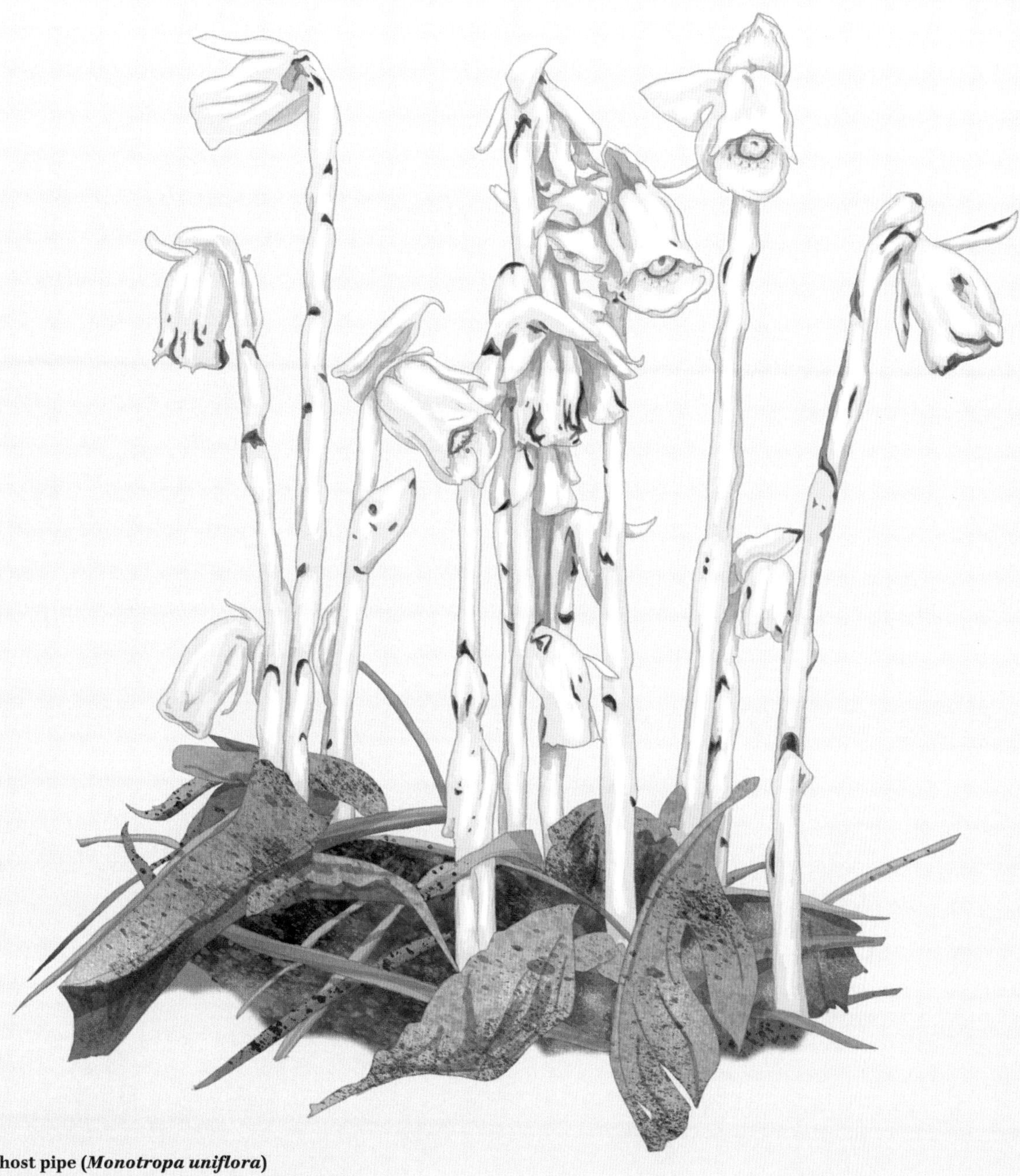

Ghost pipe (*Monotropa uniflora*)
This plant is a mycoheterotroph, meaning that it lacks functional leaves and chlorophyll, and is parasitic on a fungus. It therefore has no need of light and can grow deep in the shady forest.

Woodlands are a haven for wildflowers across the temperate world. In deciduous forests, plants appear in a succession of color, month after month.

WOODLAND WILDFLOWERS

Temperate forests are an important habitat for wildflowers across the northern hemisphere. Plants in this habitat are typically adapted to seasonal extremes of temperature—long, cold winters, brief springs, and warm summers, for example—and benefit from the shade of the tree canopy at the height of summer. Many produce flowers in the spring, taking advantage of the sunshine that comes through before the deciduous trees have developed their leaves.

Here is a selection of wildflowers that are commonly found in the woodlands of Northern Europe:

- **Bluebell (*Hyacinthoides non-scripta*)** This plant is an indicator of ancient woodland, where it dominates the floor with carpets of blue flowers, forming eponymous "bluebell woods." Northern European native plants have deep blue, nodding, fragrant flowers; the related Spanish bluebell (*H. hispanica*), which has more upright, paler blue flowers, is often grown in gardens.
- **Ivy (*Hedera helix*)** This is very familiar in gardens and uncultivated areas, on walls, fences, and trees, and even grown as a potted ornamental. Culturally significant for centuries in Western culture, it is also ecologically important, its thick growth providing habitat and its flowers fall nectar for insects.

- **Foxglove (*Digitalis purpurea*)** This familiar biennial woodland plant thrives after disturbance—large numbers sprout from dormant seeds after trees fall in storms—and for this reason it is perfectly suited to cultivation in beds as a garden plant. Although important medicinally, it is poisonous if eaten.
- **Wild garlic (*Allium ursinum*)** This common bulbous woodland plant forms vast swathes of foliage and white heads of flowers in late spring and early summer, especially on acid and clay soils. It is often found alongside bluebells in ancient woodland.

Wild garlic (*Allium ursinum*)
This plant grows in large numbers on the woodland floor and produces a strong, characteristic smell of garlic that can be detected from some distance away.

LIVING STONES

Pebble plants (*Lithops*) are masters of camouflage in the deserts of southern Africa. Hungry animals, such as tortoises, walk right over these succulent, water-rich plants, mistaking them for stones. Most of the plant remains underground, protected from the sun; the apex is translucent and acts as a window, letting in light for photosynthesis.

Deserts may seem like barren, lifeless wastelands, but nothing could be further from the truth after winter rainfall, when these habitats sing almost overnight with a million flowers.

FLOWERS OF THE DESERT

Wildflowers in the desert have evolved many adaptations to enable them to survive for months without rainfall. Many have succulent, water-storing tissues, protective waxes, or silvery hairs to reflect light and prevent water loss, and long roots to access water deep underground, long after the soil surface has baked dry.

Some desert wildflowers are annuals, for example the Arizona poppy (*Kallstroemia grandiflora*). These plants complete their life cycle rapidly during the few weeks of the year when conditions are favorable, then remain dormant in the form of seeds during the hottest, driest months. Geophytes, on the other hand, are perennials, meaning they grow back every year; these plants sit out the long summer deep underground in the form of dormant bulbs, corms, and tubers. The sego lily (*Calochortus nuttallii*) is an example of a desert geophyte.

The most enduring, steadfast desert survivors are those that grow all year round, requiring specialized adaptations to cope with extreme temperature fluctuations and prolonged drought. Many have small leaves, reducing the surface area for water loss; indeed, some (such as cacti) have lost their leaves altogether.

It can be tough at the top; plants growing in high-altitude environments must be resilient in the face of extreme conditions. To this end, they have evolved some extraordinary adaptations.

FLOWERS OF THE MOUNTAINS

Mountain habitats can be hostile. Sheer rock faces, crags, and cliffs are blasted by wind, baked dry in the summer, sluiced by rain in the winter, and, in some areas, frozen or covered in snow for months at a time. Growing seasons are short, and even then, temperature extremes and high levels of ultraviolet radiation are challenges to be faced. Yet plants have conquered this type of environment all over the world. In fact, plants from many different lineages grow at high altitude, including mosses, grasses, and so-called cushion plants from several families. Yareta or llareta (*Azorella compacta*) is a cushion plant belonging to the umbellifer family (Apiaceae; see pp.96–99) that grows in the Andes mountains in Peru, Bolivia, northern Chile, and western Argentina, at altitudes between about 10,000–17,000 ft (3,000–5,200 m). It produces tiny pink- or lavender-colored flowers that are pollinated by insects.

Trees form extensive mountain forests, and often have needlelike leaves with a waxy coating to protect against water loss (as in pines), thick bark, and flexible branches to cope with strong winds or heavy snow. They become stunted and sparse where the soil thins. Then, higher still, they disappear altogether, at a visible boundary known as the tree line. Above this point, true alpine plants dominate. The most enduring can be found as high as 20,000 ft (6,000 m)!

High mountains are refuges for rare endemic species. *Ramonda heldreichii* (opposite), for example, is found only on Mount Olympus in Greece. It is a relict species from the Tertiary period (about 66–2.6 million years ago); it was probably distributed more widely at one time, but as conditions changed, suitable habitats disappeared and it became confined to a single mountain.

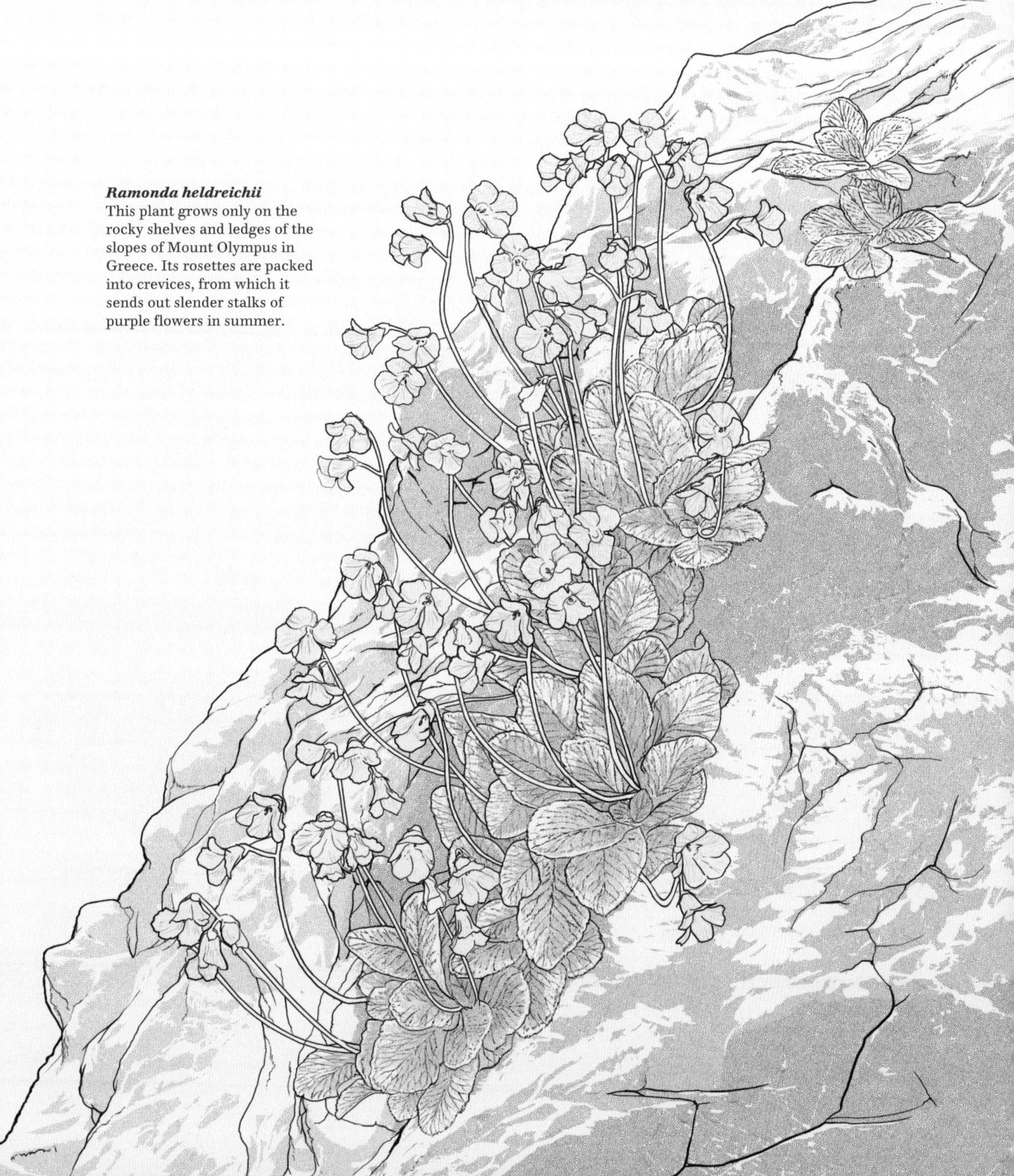

Ramonda heldreichii
This plant grows only on the rocky shelves and ledges of the slopes of Mount Olympus in Greece. Its rosettes are packed into crevices, from which it sends out slender stalks of purple flowers in summer.

Tropical rainforests are the lungs of our green planet and contain a greater diversity of wildflower species than any other habitat on Earth.

FLOWERS OF THE RAINFOREST

Tropical rainforests have a closed canopy, meaning little light penetrates the upper layer of foliage, and are dependent on constant rainfall or moist cloud. Typical vegetation includes epiphytes (see p.89), lianas (vines that travel into the canopy), and shade-tolerant plants that grow on the forest floor.

Here and opposite are some plants that grow together in the rainforests of Southeast Asia:

- **Javan cucumber (*Alsomitra macrocarpa*)** This rainforest liana produces flowers high in the tree canopy, followed by fruit called pepos that are the size of rugby balls. The suspended fruit release winged seeds that can travel over vast distances; the seeds possess the largest wings of all plants.
- **Giant taro (*Colocasia esculenta*)** This aroid has long been cultivated in Southeast Asia for its corm, which is eaten as a cooked vegetable. The leaves, said to resemble an elephant's ears, can be almost 6½ft (2m) across and are held on long stalks.
- ***Rafflesia arnoldii*** produces the largest flower on Earth, measuring 3¼ft (1m) across. It is a parasitic plant that lives within a vine (*Tetrastigma*; see right). There are about 40 species of *Rafflesia* across Southeast Asia, and many are threatened with extinction from habitat destruction.

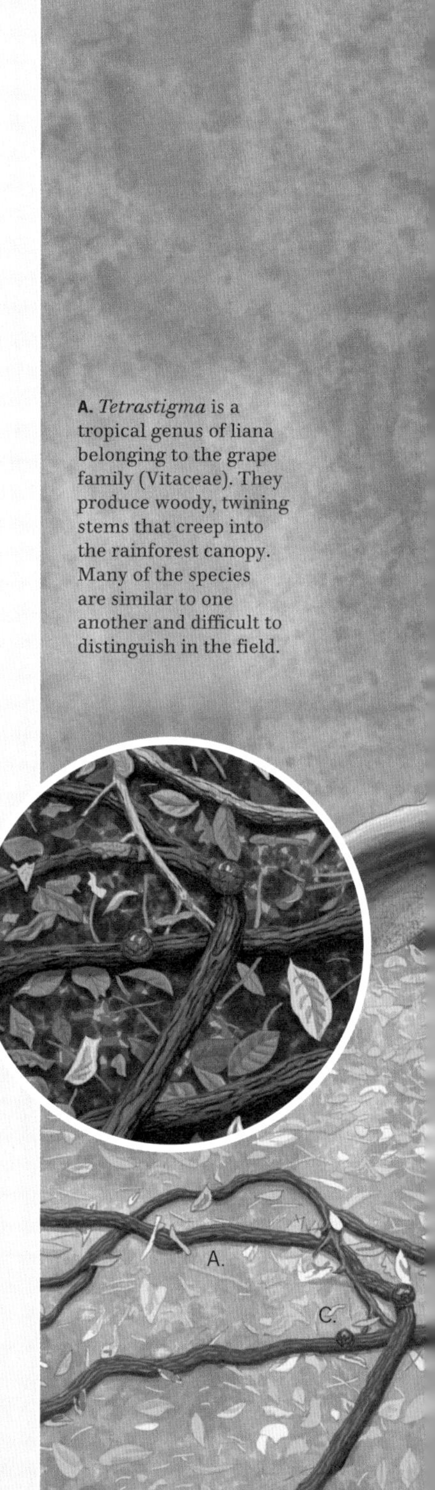

A. *Tetrastigma* is a tropical genus of liana belonging to the grape family (Vitaceae). They produce woody, twining stems that creep into the rainforest canopy. Many of the species are similar to one another and difficult to distinguish in the field.

B. *Dipterocarp* is a colossal tree belonging to a family (Dipterocarpaceae) of about 700 species in Southeast Asia. Dipterocarps have conspicuous buttress roots. Many are forest-emergent trees, meaning they grow above the canopy, reaching heights of up to 260 ft (80 m). They have historically been important for timber, and are threatened by logging.

C. *Rafflesia arnoldii* spends most of its life cycle within the tissues of the tropical vine *Tetrastigma* (see opposite), emerging only to flower and set seed. The buds reach the size of soccer balls and take months to develop.

Bathed in mist, rocks, cliffs, and tree branches at high elevation become carpeted thickly in moss. This wet, green wilderness creates the perfect conditions for some wildflowers to thrive.

MOSS FORESTS

As we saw on page 89, epiphytes are plants—such as bromeliads—that live perched in the canopy on the branches of trees. In any forest that receives fog, mist, or cloud (for example, those at high altitude), or steady rain throughout the year, the trees become draped in wet moss. This creates the perfect conditions for epiphytes, which cling to the mossy branches and receive water and nutrients from rain that trickles down the trees and is retained by the moss—so-called stem flow. In tropical rainforests, orchids often grow epiphytically on mossy branches. In the permanently wet forests (commonly referred to as temperate rainforests) of temperate regions, spore plants, such as ferns, are the most common form of epiphyte. Here are some common epiphytes that are found in the moss forest of temperate regions:

- **Filmy fern (*Hymenophyllum* spp.)** These delicate ferns are easily overlooked. They have very thin, translucent fronds—generally with tissue just one cell thick—and so are very vulnerable to desiccation. They survive only in areas that never dry out, such as on mossy branches in misty areas. There are many similar species of filmy fern worldwide.
- **Common polypody (*Polypodium vulgare*)** This fern creeps along horizontal rhizomes that burrow in moss and crevices in bark (as an epiphyte) or on rock and old walls (as a lithophyte). The undersides of the fronds bear orange spore clusters (sporangia). Similar species occur in the forests of North America and eastern Asia.
- **Hart's-tongue fern (*Asplenium scolopendrium*)** This fern produces glossy, leathery, undivided fronds. It is common in mossy forests, especially among boulders, but it occasionally grows on old walls and in gardens. It is widespread across the northern hemisphere.

Flowering forests
Moss forests in temperate regions are home to a diversity of mosses and ferns, and—in areas where sunlight infiltrates—seasonal wildflowers, such as bluebells and violets in the spring, and foxgloves and honeysuckle in the summer.

In midsummer the Mediterranean is parched and thirsty. But after rainfall in the winter and spring, the landscape blazes with wildflowers.

THE MEDITERRANEAN

The Mediterranean Basin has varied geology and topography united by its climate of hot, dry summers and mild, wet winters. The dominant form of vegetation is a spiny, shrub-dominated community of tough, drought-tolerant plants that have evolved adaptations in response to water stress. This vegetation, known by the French name maquis, includes a multitude of culinary herbs and is typically resinous and strongly aromatic. Bulbs include the fall-flowering sea squill (*Drimia maritima*) and, in the west of the region, the spring-flowering "brown bluebell" (*Dipcadi serotinum*). In gorges to the east—on Crete, for instance—dragon arums (*Dracunculus vulgaris*) are a spectacular feature. The table opposite illustrates some of the adaptations that Mediterranean plants have developed to protect them from the effects of drought, water loss, and sun damage during the region's long, hot summers.

Traditional agriculture in the Mediterranean is based on four crops that have been grown since antiquity: olive, carob, fig, and almond. These four ancient crops are a common feature of pastures and terraces across the region, and don't need intensive farming, so they create a valuable habitat for wildflowers. Traditionally farmed olive groves, in particular, are an important habitat for bulbs and perennials, and spring-flowering annuals.

ORANGES AND LEMONS

Although citrus crops originated in Asia, orange and lemon groves have also become symbolic of the Mediterranean landscape and culture. They too represent an important refuge for wildflowers.

MEDITERRANEAN PLANTS

	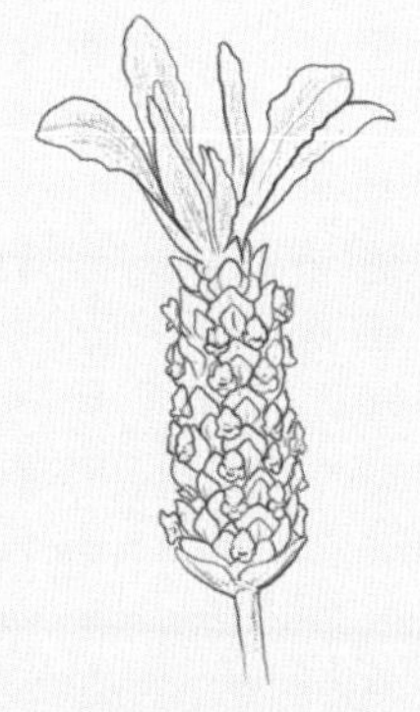 *LAVANDULA STOECHAS* FRENCH LAVENDER	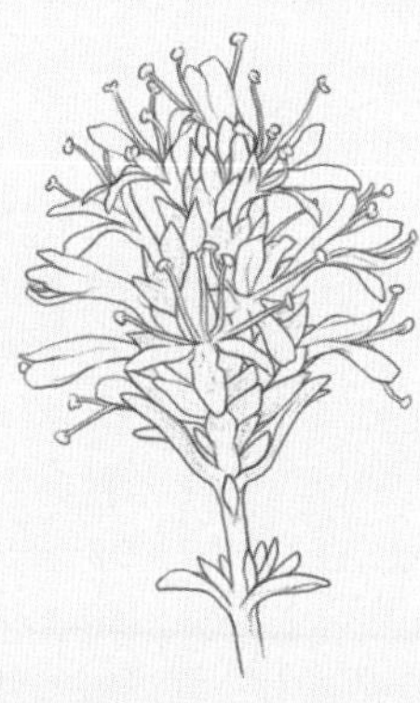 *THYMBRA CAPITATA* SPANISH OREGANO	 *STACHYS GERMANICA* DOWNY WOUNDWORT	 *QUERCUS COCCIFERA* KERMES OAK
LEAF CHARACTERISTICS	NARROW	SMALL	SILVERY COLOR	HARD SURFACE
ENVIRONMENTAL STRESSOR	Temperature Sun Wind	Temperature Sun Wind	Temperature Sun Wind	Temperature Sun Wind
ADAPTIVE TRAIT	Narrow, silvery, light-reflective leaves	Small, crowded leaves	Silvery, densely hairy (felted) leaves	Tough, leathery, waxy leaves
STRATEGY	Reflects light and reduces water loss	Reduces the surface area available for water loss by evaporation	Protects from sun damage and water loss during drought	Reduces palatability to herbivores and protects from sun damage

Archipelagos are living laboratories. The plants they contain have long been isolated from their mainland ancestors, and have undergone separate evolutionary processes, resulting in unique island floras.

ARCHIPELAGOS

In biology, "speciation" describes the evolution of new species. This involves the splitting and diverging of a single lineage (or species) into new, genetically independent ones. The form of speciation involving the diversification of an ancestral species into a multitude of new ones, each adapted to specific niches, is known as adaptive radiation. Owing to their long geological isolation, many archipelagos are hot spots for these evolutionary processes and, as a result, contain unique floras rich in endemics—species that are found nowhere else.

The Hawaiian silverswords we examined on page 108 are an example of an adaptive radiation. Tree houseleeks (*Aeonium*) are another, in the Canary Islands. There are many species of tree houseleek scattered across this archipelago. These are the result of dispersal both within and among the islands, and each species is adapted to a specific niche, such as sea cliffs, forests, and volcanic slopes. They produce flowers in cone-shaped clusters at the ends of the stems.

Dragon trees (*Dracaena*) are another genus of plants with highly restricted distributions, often island endemics. They are named for their red sap, which is thought to resemble dragons' blood. These trees are often relicts of very ancient ecosystems, now much reduced, and as such they are particularly vulnerable to environmental change. The Socotra dragon tree (*D. cinnabari*; opposite) is native to the Socotra archipelago in Yemen, in the Arabian Sea. It is thought to be a remnant of an ancient subtropical forest ecosystem that is now almost extinct following the extensive desertification of North Africa.

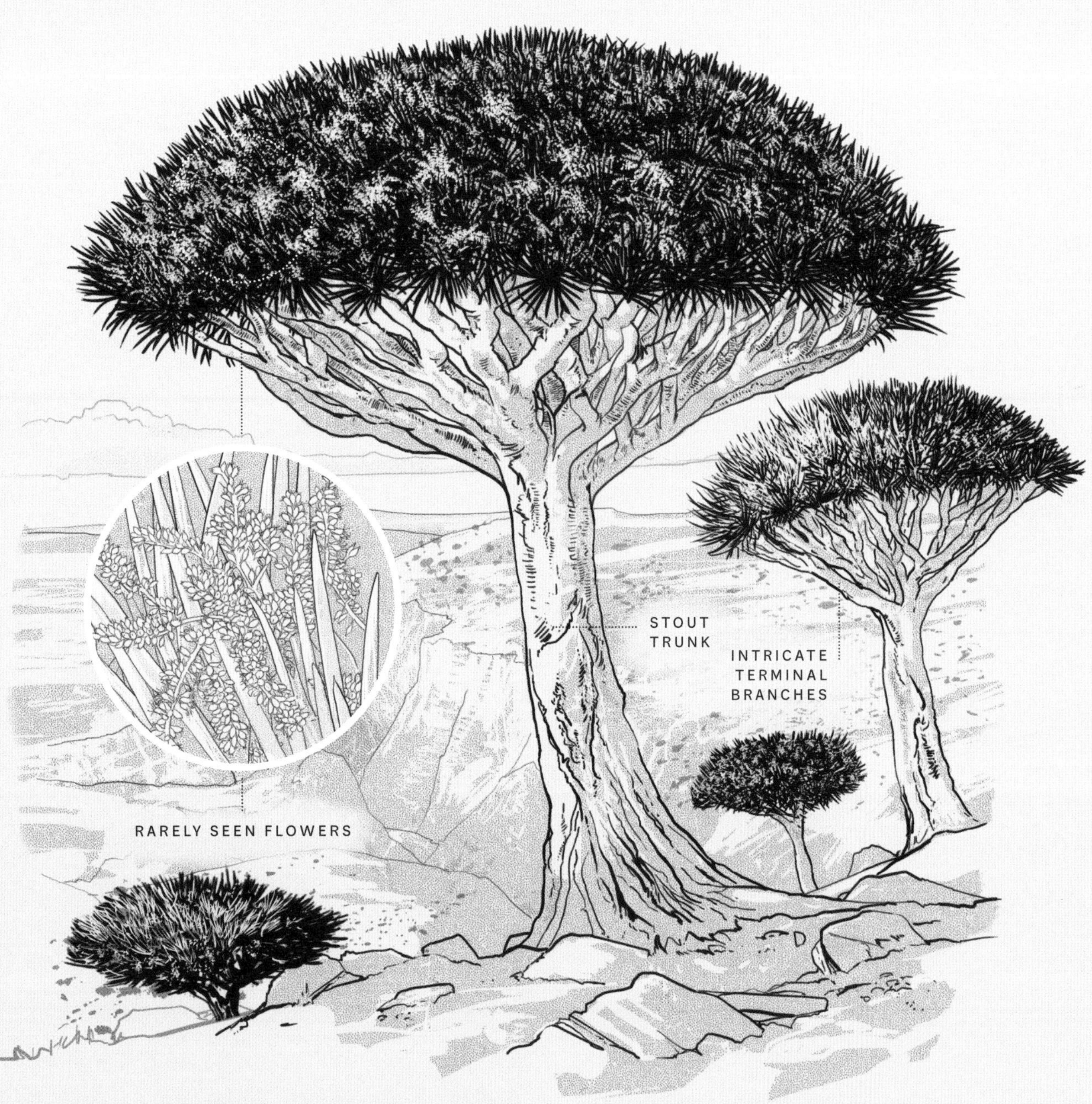

Dragon trees (*Dracaena*)
With restricted distributions, *Dracaena* species sometimes occur on just one island. The species shown here is the Socotra dragon tree (*D. cinnabari*), which grows only on the Socotra archipelago of Yemen, in the Arabian Sea.

Ragged robin (*Lychnis flos-cuculi*)
This wetland wildflower is widespread across Northern Europe and temperate Asia in areas where the ground is permanently or seasonally waterlogged, especially in wet meadows; it has also become naturalized in North America.

Wildflowers require a suite of adaptations for growing in permanently wet conditions. This gives rise to particularly distinctive and unusual floras in these habitats.

BOGS AND MARSHES

Bogs, marshes, and wetlands are either submerged or saturated with water for most or all of the year. These distinctive habitats are home to aquatic plants, known as hydrophytes, many of which are widespread across temperate ecosystems.

- **Western skunk cabbage (*Lysichiton americanus*)** is named for its distinctive fragrance, which is produced by the flowers and attracts beetles. Also known as the swamp lantern, it is a common spectacle in wooded wetlands and swamps and along streams in the Pacific Northwest. It is widely planted beside lakes and rivers elsewhere, and in the UK has become an invasive garden escapee.
- **Ragged robin (*Lychnis flos-cuculi*)** is a common wetland plant in suitable habitats across Northern Europe and temperate Asia. It is immediately recognizable owing to its distinctive dissected or "ragged" pink petals.
- **Common water-crowfoot (*Ranunculus aquatilis*)** is a relative of the buttercups. The floating mats it forms in suitable habitats around the world are an important breeding site for dragonflies, the larvae of which use the stems to climb out of the water.
- **Sundews (*Drosera*)** are a genus of carnivorous plants that thrive in acidic, waterlogged habitats, especially those in which *Sphagnum* moss is prevalent. Like the butterworts (pp.136–139), these plants lure insects with their glistening leaves; the insects are a valuable source of nitrogen for the plants.
- **Cotton-grasses (*Eriophorum*)**, also known as cotton-sedges, are a genus of sedges found across the Arctic, subarctic, and temperate regions of the northern hemisphere. They are especially abundant in Arctic tundra. Their conspicuous white, tufted seed heads are dispersed by wind.

Life on the shifting sands is far from stable. But many of the wildflowers that have adapted to exist in this challenging environment grow nowhere else.

SAND DUNES

Wildflowers that grow on sand dunes are well adapted to their environment; in fact, many occur only there. Existence in this habitat is tough, and many of the adaptations these plants possess are similar to those of desert plants (see pp.170–171). Common traits include resistance to high levels of seawater (which is toxic to most plants), such as glands to secrete excess salt; growth in response to sand burial; nitrogen fixation (in legumes); and drought-resistant characteristics, such as succulence, silvery hairs, or a waxy bloom.

Here are some of the more common or conspicuous wildflowers of European sand-dune systems:

- **Sea bindweed (*Calystegia soldanella*)** is a sprawling plant with trumpet-shaped pink-and-white flowers that point to the sky in summer; its fleshy leaves store water in dry conditions.
- **Sea holly (*Eryngium maritimum*)** has gray-blue foliage and fierce spines, protecting it from ultraviolet light and predators.
- **Sand crocus (*Romulea columnae*)** is a small bulb that grows on sand flats and has tiny, jewellike purple flowers. The bulbs remain dormant underground during the hottest, driest months.
- **Cistanche (*Cistanche phelypaea*)** is a relative of the desert hyacinths (see pp.242–243); it grows as a parasite on sand-dune and salt-marsh shrubs in the Mediterranean.
- **Sea daffodil (*Pancratium maritimum*)** is a common southern European and Mediterranean bulb that flowers in late summer. Its white flowers are a spectacle in large numbers. Like the sand crocus, its bulbs remain dormant in midsummer.

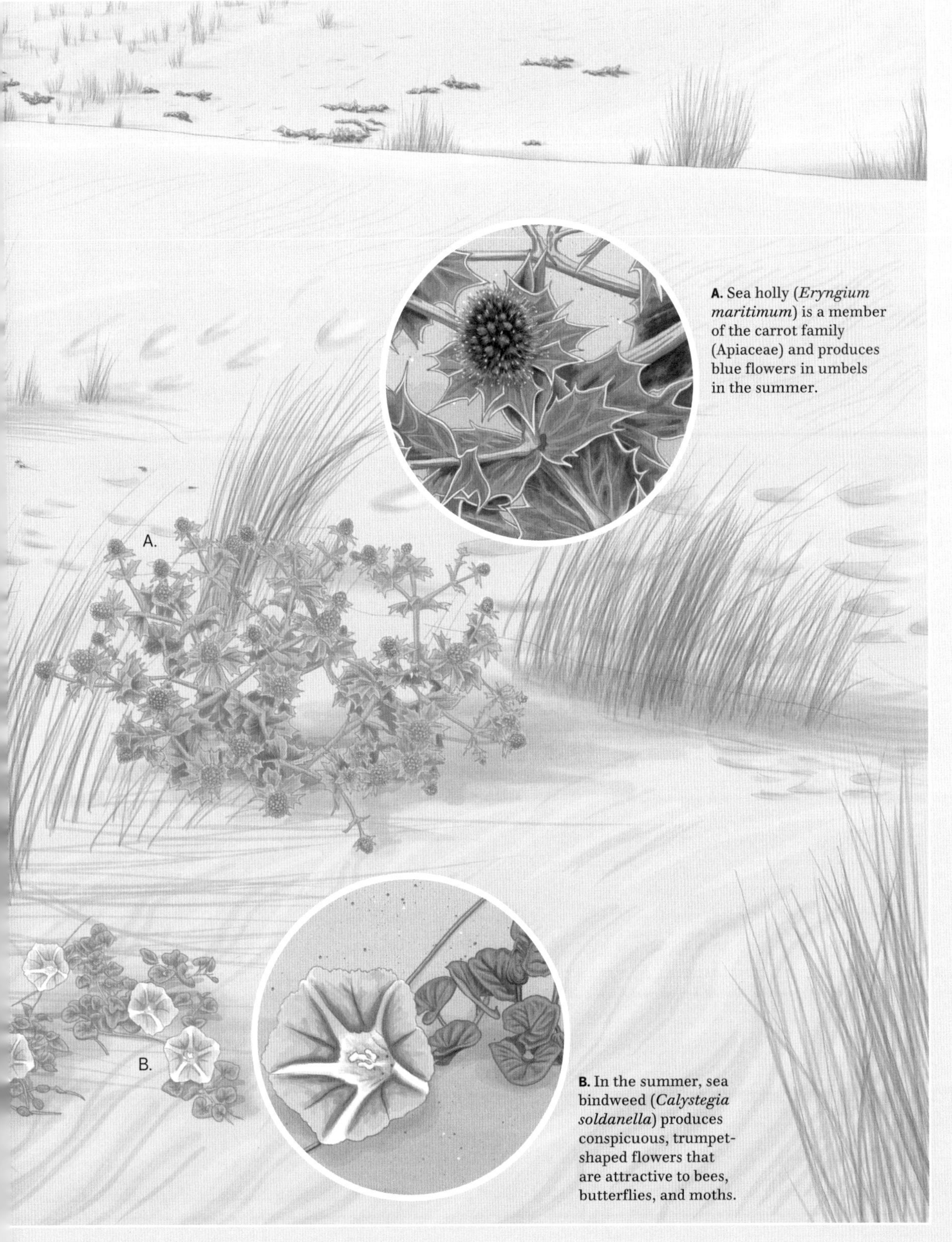

A. Sea holly (*Eryngium maritimum*) is a member of the carrot family (Apiaceae) and produces blue flowers in umbels in the summer.

B. In the summer, sea bindweed (*Calystegia soldanella*) produces conspicuous, trumpet-shaped flowers that are attractive to bees, butterflies, and moths.

Even a small piece of grassland can become home to an extraordinarily ***vivid*** *assortment of* ***wildflowers****, each one valuable to pollinating* ***insects*** *and other* ***wildlife****.*

Ancient and undisturbed grassland habitats are havens for all sorts of wildflowers; in fact, any area of unmown grass can contain fascinating plants.

GRASSLANDS

Seasonal grasslands across the temperate world hum with life in the summer. European chalk and limestone (calcareous) grasslands and meadows are rich in calcium and home to wildflowers including mint relatives, such as wild thyme and marjoram; legumes, such as bird's-foot trefoil and various vetches; and a plethora of orchids. Pasqueflower (*Pulsatilla vulgaris*) is a rarer species of calcareous turf. Lowland meadows, with their deeper, moister soils, play host to a different community of plants, including ox-eye daisy, meadowsweet, and great burnet. Drier pastures support knapweed, the adaptable ox-eye daisy, and lady's bedstraw. Similar species are found on roadsides (see pp.190–191).

Prairies are flat, temperate grasslands in North America. As with European grasslands, the vegetation they support is predominantly made up of grasses, interspersed with other wildflowers. These habitats can be subdivided into tallgrass prairies in the central North American plains; central midgrass prairies made up of bunchgrasses and sod-forming grasses; and shortgrass prairies, the warm, dry plains dominated by buffalo grass and grama grasses. Each supports a different collection of wildflowers. The North American prairies are home to a vast range of species, including wild lupin, purple coneflower, and butterfly weed.

You don't have to go to a tropical rainforest, desert, or mountain to find wildflowers. Many are likely to be growing in your local park or garden—or even lawn!

GARDENS AND LAWNS

Mowed lawns are challenging environments for wildflowers to thrive in, but a few grow very close to the ground, or produce fast-growing stalks that flower and set seed quickly, between mowings. Others send out runners or form loose carpets among the grass. Mowing infrequently can encourage wildflowers that, in turn, attract other wildlife. Here are some wildflowers that are native to Eurasia, but commonly found in lawns in temperate regions worldwide:

- **White clover (*Trifolium repens*)** A patch-forming perennial. Bees visit the white flowers and numerous insects feed on the leaves. As in all clovers, root nodules fix nitrogen, helping to fertilize the soil.
- **Ribwort plantain (*Plantago lanceolata*)** A rosette-forming plant with a fibrous root system, enabling it to regenerate and survive mowing. Identified by its long, narrowly ovate leaves and flowers that grow in spikes atop long stems.
- **Creeping buttercup (*Ranunculus repens*)** One of the most common buttercups found in lawns and meadows, this species prefers damp ground. It produces golden-yellow cup-shaped flowers in the spring.
- **Self-heal (*Prunella vulgaris*)** Also known as heal-all, woundwort, or heart-of-the-earth, this is one of the few plants that can flower prolifically even in grass that is mowed regularly. It has toothed leaves and small heads of purple flowers.

A LOCAL CELEBRITY

In the English village of Sandwich, Kent, the lizard orchid (*Himantoglossum hircinum*)—which is otherwise rare—grows in the golf-course rough and makes sporadic appearances in lawns. Local gardeners mow around it, recognizing its importance.

- **Cat's-ear (*Hypochaeris radicata*)** This rosette-forming plant has coarse-haired leaves and a long taproot, and produces yellow flower heads in the summer. Cat's-ear is common on verges and in short turf and lawns.
- **Yarrow (*Achillea millefolium*)** This plant is difficult to eradicate from lawns because of its creeping underground rhizomes. It has feathery leaves and produces clusters of white flowers in summer.

Lawn daisy (*Bellis perennis*)
Lawns are challenging environments for wildflowers. Low-growing perennials such as daisies, however, can form carpets that are resistant to being mowed or even walked on.

There are few habitats that remain completely untouched by human-induced change. Roadsides are a highly artificial habitat that may seem an unpromising place to look for wildflowers—but they can be a rich hunting ground for the botanist.

ROADSIDES

Many wildflowers thrive on roadsides; given the hundreds of thousands of miles of roads in many countries, this is a significant habitat. Low-growing plants, such as clovers, black medic, stonecrops (see p.203), and bird's-foot trefoil, are all common on Northern European roadsides, and spill out on to the asphalt. Bee orchids (see pp.70–71) are more common on chalk roadsides as summers become warmer in Northern Europe.

Although roadsides are important habitats, these plants are at risk from air pollution, especially excess nitrogen, which encourages nettles that displace other species. They are also easily damaged by mowing before they have bloomed and set seed. Mowing just twice a year, in the spring and late summer, is the best regimen for encouraging sustainable wildflower displays on roadsides.

There are a few wildflowers that are found almost exclusively on roadsides. They include the following:

- **Crested cow-wheat (*Melampyrum cristatum*)** A hemiparasite found mainly on grassy road verges in Cambridgeshire.
- **Spiked rampion (*Phyteuma spicatum*)** A woodland plant found in just a handful of sites, including wooded lane verges.
- **Sulphur clover (*Trifolium ochroleucon*)** A low-growing perennial that has suffered habitat loss and now grows mainly on verges.

A. Yarrow broomrape (*Phelipanche purpurea*) is a parasitic plant that grows in grassy habitats where yarrow is abundant, including road verges, especially in coastal areas.

B. One wildflower that occupies a similar niche in North America is the American basket flower (*Centaurea americana*), an annual native of the southern central United States and northeastern Mexico. It can form dense, tall colonies along roadsides.

Life in, on, or under water requires special adaptations for plants, just as it does for animals—whether for keeping afloat or remaining anchored in the mud.

RIVERS AND LAKES

Plants growing in ponds and lakes possess a suite of adaptations that enable them to grow in or by water. Many have spongy, air-filled tissues in their leaves and stems that enable buoyancy and oxygenation. Horizontal floating leaves (such as those of waterlilies) maximize surface area for photosynthesis. Some, such as hornwort, live permanently submerged beneath the water's surface; others are "amphibious," alternating between the surface and the pond-bed. The water soldier (*Stratiotes aloides*), for example, lives underwater for most of the year, but pushes its pineapple-top-like rosettes of leaves to the surface in the summer, when the flowers are produced.

Marginal wildflowers are those that live in the permanently wet mud found along the banks of standing water. Such plants often have creeping rhizomes and stands of upright, sword-shaped leaves that can cope with fluctuating water levels. Bulrushes and irises are common examples.

The sacred lotus (*Nelumbo nucifera*) floats unblemished above muddy river water, and is regarded as sacred by Hindus and Buddhists. It is an aquatic marginal of ponds, lakes, and slow-moving rivers across much of subtropical and tropical Asia, where its roots anchor in the mud and its leaves and flowers emerge above the water's surface on long stems. It has been introduced around the globe and is now widespread in warmer regions. The sacred lotus has "self-cleaning" leaves covered in a waxy, water-repellent (hydrophobic) surface upon which water forms spherical beads that roll off, carrying away dirt and impurities. This hydrophobic surface is of interest to materials scientists seeking to develop new commercial applications based on natural surfaces (see p.261).

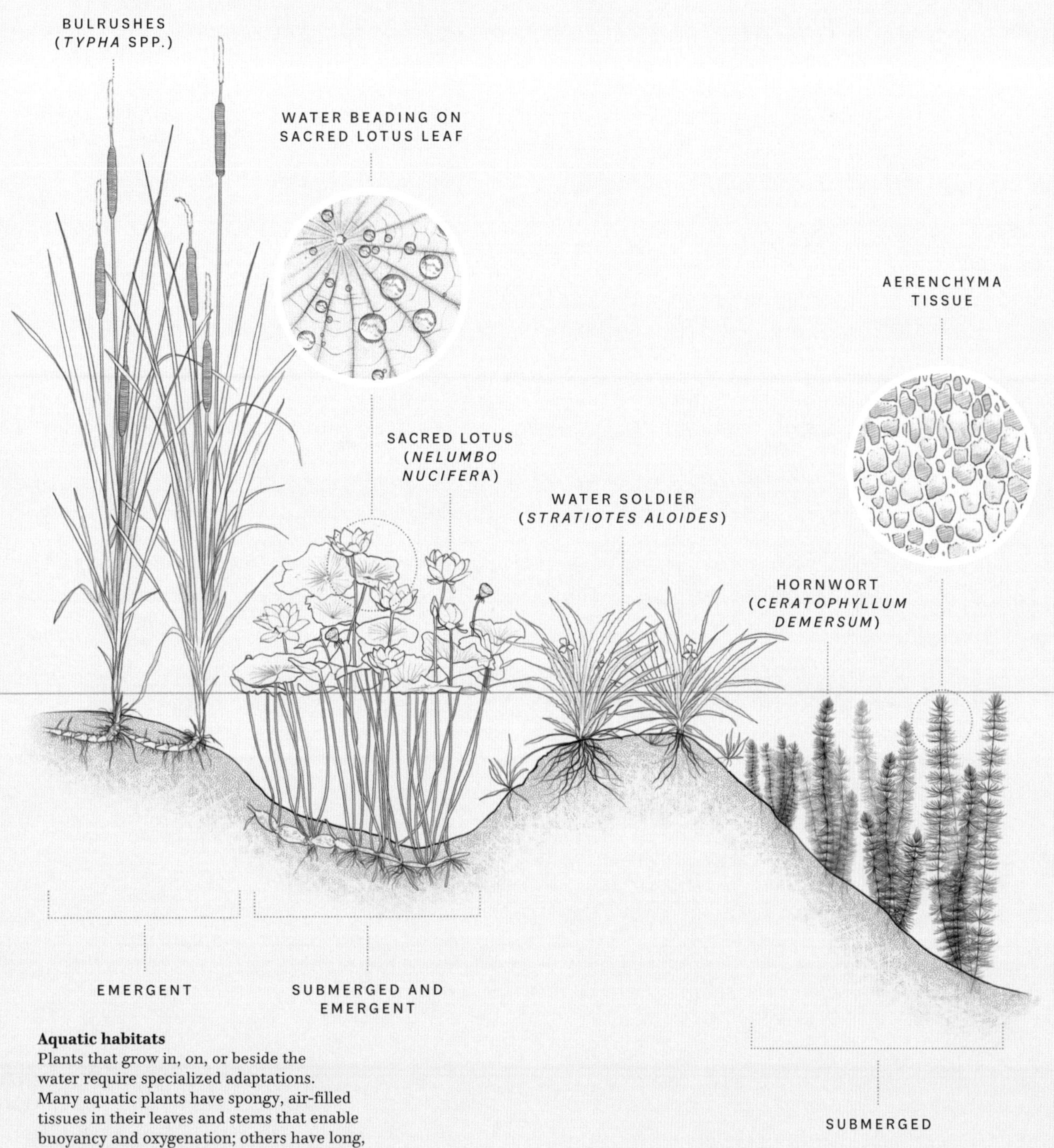

Aquatic habitats
Plants that grow in, on, or beside the water require specialized adaptations. Many aquatic plants have spongy, air-filled tissues in their leaves and stems that enable buoyancy and oxygenation; others have long, sword-shaped leaves that can withstand fluctuating water levels.

Life between the tides isn't easy. High salt levels and strong currents create a hostile set of conditions that most plants cannot survive. But some flowering plants have managed it.

SEAS AND OCEANS

Marine flowering plants are an important part of underwater ecosystems because they provide shelter and food for a variety of marine animals, and secure loose and unstable seabeds. Commonly called seagrasses or eelgrasses, these plants form what look like vast underwater lawns, sometimes called eelgrass beds. They produce ribbonlike leaves, spread by way of rhizomes, and have small, inconspicuous flowers that are pollinated via water currents. There are four families of eelgrass that appear similar at a glance: the Zosteraceae, Cymodoceaceae, Ruppiaceae, and Posidoniaceae. *Posidonia oceanica*, commonly known as Neptune grass, belongs to the family Posidoniaceae, and produces balls of fibrous material that wash up on to the beach. These are known as Neptune balls. Its life cycle is described on the opposite page.

Unlike land grasses (an unrelated family called the Poaceae; see pp.236–237), eelgrasses lack stomata, the pores used by most plants for gas exchange. Instead, they contain pockets of air in the veins along their leaves, and these pockets hold them afloat to optimize photosynthesis.

The tape-grasses (*Halophila*) are a genus of marine flowering plants that are widespread worldwide in warm seas, extending to temperate waters, including the Mediterranean. They are unrelated to eelgrasses, but are superficially similar in appearance. Tape-grasses are also important components of marine underwater ecosystems, especially in the tropics.

LIFE CYCLE OF NEPTUNE GRASS

Neptune grass (*Posidonia oceanica*)
This plant forms extensive beds in shallow waters of the Mediterranean, forming an important habitat for many marine animals.

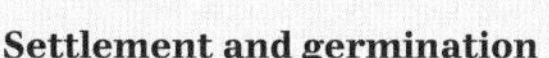

Settlement and germination
The released seed sinks to the seabed, where, under favorable conditions, it germinates and gives rise to a new Neptune grass plant.

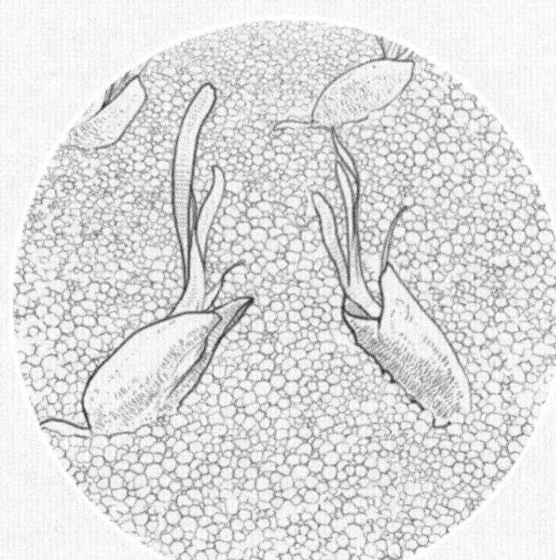

Flowering and fertilization
The flowers are inconspicuous and release pollen that is carried among plants via water currents, enabling cross-pollination and fertilization.

"NEPTUNE BALLS" PRODUCED FROM FIBERS

Fruit production
The small, fleshy fruits, known as "sea olives," are released into the current when mature.

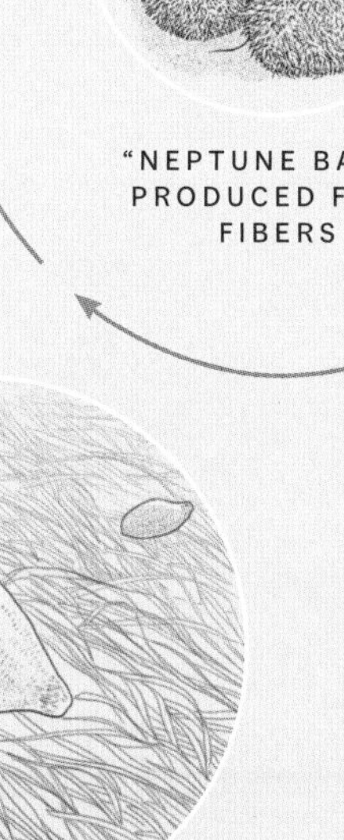

Fruit and seed dispersal
The fruit is buoyant and can travel long distances on the current. Eventually the outer layer (pericarp) rots to release the seed.

Some plants can subsist on water vapor in the air, rainwater run-off—and little else! These "air plants" truly live up to their name.

WILDFLOWERS IN THE AIR

Air plants belong to a group of plants called the bromeliads (the Bromeliaceae), a family that includes the pineapple. The air plants live high in the forest canopy, where they grow as epiphytes, typically perched high up on the branches of trees in the forests of North, Central, and South America. A few grow on damp, rocky cliffs, while some cling to roofs and even telephone wires in hot, humid climates. Air plants produce rosettes of leaves and tubular or funnel-shaped flowers that are often borne in double-ranked spikes with brightly colored bracts.

Most air plants are reliant on animals for cross-pollination. Plants in the genus *Tillandsia* typically produce tubular flowers, with protruding stamens and stigmas, which are pollinated by hummingbirds. Some possess brightly colored (pink, red, or yellow), odorless flowers that are highly attractive to a variety of birds that visit the forest canopy.

Miraculously, air plants lack roots. Rather than absorbing water and nutrients from the soil, they extract them directly from the air, hence their name. Dust and minerals in the atmosphere dissolve into rainwater and dew, along with minerals that wash off the bark to which the air plants cling, and these are absorbed by microscopic hairs (called trichomes) on the plants' leaves.

A. Spanish moss (*Tillandsia usneoides*) is a particularly popular air plant in botanic-garden hothouses. Hanging from tree branches in silver-gray, threadlike masses, it resembles mosses and lichens more than it does a true flowering plant.

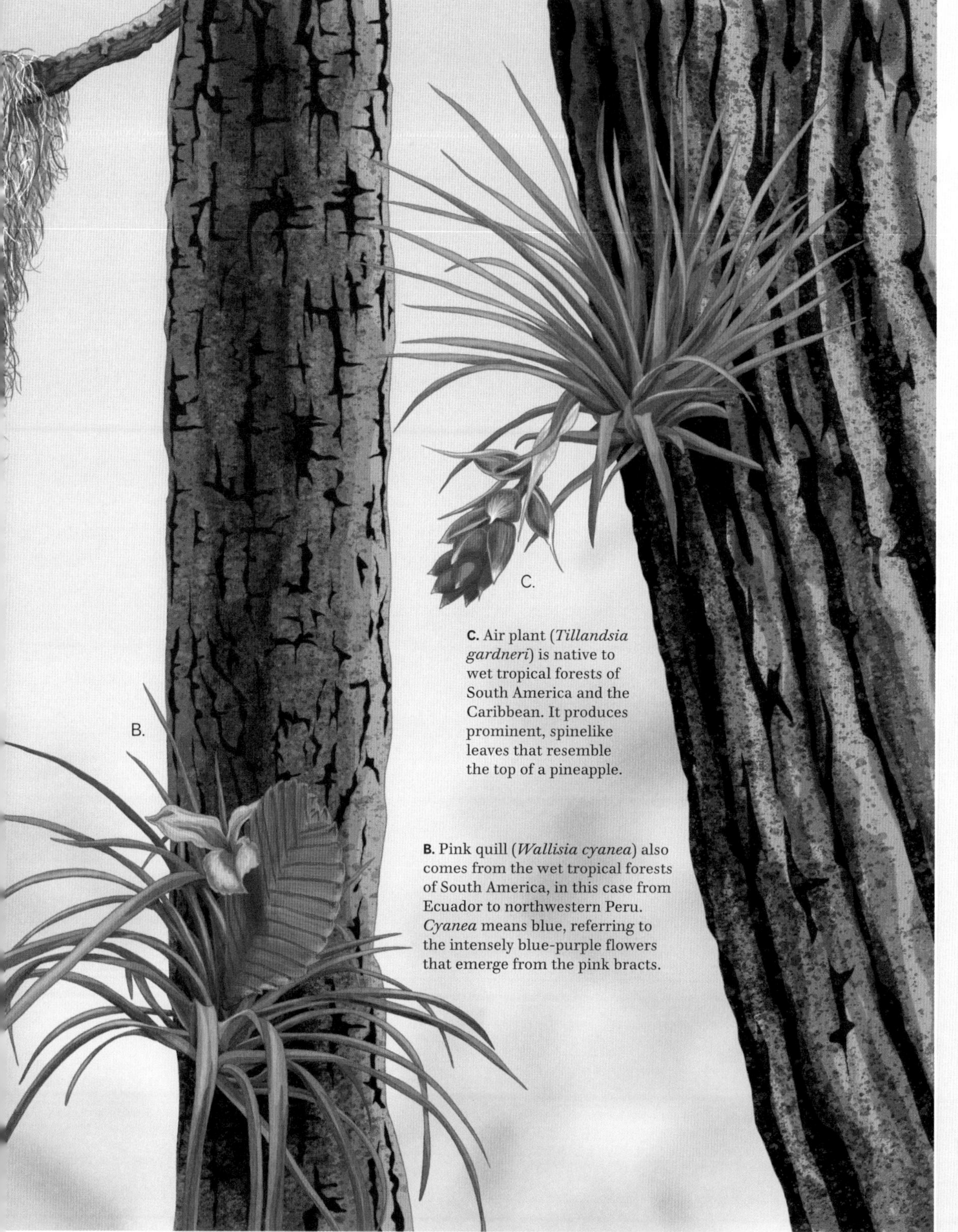

C. Air plant (*Tillandsia gardneri*) is native to wet tropical forests of South America and the Caribbean. It produces prominent, spinelike leaves that resemble the top of a pineapple.

B. Pink quill (*Wallisia cyanea*) also comes from the wet tropical forests of South America, in this case from Ecuador to northwestern Peru. *Cyanea* means blue, referring to the intensely blue-purple flowers that emerge from the pink bracts.

Fire is a destructive force. While many habitats cannot withstand fire, there are some plants that benefit from its effects; in fact, a few are utterly dependent on it.

WILDFLOWERS AFTER FIRE

Perhaps surprisingly, many plants and plant communities are well adapted to survive fire and its cycles of burning and regrowth, and some even require it to grow and disperse. Fire-tolerant plants are called pyrophytes. Habitats containing pyrophytes are often found in Mediterranean climates, for example in southern Europe, South Africa, and parts of the US and Australia.

Some plants, including many pines and cork oaks, resist low-intensity fire using such features as deep roots and thick bark. They are known as passive pyrophytes, because they can withstand fire but do not require it for their life cycles.

Some seeds are dependent on fire, either directly for germination, or indirectly because fire creates bare, nutrient-rich patches that they can colonize with minimal competition for resources. Shrubs may die back above ground after fire, but later sprout from deep rootstocks; some species of oak, cistus, and South African sugar bushes, such as the king protea (opposite), often bounce back quickly after fire, their new growth pushing through the dead, blackened branches.

Plants that require fire to reproduce often contain volatile, flammable oils that help fires establish and spread; these plants are sometimes known as active pyrophytes. Eucalyptus and some cistus species are notable examples.

WILDFIRE RENEWAL

Fire
Some plants—such as this king protea bush (*Protea cynaroides*), which grows in the Cape Floral Region of South Africa—require fire to complete their life cycles.

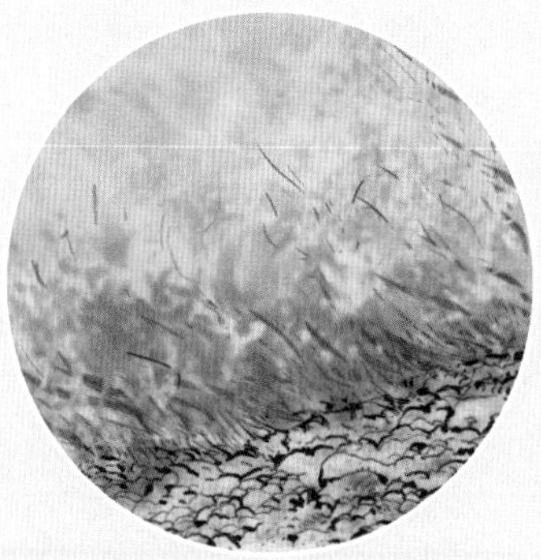

Cones store fertile seeds in the protea canopy seed bank

Flowering and seed production

Fire kills adult plants, triggers seed release and dispersal
Wildfires trigger the release of seeds from the long-lived cone-like structures in the protea canopy.

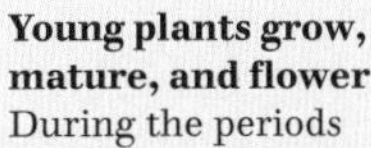

Young plants grow, mature, and flower
During the periods between fires, protea bushes develop and, when mature, flower every year. The blooms are followed by long-lived cone-like structures that contain the seeds.

Seedlings emerge several months after fire
Soon after the wildfires have passed, the protea seeds germinate and the seedlings develop quickly.

Plants tend to thrive where people don't. Crags, cliff edges, and precipices have remained untouched by human progress for millennia and are refuges for rare wildflowers.

LIFE ON THE EDGE

Cliffs and vertical rock faces are places where rare and unusual flora can thrive undisturbed. In fact, there are some plants that grow in this habitat and nowhere else; these plants are known as chasmophytes (the term "lithophyte" has a similar meaning, referring to plants that are adapted to growing out of rock, and the two are often used interchangeably).

Many chasmophytes have similar adaptations to mountain-dwelling plants and those dwelling in deserts and other arid habitats, because living on cliff edges leads to exposure to drought and high levels of ultraviolet light. Therefore, these plants possess waxy or hairy surfaces, and a compact or sometimes succulent form.

- **Sea thrift (*Armeria maritima*)** is a compact evergreen plant that produces domed clumps and sends up long stems carrying globes of pink flowers. It is found on sea cliffs across the northern hemisphere.
- **Rock samphire (*Crithmum maritimum*)** is a member of the umbellifer family (Apiaceae) and a distant relative of the carrots. As well as being well adapted to life on a cliff, it is also highly salt-tolerant; such plants are referred to as halophytes. It is found across Europe and western Asia.
- ***Aeonium tabuliforme*** is one of many species of tree houseleek that occur on the Canary Islands (see p.180). This particular species lacks stems and grows hunkered down in clifftop crevices. Its succulent leaves are adapted for water storage.

The eastern Mediterranean islands Crete and Cyprus harbor a rich chasmophyte flora because they contain many canyons and gorges that have remained protected as the vegetation changed around them. *Verbascum arcturus* is a rare Cretan endemic that grows only on vertical limestone faces that are almost entirely inaccessible to people.

Hold tight
The four plant species shown here are all well adapted to growing in the crevices of cliffs and rock faces.

Houseleeks *have long been grown on* ***rooftops****, and have become associated with certain* ***beliefs*** *and* ***folklore****, such as protecting a house from* ***lightning****.*

Plants were colonizing the roofs of buildings long before "green roofs" came into fashion. But they are sluiced by rain during storms and baked dry in the summer, so only the toughest wildflowers can prosper in this artificial habitat.

LIFE ON THE ROOF

The houseleeks (*Sempervivum*) are a genus of succulents that are well adapted to drought-prone, exposed habitats, such as those of a rooftop or old wall. Their scientific name means "always living," referring to their resilience. They are native to the mountaintops of Europe and Asia Minor, and their compact rosettes of succulent leaves are adapted to dry, stony environments; rooftops are similar to the mountain scree in which they thrive in nature. These plants form clumps, producing offsets, and each mature rosette sends up a robust spike of flowers. After blossoming, the main plant dies. One species (*S. arachnoideum*) produces cobweb-hairy rosettes, and the hairs shield the plant from exposure to sunlight and extreme temperature fluctuations.

The stonecrops (*Sedum*) are another genus of succulents that grow on old rooftops. They produce small, crowded leaves along creeping stems that eventually form mats or carpets. Sedum roofs are planted with these wildflowers because of their resilience to extremes of weather. Biting stonecrop, also known as gold moss and wall-pepper (*Sedum acre*), is commonly found growing spontaneously on bare sand, shingle, roadsides, walls, and sidewalks—as well as old roofs.

Arctic tundra is one of the most inhospitable habitats imaginable. And still, blasted by wind, frozen, and deprived of sunlight for months, some wildflowers are able to prosper there.

LIFE ON THE ICE

The Arctic conjures up thoughts of blank landscapes, glaciers, and polar bears. But, perhaps surprisingly, there are plants that can survive there. Wildflowers of the Arctic endure some of the harshest conditions of all plants. Many are small and grow in fjords and crevices fed by meltwater. Low-growing plant communities are able to withstand significant snowpack and strong winds.

- **Dwarf birch (*Betula nana*)** is a miniature tree of the Arctic tundra, with small leaves that turn orange-red and a compact, mat-forming habit that is well adapted to the inhospitable conditions of its natural habitat.
- **Compass plant (*Silene acaulis*)** is a ground-hugging, cushion-forming plant that grows on rocky outcrops and ridges. In the brief Arctic summer the green domes become covered in blossoms, forming pink splashes on the cliffs.
- **Mountain sorrel (*Oxyria digyna*)** is an alpine stalwart that is native to Arctic regions and the mountains of the northern hemisphere, and related to the more familiar sorrels and docks that grow at lower altitudes. A deep taproot anchors it firmly in unstable, scree-like habitats, and the plant produces congested red flower heads.
- **Polar campion (*Silene uralensis*)** is a perennial capable of withstanding extreme cold, and is found across Greenland, northern Canada, Alaska, East Asia, and Siberia. It has basal tufts of leaves and distinctive inflated, dark-striped calyces.

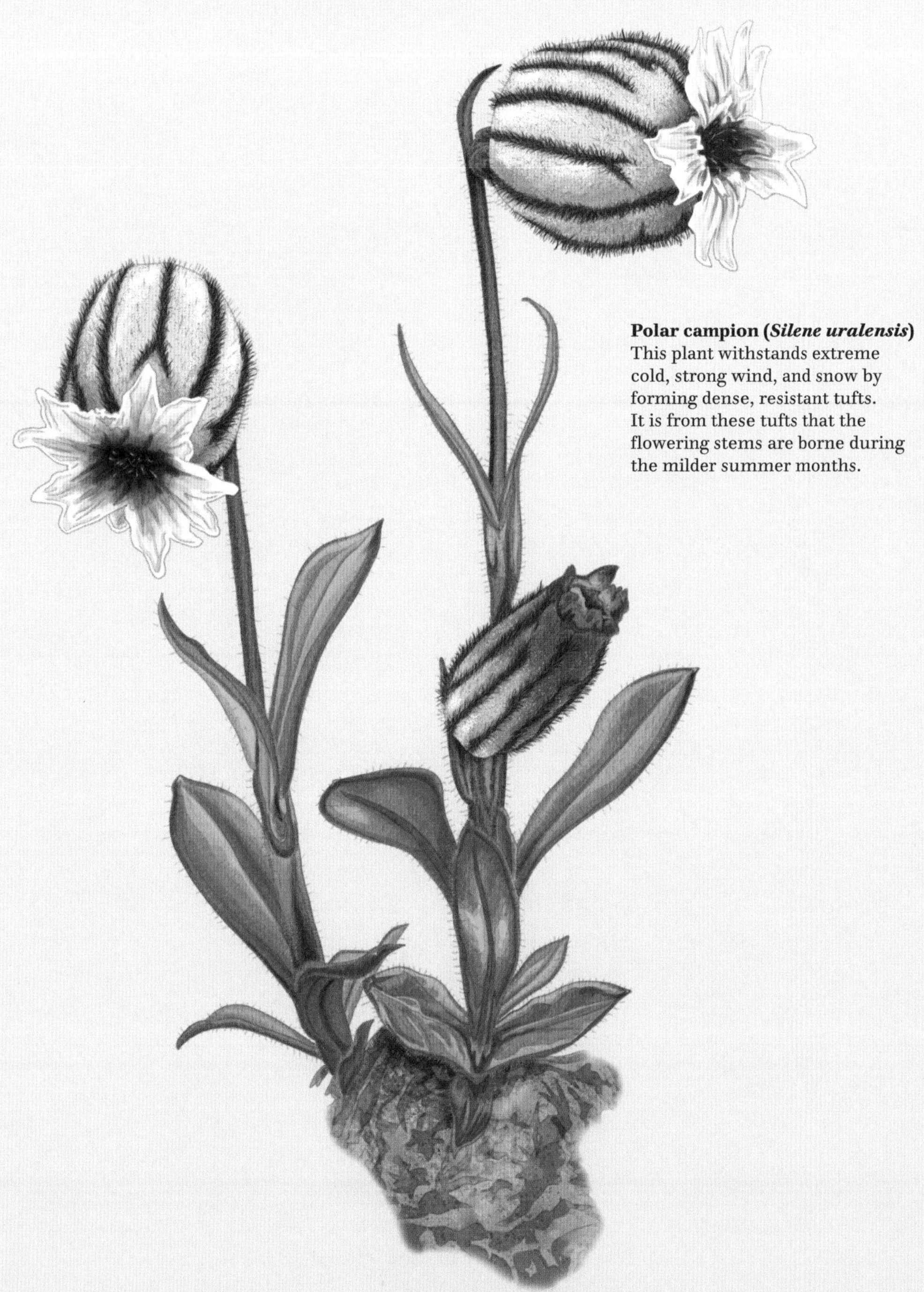

Polar campion (*Silene uralensis*)
This plant withstands extreme cold, strong wind, and snow by forming dense, resistant tufts. It is from these tufts that the flowering stems are borne during the milder summer months.

Oxford ragwort
(*Senecio squalidus*)
This hybrid species is well adapted to growing in British railroad beds because they resemble the volcanic scree of Mount Etna, Sicily, where the parent species originated.

Railroad tracks might not immediately spring to mind as an ideal habitat. However, their dry, stony beds resemble shingly shores or rocky scree—and they have become a home from home for wildflowers that originated in such habitats.

LIFE ON THE RAILS

Artificial environments can be surprisingly rich in wildflowers. Colonists and opportunists find new habitats, then spread via such networks as water systems, roads, or railroads, depending on the plant.

Oxford ragwort (*Senecio squalidus*; opposite) has an interesting history associated with the railroads in the UK. Two species of ragwort (*Senecio*) were introduced to Britain by the botanists Francesco Cupani and William Sherard, probably between 1700 and 1702, each collected from different altitudes on Mount Etna in Sicily. Where the two plants grew together in the Badminton garden of Mary Somerset, Duchess of Beaufort, they hybridized. Plants from this hybrid offspring were later transferred to the University of Oxford Botanic Garden by its curator Jacob Bobart the Younger. The plant colonized the city's old walls and stonework (hence the common name), eventually reaching the train station. Then, during the Industrial Revolution, Oxford ragwort spread along the rail network, its journey accelerated by its wind-carried seed and the movement of the trains. The railroad system's beds were similar to the volcanic scree of Mount Etna, where the plant originated.

Buddleia davidii, a shrub that is native to central China, is a garden escapee that has spread by similar means throughout many parts of the world. Again, the disturbed, shingly habitat of rail lines and disused sites resembles the rocky scree upon which it first evolved. The plant's nectar-rich blossoms are well known for being attractive to butterflies, hence the plant's common name, butterfly bush.

Volcanic landscapes are good hunting grounds for endemic wildflowers. These mineral-rich, loose, dry environments require a unique set of adaptations in the plants that grow there.

VOLCANIC LANDSCAPES

Landscapes with volcanic origins often have very distinct floras. The Canary Island archipelago, in the Atlantic Ocean off the northwest coast of Africa, comprises eight major islands and their associated islets. The main archipelago originated as submarine seamount volcanoes on the sea floor. As we saw on page 180, this collection of islands is home to many endemics—plants found nowhere else—including many species of *Aeonium*.

Malpaís (meaning “bad land”), a barren, rocky landscape derived from lava fields, is a dominant habitat on much of the islands at low altitude. These lava fields are rough and difficult to walk over, and form undulating rocky swathes. Malpaís is particularly rich in lichens, which give a distinct greenish tint to the landscape. Mature malpaís landscapes (deposited many centuries ago or earlier) are often dominated by *Euphorbia* scrub vegetation. This vegetation has an ancient dry-tropical origin and occurs on all the islands. It is typically dominated by gnarled, twisted stands of *Euphorbia balsamifera* and *Kleinia neriifolia*, the imposing candelabra-like stems of *E. canariensis*, and an assemblage of other endemic succulent shrubs.

Canary Island spurge (*Euphorbia canariensis*)
This impressive plant grows in imposing stands that resemble organ pipes. The succulent stems store water and can withstand long periods with scarcely any rainfall.

Tiganophyton karasense

CHANGE

CHAPTER VI

WILDFLOWERS ARE UNDER THREAT. Plants have dominated the land for hundreds of millions of years, but habitats are vanishing and climate change is driving concerning shifts in the Earth's vegetation. Yet in the face of change, plants hold many of the answers to the world's problems. Appreciating them has never been more important.

TULIPS UNDER THREAT

Some species of wild tulip, such as those growing in the mountains of Central Asia, are well adapted to growing in seasonally cool environments. Combined with other threats, such as livestock overgrazing, urbanization, wild collection, and mining, climate change is believed likely to drive the extinction of vulnerable tulips in the wild.

Shrinking habitat
Tulipa dasystemon is a popular garden plant. In its native range in Central Asia—for example, the mountains of Kyrgyzstan—it is currently widespread but threatened by the loss of suitable habitat brought about by climate change.

Climate change is driving alarming shifts in our green planet's vegetation. But plants hold many of the answers to the world's greatest problems.

CLIMATE CHANGE

Climate change affects which plants can grow where. It can drive local extinction through extreme weather events, for example, or drive species into habitats at higher altitudes, thus changing the composition of vegetation. As well as influencing where species can survive, it also affects the phenology of plants: when the various life stages occur, such as leaf emergence, flowering, or seed-set. This can decouple plants' flowering times from the emergence of pollinators, meaning they can no longer set seed.

Changes in temperature and other climatic shifts have a direct influence on all types of plant in cultivated as well as wild environments. In the UK, the area on which grapevines are cultivated has doubled, and new crops are being grown, such as soy—which has traditionally been grown in South America.

Plants hold many of the answers to the world's greatest problems, such as food security and climate change. Plant-rich diets reduce harm to the land and environment, and—if adopted on a global scale—they might mitigate climate change significantly. Meanwhile, trees remove significant quantities of carbon dioxide from the air over their lifetime; the carbon is stored by the tree and held in the surrounding soil. While tree-planting alone is not enough to combat the climate crisis, it is certainly beneficial.

Plants that have been introduced from one part of the world to another can become invasive, displacing the local flora. This is a less obvious threat than habitat loss, but it can be very damaging.

INVASIVE SPECIES

People have been moving plants around for thousands of years. Most of the plants we grow in our gardens originate in other countries. Of the many nonnative plants growing in the wild, most cause little or no harm to ecosystems. But some are extremely problematic, and these are known as invasive. They can displace the native vegetation.

It isn't always obvious whether a wildflower is native, or indeed whether it is invasive or not. Well-known examples of invasive wildflowers in the US are purple loosestrife (*Lythrum salicaria*), Japanese honeysuckle (*Lonicera japonica*), kudzu (*Pueraria montana var. lobata*), and ox-eye daisy, (*Chrysanthemum leucanthemum*).

But there are other, lesser-known examples of wildflowers that are invasive elsewhere. They include the Hottentot fig (*Carpobrotus edulis*), a South African succulent that is grown in mild temperate regions as an ornamental, and to control soil erosion and stabilize sand dunes. It may be attractive, but it forms dense mats that change the soil characteristics over time and choke out native vegetation. Two more examples are illustrated opposite.

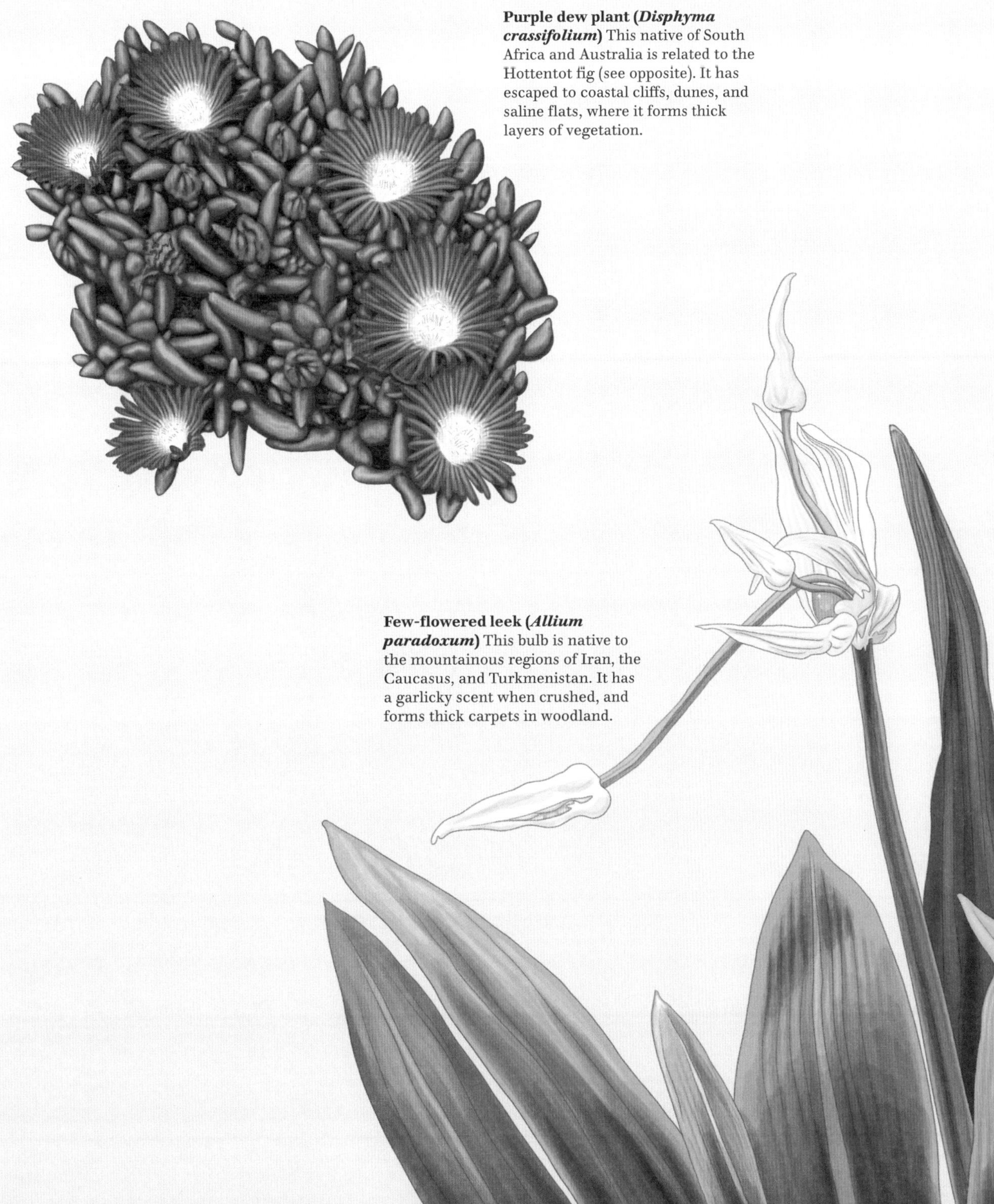

Purple dew plant (*Disphyma crassifolium*) This native of South Africa and Australia is related to the Hottentot fig (see opposite). It has escaped to coastal cliffs, dunes, and saline flats, where it forms thick layers of vegetation.

Few-flowered leek (*Allium paradoxum*) This bulb is native to the mountainous regions of Iran, the Caucasus, and Turkmenistan. It has a garlicky scent when crushed, and forms thick carpets in woodland.

In a ***fast-changing*** *world, many wildflowers are in peril.* ***Conservation*** *is just as important for* ***plants*** *as it is for* ***animals****.*

Habitat loss is the single biggest threat to wildflowers, and, coupled with climate change, is driving unprecedented levels of plant species to extinction today.

HABITAT LOSS

Plants exist in a dazzling array of forms. But quantifying their diversity is just part of the challenge faced by botanists; what drives their diversity is another question. Various factors in combination, including geology, interaction with other organisms, and climate, are believed to have shaped the habitats that are available to plants today, driving their diversity. As we have seen, from the Arctic to the tropics, plants have adapted to enable them to survive in environmental conditions of all kinds, resulting in an array of growth forms in different habitats.

Habitat loss is a significant threat to plants and species diversity worldwide. But plant diversity is not distributed equally around the planet. This means that habitat destruction in one place—a tropical rainforest, for example—can have a greater impact on overall levels of extinction than in another. Meanwhile, although trees make up most of the biomass of habitats in the northern hemisphere, they make up only a small amount of the overall diversity of wild plant species; there, herbaceous plants make up most of the diversity.

PLANT LORE LOSS As humans colonized new environments, their historical interaction with the local flora led to a wealth of traditional wisdom about the distribution of plants and their uses. We are losing plant species to extinction at an alarming rate, and at the same time we are losing our local knowledge of plants, our "plant lore."

Frying pan plant (*Tiganophyton karasense*)
This species is new to science; it was probably overlooked because it is so rare and has been seen by so few people. Not only is it a new species, but also it belongs to a plant family that was hitherto completely unknown.

When we think of endangered species, extinction, and biodiversity loss, animals tend to spring to mind. But animals—including humans—depend on plants for their existence; and plants too are in peril.

THREATENED SPECIES

Botanists are in a race to document, describe, and name new species of wildflower before they are lost to extinction. Here is a selection of plants that have been described since 2020 and are extremely rare or threatened in the wild:

- **Frying pan plant (*Tiganophyton karasense*)** This is not only a new species; it also belongs to a whole new genus and family (the Tiganophytaceae). It grows in the arid ||Karas Region of southern Namibia in violently hot salt pans, hence its common name.
- ***Sternbergia mishustinii*** The discovery of this plant can be traced back to 1997, when a Ukrainian explorer collected the seed of an undocumented bulb in southern Türkiye. The species was officially described only in 2022, and is believed to be critically endangered.
- ***Lophopetalum tanahgambut*** An Indonesian botanist and his team swam across a muddy river, avoided wild tigers, and climbed this giant tree with knotted roots to examine what they suspected to be a species new to science, which indeed turned out to be the case.
- ***Rafflesia banaoana*** The author and a team of Filipino botanists reinstated this species in 2023, raising the total number of *Rafflesia* species (possessing the world's largest flowers) in the Philippines to 15. The plant had previously been confused with a similar *Rafflesia* species that occurs farther east. Most species in the genus *Rafflesia* are threatened by habitat destruction.

Botanists can measure how habitats have changed over space and time by examining dried, pressed plant specimens housed in collections known as herbaria.

PRESSED FOR TIME

Much of our knowledge about the diversity of wildflowers that exist today comes from herbaria: collections of dried, pressed plants, amassed over the course of centuries. The earliest herbaria were founded in Europe in the seventeenth century by traveling botanists. At this time, knowledge of the world's plants outpaced the rate at which botanic gardens could grow them, so repositories of dried specimens were made.

Today, herbaria are key to the documentation of the world's flora. They help us understand the relationships among and distribution of wildflowers, as well as informing potential uses for the plants in a changing world.

Most known wildflowers worldwide are represented in an herbarium. Each is mounted on a sheet of archival paper, labeled with information about when and where the plant was collected, along with key details, such as its habitat or color. The specimens are then stacked and stored on shelves in cabinets that can be browsed like books in a library. Among the most important are the so-called type specimens. In biology, a type is a specimen with which the scientific name of a particular species is formally associated—in other words, the go-to reference.

WHAT'S IN A NAME?

The first step toward understanding, protecting, and potentially benefiting from plant diversity is to identify and describe it scientifically. New wildflower species are documented using the long-established naming protocol (see p.224), then a type specimen is created and preserved in an herbarium.

THE HISTORY OF HERBARIA

Keeping a record
An herbarium (plural: herbaria) is a collection of preserved (typically pressed) plant specimens and associated information. The amassing of herbaria dates back at least six centuries; techniques have changed little, but today these collections make available plant material from across place and time, and are important in a fast-changing world. Some herbarium specimens constitute the only remaining record of an extinct plant.

PRE-1500

Evidence of dried plant specimens is mailed in letters and pasted into manuscripts in Italy; these are not amassed as collections, but they pave the way for early herbaria.

1543

The botanist Luca Ghini in Bologna founds a botanic garden at Pisa and, at around the same time, amasses the first true herbarium (although this has not survived).

1600

By now the art of compiling herbaria has developed and spread across Europe; specimens are exchanged among scholars in different countries, becoming a source of shared knowledge.

1700s

The Linnaean Herbarium, containing 13,000 dried plant specimens, is assembled by the Swedish taxonomist Carl Linnaeus; from 1829 it is housed at the Linnean Society of London.

1990–2010s

Herbaria become a useful source of plant DNA for taxonomy and molecular systematics (understanding the relatedness of plants).

2020s

Specimens in herbaria help environmental scientists track changes in climate and human impact as plant distribution changes over time.

Canarina canariensis

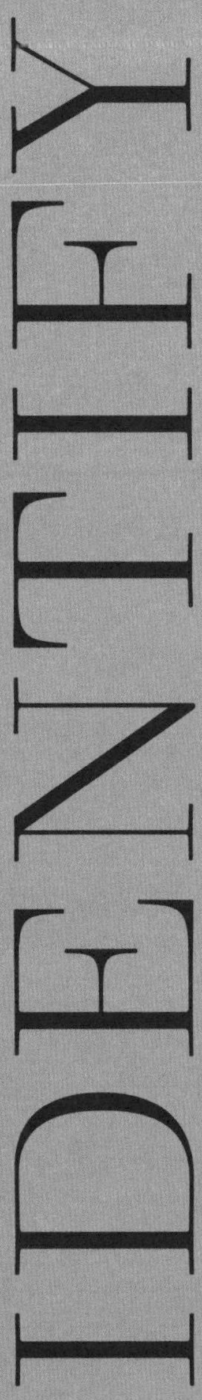

CHAPTER VII

WHEN CONFRONTED WITH a bewildering array of wildflowers, it can be a challenge to know where to begin identifying them. Understanding their key forms and characteristics—and which plant family each belongs to—is a good start. This chapter highlights the most important features, from flower form to leaf surface characteristics.

It is useful to begin identifying wildflowers by understanding the key forms and characteristics, and which species belong to a particular plant family.

WHERE TO START

Identifying wildflowers can be a rewarding hobby wherever you live in the world. It is also important for measuring and quantifying biodiversity in a given area, and to inform priorities for conservation. A basic grasp of plant taxonomy, as well as an understanding of flower and leaf characteristics, is important. Here are some simple questions for the beginner to consider:

1. **Is it a spore plant or a seed plant?** Seedless plants (**cryptogams**) include algae, mosses, liverworts, and ferns. Seed plants (**phanerogams**) include **gymnosperms** (such as conifers) and all flowering plants (**angiosperms**).
2. **Is the plant a monocot or an eudicot?** As we saw on pages 36–37, the vast majority of flowering plants fall into one of these two major groups. Knowing which group a plant belongs to can help guide family, genus, and finally species-level identification.
3. **To which genus does the plant belong?** A particular group of related species that evolved from a common ancestor is called a genus (plural: genera). Once you have identified the genus, a comparison of flower and leaf characteristics among its different representatives can be used to identify a plant to species level (using a dichotomous key, for example; see pp.226–227).
4. **To which family does the plant belong?** Related genera are, in turn, organized into families. Families vary in size and characteristics. The grass family (Poaceae) is a large and diverse example (pp.236–237), in which species are united by their typically linear leaves and inconspicuous, wind-pollinated flowers.

BINOMIALS

Every plant species name is made up of two parts: the generic name and the specific name. Let's take *Hibiscus tiliaceus*. *Hibiscus* is the generic name, and *tiliaceus* the specific. There are many species of *Hibiscus*, but only one called *Hibiscus tiliaceus*. Scientific names are important if we are to avoid confusion when a plant has many common names.

KINGDOM PLANTAE

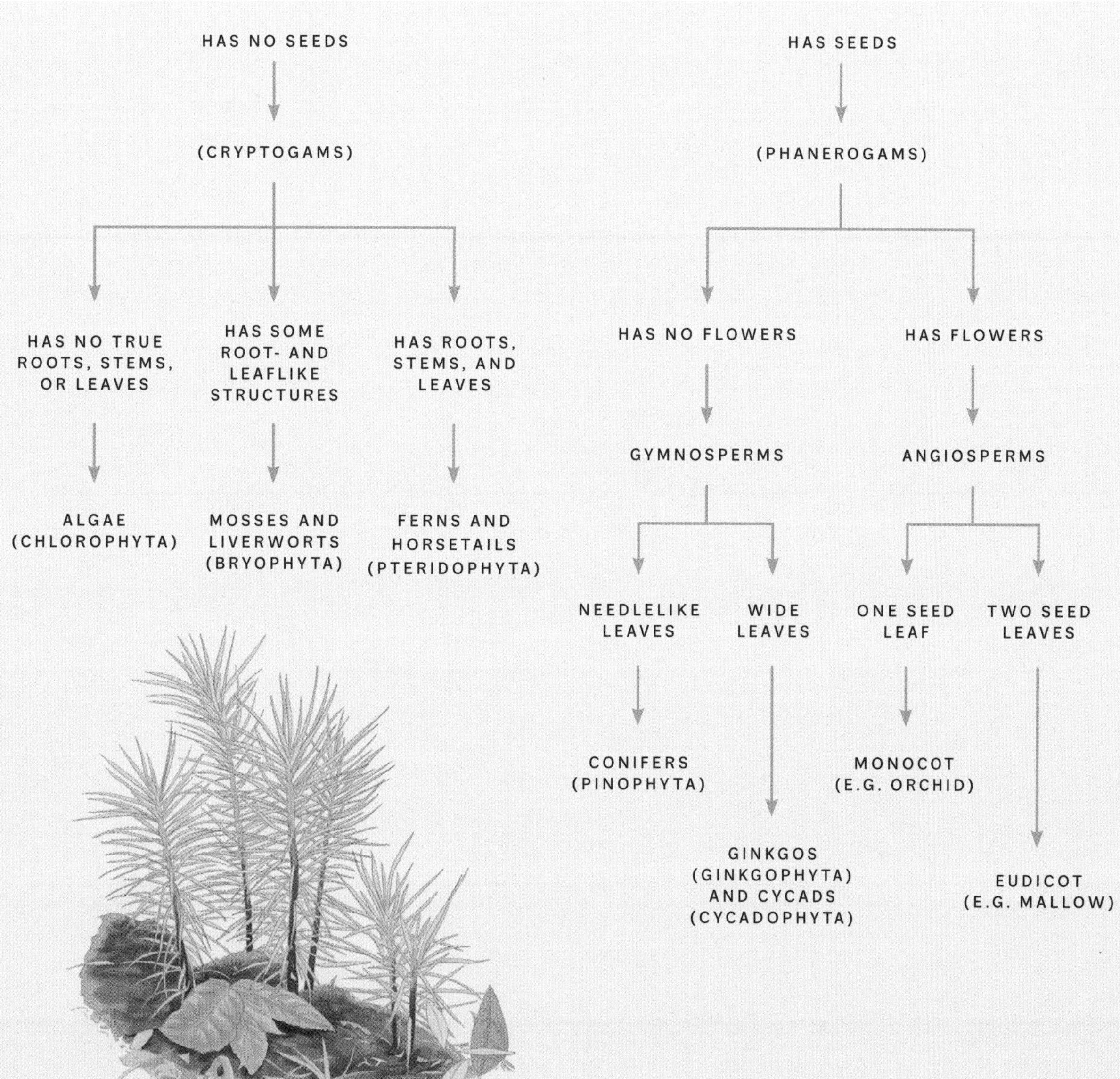

DAWSONIA MOSS

A dichotomous key is a method of identification by which descriptions are repeatedly divided into pairs, presented as choices. With each choice the user makes, more information is revealed about the plant, until a positive identification is reached.

DICHOTOMOUS KEYS

Once you have a grasp of the basic anatomy of wildflowers, you can use this knowledge to follow a key, which will allow you to identify a plant systematically down to species level, even from a long list of similar species. Dichotomous keys appear in books, floras, and scientific papers, and are used by all taxonomic botanists as an identification tool. They comprise a series of statements, each with two choices in every step that ultimately lead to the correct identification. They can be presented in one of two ways: diagrammatically, as a branching flowchart; or (more commonly in floras) descriptively, as a numbered sequence of paired statements.

Opposite is a simplified dichotomous key to some deciduous trees. To identify one of the trees included in this key, you would start with the first pair of statements, then go to the number each choice takes you to, until you reach a match.

LEAVES OPPOSITE OR ALTERNATE

LEAVES ALTERNATE

LEAVES OPPOSITE

LEAVES COMPOUND

LEAVES SIMPLE

LEAVES COMPOUND

LEAVES SIMPLE

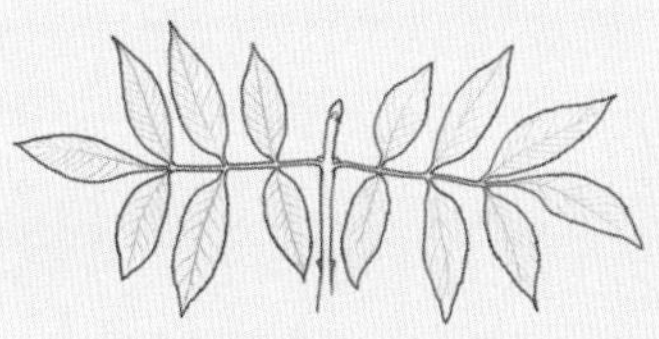

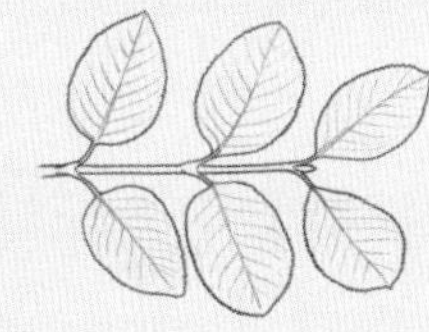

CARYA GLABRA
PIGNUT HICKORY

ALNUS RHOMBIFOLIA
WHITE ALDER

FRAXINUS EXCELSIOR
ASH

CORNUS SANGUINEA
DOGWOOD

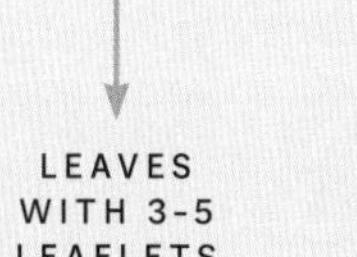

LEAVES WITH 3-5 LEAFLETS

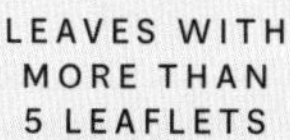

LEAVES WITH MORE THAN 5 LEAFLETS

CARYA OVATA
SHAGBARK HICKORY

JUGLANS CALIFORNICA
CALIFORNIA BLACK WALNUT

KEYING OUT

Dichotomous keys can used to identify plants, animals, fungi, and even rocks and minerals, based on their observable traits. This example shows trees with different leaf arrangements. It has been simplified to act as a visual guide to the principles of following a key, and the species chosen for this purpose are unlikely to be found growing together. The process of identifying species by key is known as "keying out."

Wildflowers face threats from human-mediated change. Recording them is an important way of monitoring this change, and ultimately informs when and where we should focus our efforts on protecting them. You can easily record and preserve wildflowers at home.

RECORDING AND PRESERVING

Picking wildflowers (or at least parts of them) responsibly and sustainably can play an important role in identification. For example, it can be necessary for confirming minute features buried deep within a flower. Picking flowers can also help children learn and become enthusiastic about plants, and eager to protect them. Be sure not to pick anything rare or on protected land, nor to uproot a whole specimen.

You can also preserve the specimens you gather and record. Specialized flower-pressing kits are available, but it's easy to do using simple materials that you probably already have at home. See opposite for instructions.

GREEN BEAUTIES

Fern fronds make excellent pressed specimens that maintain their shape and form well. However, when exposed to direct sunlight, they soon lose their green color.

PRESERVING WILDFLOWERS

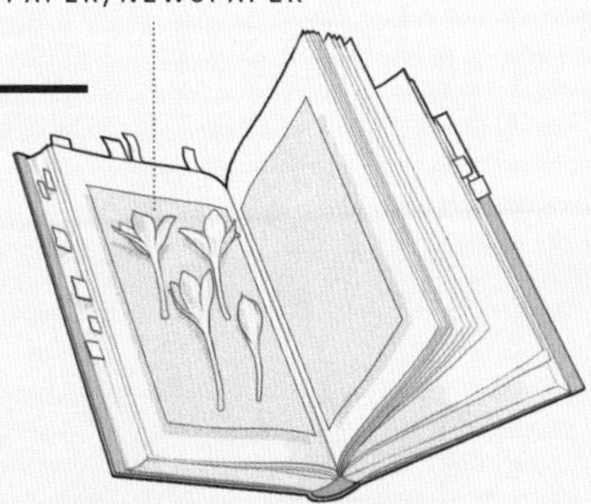

1. Cut away any unwanted leaves or stems so the specimen lies flat.

2. Sandwich the specimen between sheets of paper or newspaper (this is especially important for plants that contain a lot of moisture).

3. Flatten the specimen inside a large book or between or underneath several books (the more weight on top, the better). Be sure to press the whole plant; anything left exposed and without weight on it will shrivel.

4. Leave the specimen and book(s) in a warm, dry place for about four weeks, until the plant is completely dry.

5. Remove the specimen with forceps (tweezers) and glue it onto cartridge paper or mounting board.

6. Frame your specimens, or collect them in a book, along with details of what they are, and when and where they were collected. Or why not use them to create a mini herbarium recording the wildflowers in your yard?

Leaves do not simply vary in shape, size, and color; they also possess a range of textures and surface characteristics, from waxy to hairy, and wrinkled to smooth.

LEAF CHARACTERISTICS

Leaves come in a bewildering assortment of shapes and sizes, as we examined on pages 46–47. Their surface characteristics, as well as their shapes and arrangements, are important diagnostic tools. Many leaves are pubescent, meaning they possess an indumentum (a covering of hairs called trichomes); this in turn comes in many forms, which can be a useful guide to identification—although some can seem very similar at first glance.

The various leaf surface characteristics and their identifying features are described and illustrated opposite.

Leaf surfaces
Examining the surface characteristics of leaves is important for identifying wildflowers. For example, the level of hairiness and what type of hairs—the degree of waxiness, and the color are all important diagnostics. Here are some of the most commonly encountered surface characteristics.

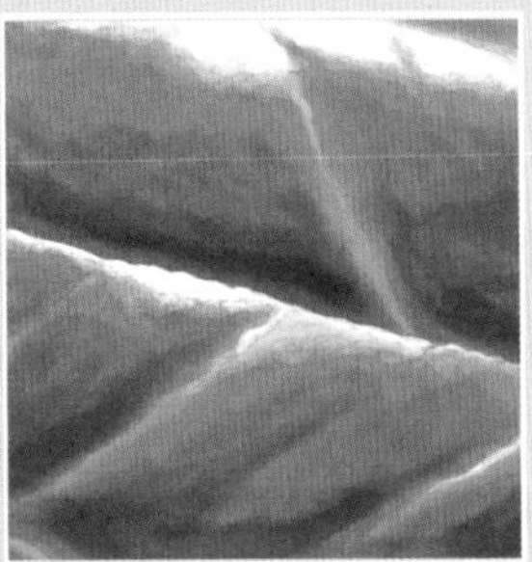

Glabrous
Hairless

Glaucus
Covered with a blue or silvery waxy covering

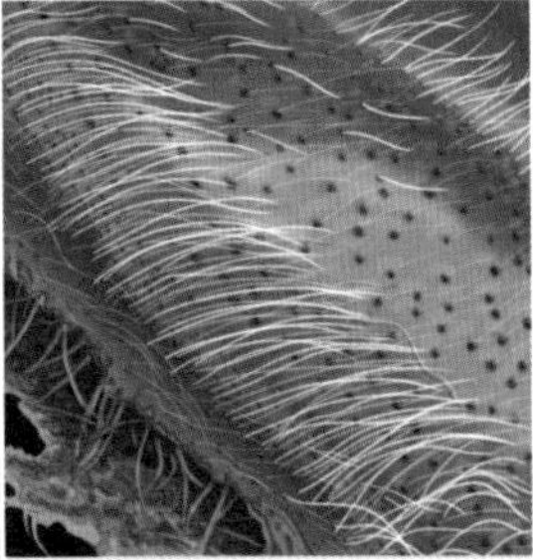

Hirsute
Covered with long, straight, rather stiff hairs

Lanate
Covered with long, interwoven, cottony hairs

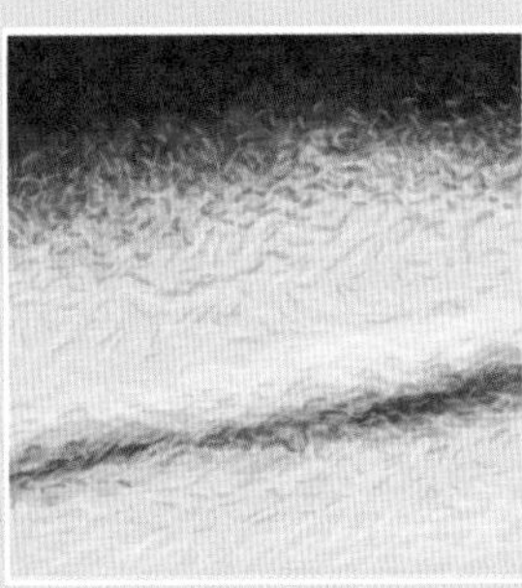

Pannose or felted
Covered with a matted, felt-like layer of hair

Pubescent
Covered or scattered with more or less dense hair

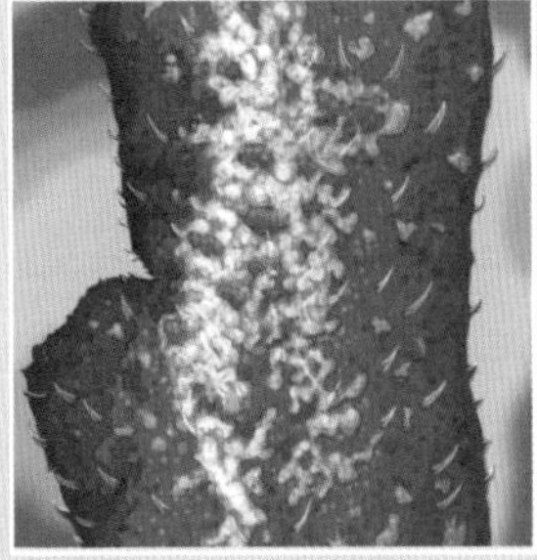

Scabrous
Rough to the touch

Sericeous
Covered with long, silky hairs, usually pressed to the surface

Stellate
Referring to star-shaped hairs

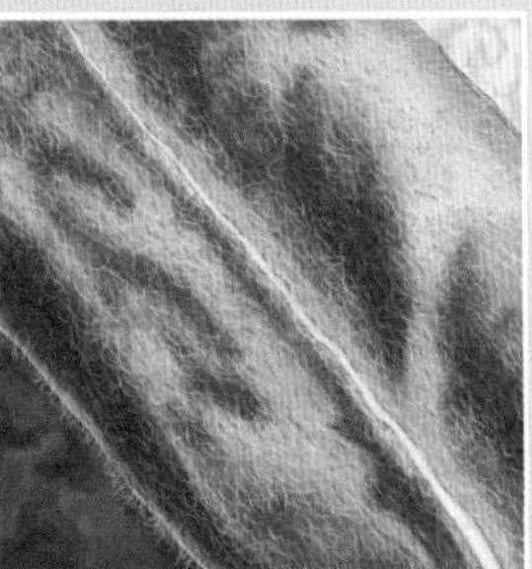

Tomentose
Covered with dense, interwoven hairs

The roughly 300,000 species of wildflower that bedazzle our planet come in a bewildering array of shapes, sizes, and colors. Recognizing some of the common forms is important in wildflower identification.

FLOWER FORMS

On pages 40–41 we saw that flowers are made up of whorls, typically comprising a calyx, corolla, androecium, and gynoecium. Not only is recognizing the parts of flowers fundamental to wildflower identification, but also understanding how they are arranged is important. On the facing and next pages are some of the forms that are commonly encountered.

Typically, closely related species of wildflower share common characteristics; for example, most plants in the pea family possess distinctively shaped papilionaceous flowers (see opposite). However, unrelated plants can also produce very similar flower forms that can be confusing in the field. For this reason, it is important to examine a range of characteristics—including leaves, flowers, and surface characteristics (such as hairiness)—when identifying wildflowers.

Actinomorphic
A flower that is radially symmetrical, such as a tulip.

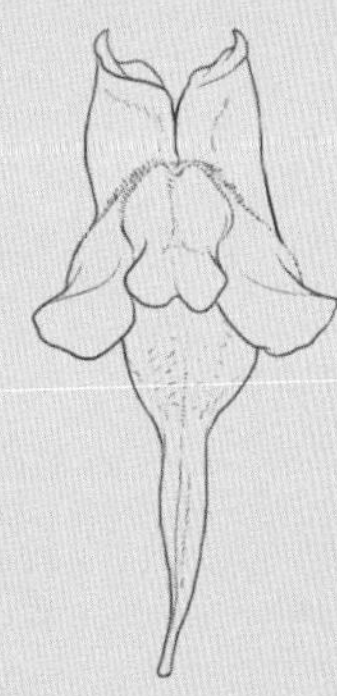

Zygomorphic
A flower that is bilaterally symmetrical, such as a toadflax.

Campanulate
A bell-shaped flower with a broad tube and reflexed lobes (tips), typical of the bellflower family (Campanulaceae).

Cruciform
A cross-shaped, four-lobed flower, typical of the cabbage family (Brassicaceae).

Funnelform
A flower in which the corolla lobes are fused, and that widens gradually from the base, opening in a flared manner, like a funnel.

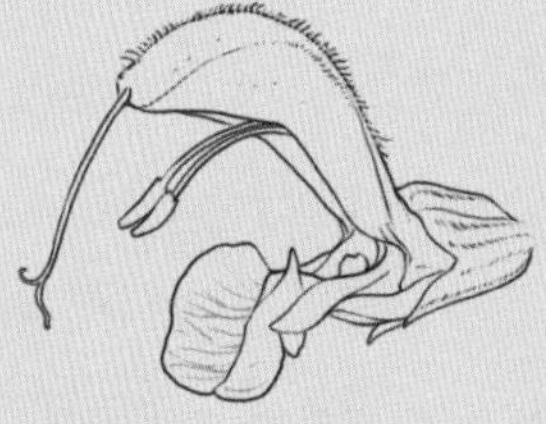

Labiate
A flower with petals fused into an upper lip (or hood) and a lower lip, typical of the mint family (Lamiaceae).

Papilionaceous
A flower with an upper petal (the standard), two lateral petals (wings), and two lower petals (the keel; often fused), typical of the peas (Fabaceae).

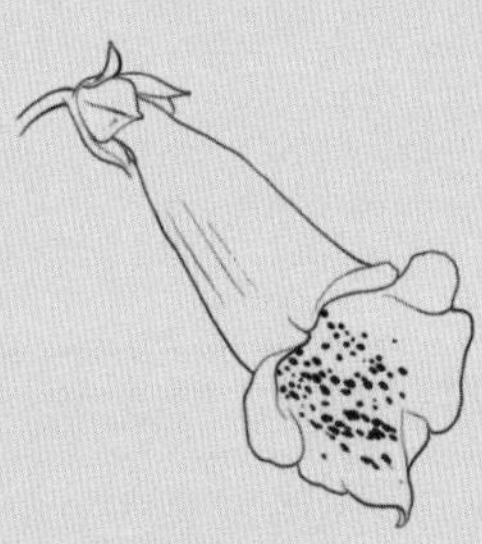

Tubular (tubulate)
A flower with the corolla fused to form a narrow tube.

Urceolate
An urn-shaped flower in which the petals are fused into a tube and contracted at the opening to form a partially enclosed structure.

*Besides being able to **identify** the forms of **individual** flowers, it's also important to **recognize** how flowers are arranged into **groups**.*

Flower collectives

Below are some commonly encountered forms of inflorescence (a group or cluster of flowers). Note that some of these structures and terms can be used in combination, for example an **umbellate cyme**, **capitula in cymes**, or even a **cymose capitulum**. You will find it easier to grasp the more complicated terminology if you understand each term individually first.

Capitulum (plural: capitula)
A close-packed cluster of stalkless flowers arising on a flattened axis, all at the same level and surrounded or subtended by an involucre (ring of bracts), appearing as a single flower—typical of the daisies (Asteraceae).

Compound umbel
Several individual umbels arising from a common point and maturing at about the same level—typical of many umbellifers (family Apiaceae; see pp.96–99).

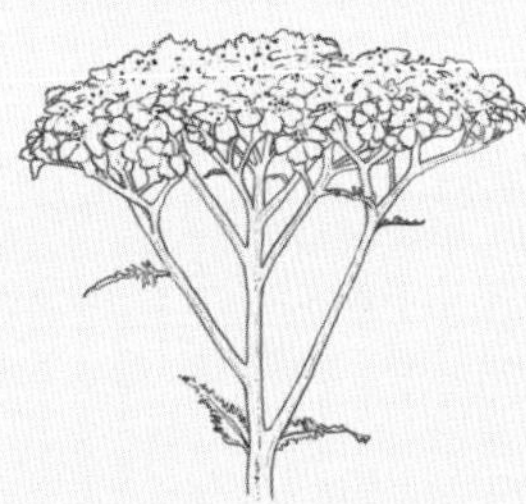

Corymb
A cluster of flowers in which the lower stalks are proportionally longer than the uppermost, so the flowers form a more or less flat head.

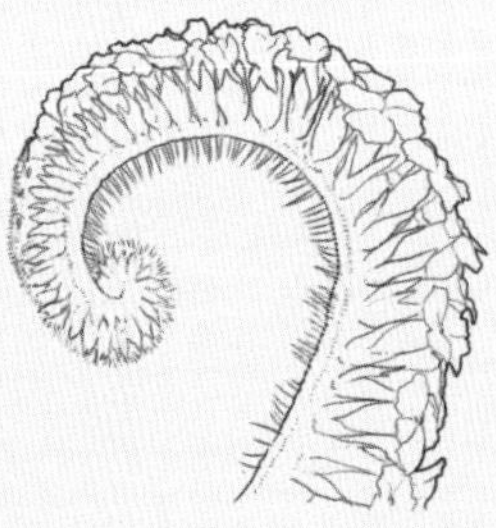

Cyme
A (cymose) inflorescence in which the central or terminal flower opens first, followed by the peripheral or lower flowers. There are different types of cyme; for example, **helicoid cymes** develop in a coiled structure.

Umbel
A cluster of flowers with short stalks (pedicels) that rise from a common point to form an umbrellalike structure; several together form a compound umbel. The example shown here could also be described as an **umbellate cyme**.

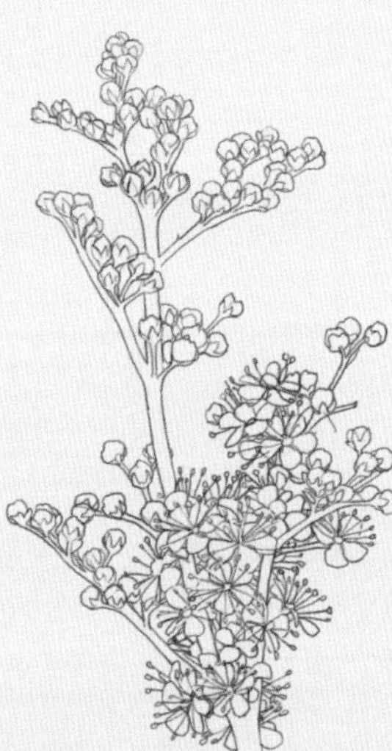

Panicle
A much-branched inflorescence in which each branch has more than one flower.

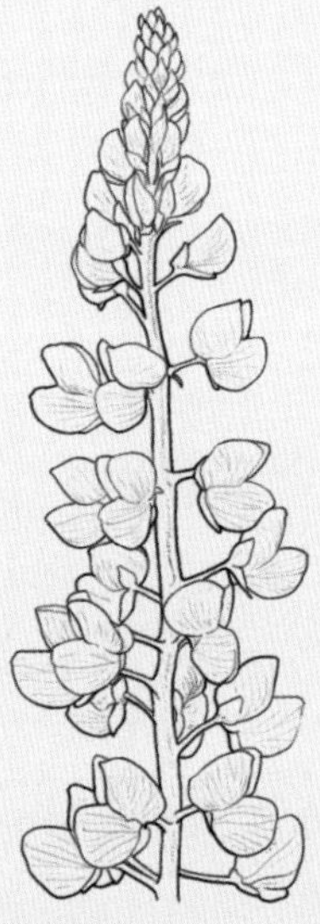

Raceme
An unbranched inflorescence in which each flower has a short stalk, with the oldest flowers at the base.

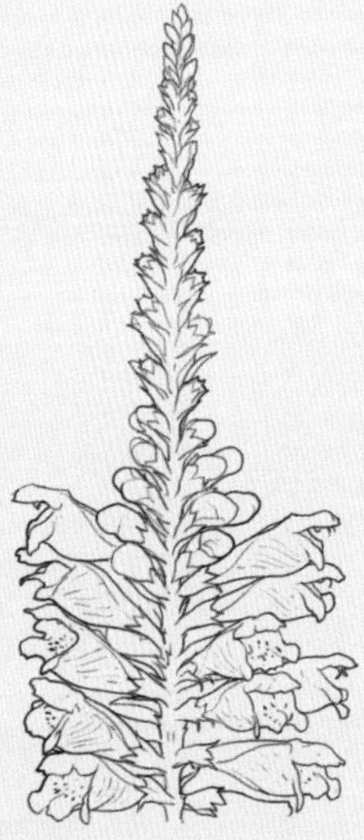

Spike
An unbranched inflorescence in which each flower is stalkless, with the oldest flowers at the base.

Grasses are not the most conspicuous wildflowers, but what they lack in vibrancy, they make up for in diversity.

IDENTIFYING GRASSES

Here are some of the key diagnostic features to examine when identifying grasses. Some are very small, so it can be beneficial to use a magnifying glass.

1. STEMS Flowering stems in grasses are called culms.
- **Leaf blade** The expanded, distal part of the grass leaf (a blade of grass).
- **Leaf sheath** The basal part of the grass leaf, which normally encloses an internode (a joint).
- **Ligule** A membrane or fringe of hairs on the inner side of the junction between the leaf sheath and leaf blade.

2. INFLORESCENCES Flowering heads in grasses consist of lots of tiny flowers called spikelets.
- **Spikelet** The basic unit of a grass inflorescence, usually composed of two glumes (see below) and one or more florets.
- **Floret** The individual unit of a spikelet, each comprising a lemma and palea (see below) enclosing reproductive organs.

3. SPIKELET
- **Palea** The upper inner scalelike bract that, together with the lemma, encloses the floret; often two-keeled.
- **Lemma** The lower of the two bracts enclosing the grass floret that, together with the palea above it, encloses the floret.
- **Awn** A bristle, sometimes long and conspicuous, arising from the spikelet.
- **Glume** One of a pair of empty scales at the base of a grass spikelet.
- **Rachis** The axis of the raceme (the flower stem).

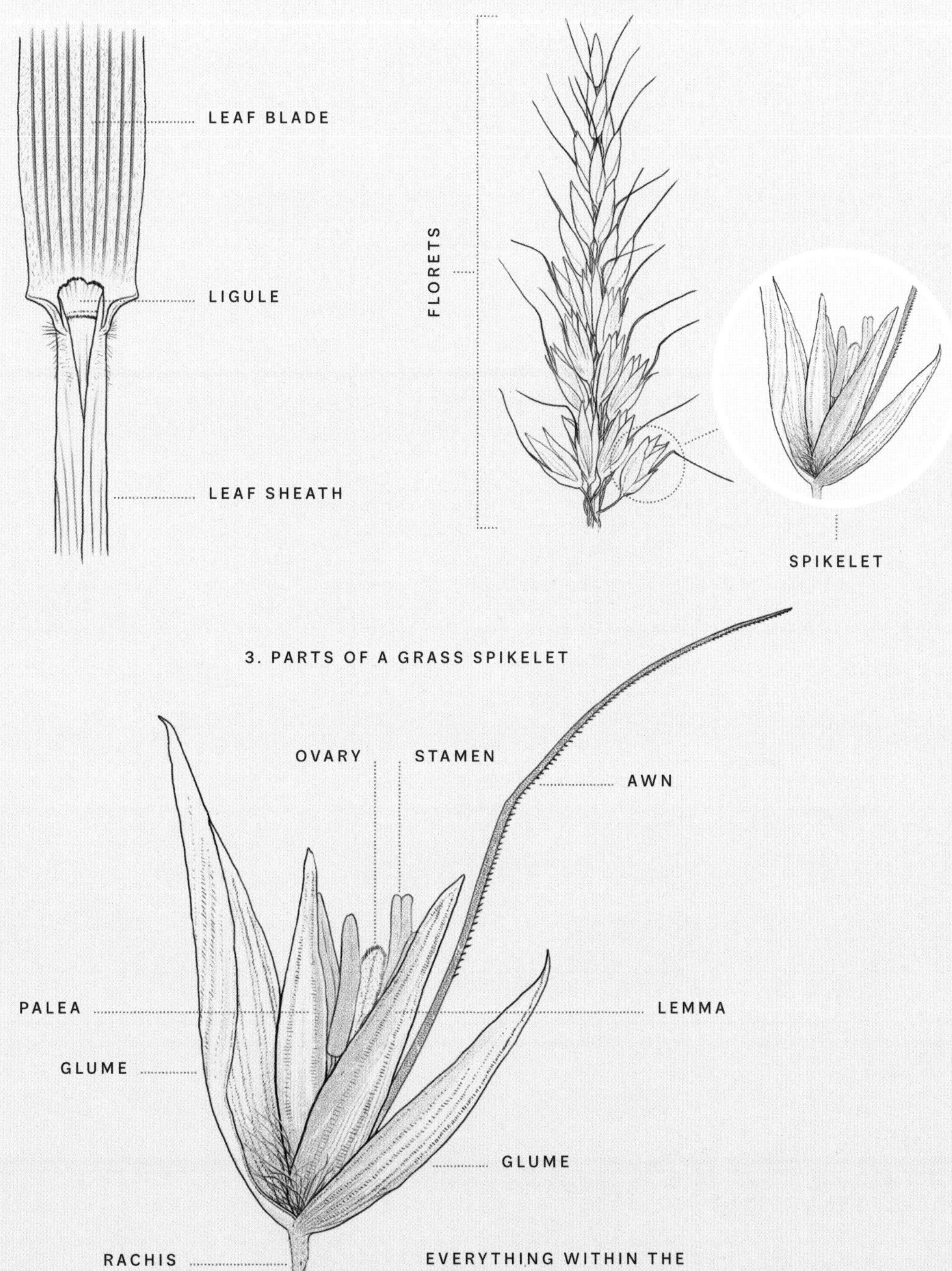
1. PARTS OF A GRASS STEM
LEAF BLADE
LIGULE
LEAF SHEATH
2. GRASS INFLORESCENCE
FLORETS
SPIKELET
3. PARTS OF A GRASS SPIKELET
OVARY
STAMEN
AWN
PALEA
LEMMA
GLUME
GLUME
RACHIS
EVERYTHING WITHIN THE GLUMES IS ONE FLORET

Ferula drudeana

CHAPTER VIII

THE LIVES OF WILDFLOWERS and people have always been closely intertwined. The people of ancient civilizations depended on plants for their very existence—just as we do still. Today, plants inspire solutions to technological challenges and technical applications that we use in our everyday lives, from self-cleaning paint to ways of fastening our shoes.

Thyme (*Thymus* sp.)
People have always used plants in their daily lives. Ancient herbals record how plants were used thousands of years ago. Not only was thyme used as a culinary herb, but also it was taken as a source of courage.

The lives of plants and people have been closely intertwined for thousands of years. Ancient civilizations relied on wildflowers for use in many areas of everyday life.

ANCIENT HERBAL MEDICINE

People's lives have always depended on plants. Ancient cultures wrote about the plants they used for food and medicine on scrolls or in books called herbals, and depicted them in tomb illustrations or on clay tablets. In Mesopotamia, the study of herbs dates back more than 5,000 years to the Sumerians, who created clay tablets with lists of hundreds of medicinal plants (such as myrrh and opium).

The earliest surviving comprehensive herbals are those of the ancient Greek philosopher Theophrastus of Eresos (371–287 BCE), who documented the wildflowers he encountered, and how they were used by local people. His herbals represented the first systematization of plants, and informed later texts in the region; Pliny the Elder (c. 23–79 CE) wrote a guide to nature with an extensive catalog of medicinal herbs, and this was followed by the *De Materia Medica*, written by the physician and botanist Dioscorides (c. 40–c. 90 CE). Together these early texts describe a rich history of early herbal medicine.

ANCIENT HERBAL CURES

- **Rosemary (*Salvia rosmarinus*)** was used in wreaths given to ancient Greek students, and reputed to aid memory.
- **Thyme (*Thymus* spp.)**, reputedly a source of courage, was used in infusions for bathing and to flavor food and drink.
- **Sage (*Salvia officinalis*)** conferred wisdom, and was a symbol of fertility and a long and healthy life.
- **St. John's wort (*Hypericum perforatum*)** was believed to ward off evil spells and demons.

Wildflowers have been used as a source of traditional herbal medicine for thousands of years, for example in China. In a changing climate, some now have the potential to be grown at scale to feed a growing population.

FOOD FOR THOUGHT IN A CHANGING WORLD

Desert hyacinths (*Cistanche* spp.) are widespread across the desolate sandy tracts and dunes of Asia and North Africa. They are related to the broomrapes (pp.148–151), and, like them, are parasitic, and devoid of leaves and green pigments (chlorophyll).

There are some thirty or so known species of desert hyacinth. A handful of species are traded around the world for herbal medicine, or have historical importance as food plants, for example *C. deserticola*. In traditional Chinese medicine the plants are dug up and their fleshy underground stems traded as products called "Rou Cong Rong" or "Guan Hua Rou Cong Rong." The plants have been used in China for more than 2,000 years and are still valued as tonic herbs (functional health foods). This rare plant has purported "trophy" attributes (properties reputed to bestow longevity, stamina, and even sexual vigor).

FOOD FOR THE FUTURE Some desert hyacinth species are now farmed at industrial scale in China to satisfy the demands of traditional herbal medicine at low cost. Recently these plants have been cultivated alongside "shelter forests," long ribbons of drought-tolerant trees planted to halt land degradation—a growing problem in the world's deserts. This suggests that desert hyacinths could be grown as an ancillary crop in arid regions, where they can be cultivated without irrigation. The plant may be an important new crop in a warming world.

Denizens of the desert
Desert hyacinths grow in barren plains and deserts. They are leafless, parasitic plants that feed from the roots of desert shrubs, forming connections with them deep below the sand's surface.

HALOXYLON AMMODENDRON
HOST PLANT

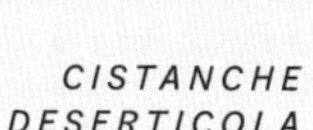

Winter blossom
After winter rainfall, the desert hyacinths force their way through the bare earth to blossom in an explosion of yellow, white, or mauve.

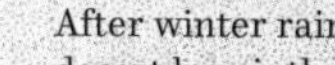

ATTACHMENT TO HOST

The Romans knew their wildflowers. They had an herbal cure for just about every ill, from rheumatism and slow digestion to nervous pains.

ROMAN HERBS

In most cultures throughout history, the medicinal and culinary herb garden played an important role in daily life, and the Romans were no exception. Before the grocery stores and pharmacies of the present day, people relied on wildflowers and cultivated herb gardens for food and herbal cures.

- **Rue (*Ruta graveolens*)** is a blue-gray shrub with sap that yields a sharp, pungent aroma that is distasteful to most people today. Romans used the plant in a similar way to parsley, as a garnish, and as a pickle. In moderation, it seems the plant was used in all kinds of food and drinks.
- **Roman chamomile (*Chamaemelum nobile*)** was used for its volatile oil to clear and treat infected wounds. Chamomile is one of the most ancient medicinal herbs. Today German chamomile (*Matricaria chamomilla*) is commonly used in teas.
- **Garlic (*Allium sativum*)** was so popular with the Roman army that the path of Roman legions around Europe reputedly overlaps with the range of the plant.
- **Silphium** was a plant in the carrot family (Apiaceae), the exact identity of which is unclear. Used variously as a contraceptive, a spice, and a panacea for medical ailments, it was harvested from the wild and may have become extinct from overuse. Its identity has long been debated, and recently it has been proposed that *Ferula drudeana* (see opposite), a plant from Türkiye, might be the plant used by the ancient Greeks and Romans.

ORCHID ODYSSEY

Orchids have fascinated humans since antiquity. Their unique flowers have inspired myths, legends, and popular traditions in many cultures around the world—the Romans included. Orchid flowers feature in Roman cornices and ceilings, in representations that seem to refer to a symbolism of fertility and sexuality.

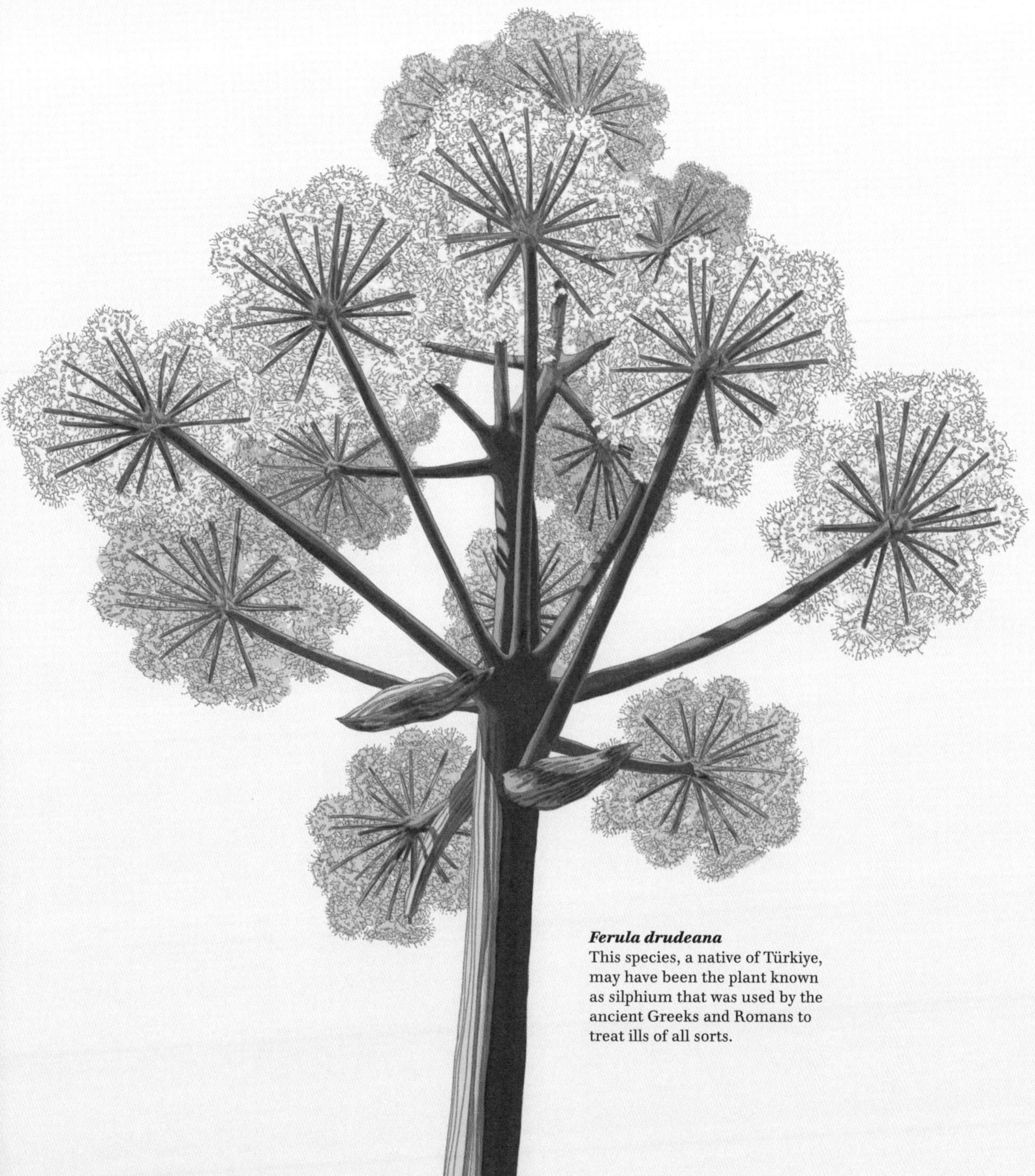

Ferula drudeana
This species, a native of Türkiye, may have been the plant known as silphium that was used by the ancient Greeks and Romans to treat ills of all sorts.

*It was believed in the **ancient world** that some plants were marked with a **sign** or "**signature**" linked to their **purpose**.*

Before the advent of science and technology, practitioners of herbal medicine believed—sometimes with disastrous consequences—that the appearance of a plant was linked to its properties and use.

THE DOCTRINE OF SIGNATURES

The Doctrine of Signatures dates back to ancient Greece. It purported that an herb's resemblance to a part of the body denoted its use; for example, a plant exuding a red sap might be considered to be an herbal cure for a blood disorder. This was dangerous in some cases, since it is not always clear that a plant is chronically poisonous. Birthwort (*Aristolochia clematitis*; see p.32), for instance, was prescribed for pregnant women because its flowers were believed to resemble a uterus. It is now known to be toxic.

Here are some other wildflowers that were made use of according to the Doctrine of Signatures:

- **Eyebright (*Euphrasia* spp.)**, a genus of small, hemiparasitic annuals of grassland habitats, was used to treat eye infections.
- **Woundwort (*Stachys sylvatica*)** and related plants were used for treating wounds, owing to their reputed antiseptic properties.
- **Liverworts (Marchantiophyta)**, also known as hepatics, were used to treat liver disorders.
- **Spleenwort (*Asplenium trichomanes*)** is a small fern with fronds that resemble the outline of a spleen, so it was used in association with this organ.
- **Lungwort (*Pulmonaria* spp.)** has leaves with white spots, thought to symbolize diseased or ulcerated lungs; the plant was used for pulmonary infections (hence its scientific name).

Some plants have a long, rich history of use. But the uses of some were far from conventional.

MALTESE FUNGUS

Maltese fungus (*Cynomorium coccineum*), also known as desert thumb and tartuth, is a parasitic plant that scarcely resembles a plant at all. It has no leaves or chlorophyll, just a congested, blackish spike of minute flowers. This wildflower is distributed in dunes and deserts from the Canary Islands eastward to China, and also occurs sporadically on rocky cliffs and in mudflats and saline areas around the Mediterranean. It feeds from the roots of shrubs in the family Amaranthaceae, and in the spring it sends up fat, blackish sprouts that are pollinated by flies.

Maltese fungus has a long and interesting history of use in European, Arabian, and Chinese herbal medicine. The plant has for centuries been recorded as growing on a remote sea cliff off the coast of Malta, on the island of Gozo, where it earned its popular name in the Middle Ages. The plant was reputedly highly prized for its purported properties by Maltese knights, who protected it by armed guard. It yields a reddish sap, which is perhaps why it was believed to solve blood-related problems (an example of the Doctrine of Signatures; see pp.246–247). It was used to treat dysentery, and—linked to its stature—was given as a remedy for "sexual problems." Maltese fungus has also long been prized in the Middle East, and in traditional Chinese medicine.

DNA sequence analysis shows that, despite its unique appearance, Maltese fungus is in fact a distant relative of the stonecrops (see p.203).

Maltese fungus
A parasitic plant that lacks functional leaves, roots, and chlorophyll, Maltese fungus steals its food from the roots of desert or salt-marsh shrubs. Its curious, spikelike form has long attracted the attention of herbalists, and it has a rich history of use.

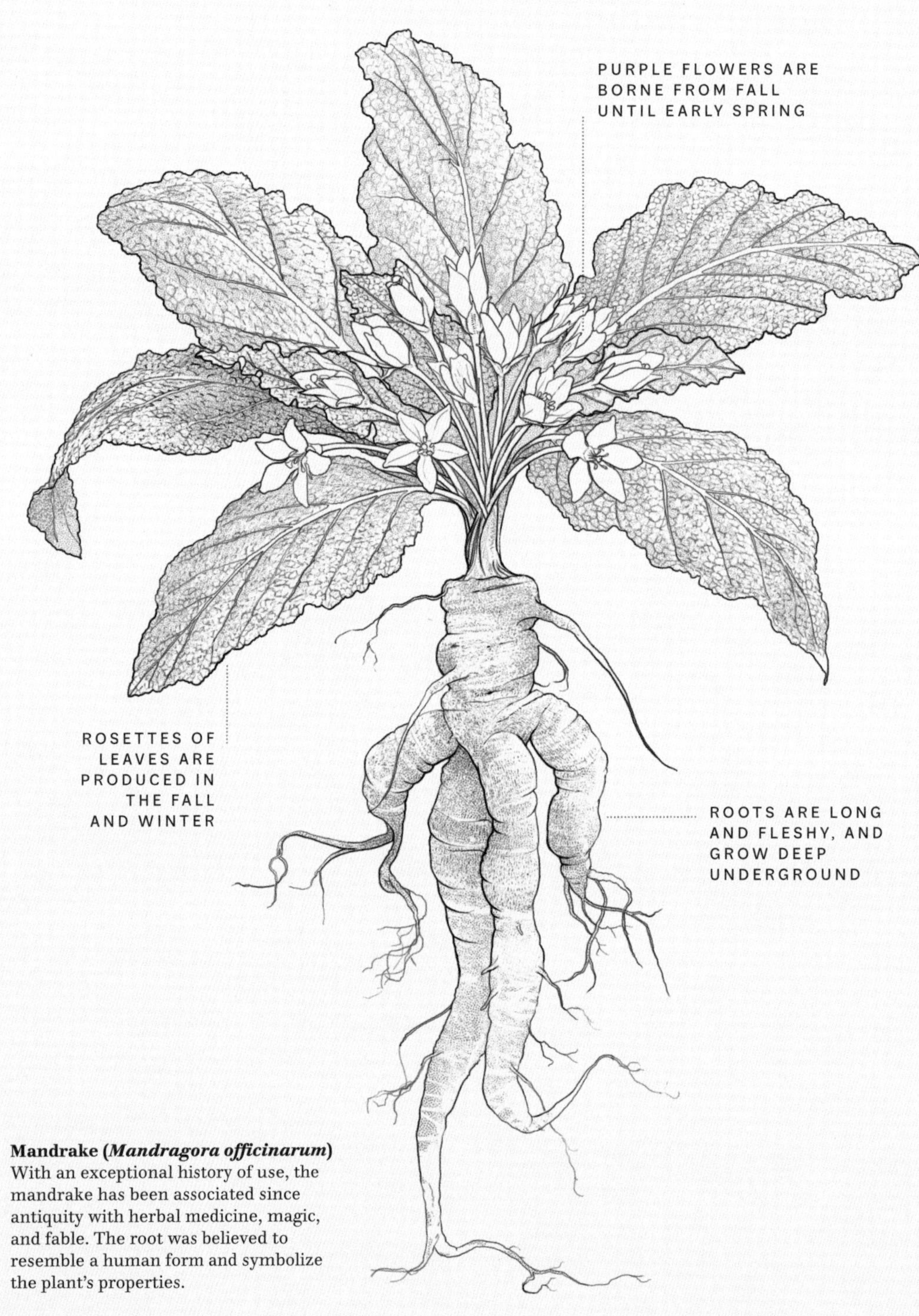

Mandrake (*Mandragora officinarum*)
With an exceptional history of use, the mandrake has been associated since antiquity with herbal medicine, magic, and fable. The root was believed to resemble a human form and symbolize the plant's properties.

Few wildflowers can have a greater claim to association with local culture, folklore, and magic than the "screaming mandrake."

MANDRAKE MAGIC

The screaming mandrake is celebrated as a plant that famously features in the *Harry Potter* novels. But this fabled plant is in fact real, and has long been associated with magic.

The mandrake (*Mandragora officinarum*) grows in the Mediterranean and parts of West Asia, and is a member of the nightshade family (Solanaceae; see pp.156–159). It has a rosette of leaves, purple flowers, and a branched, distended taproot. Historically, the root was believed to resemble the outline of a human figure, and this—combined with the mandrake's potent pharmacological properties—led to the plant's longstanding association with magic in popular folklore. Mandrake was once used as a narcotic, a sleep-inducing makeshift anesthetic. This was useful thousands of years ago, when medical interventions could be brutal. The plant was also used as an aphrodisiac and in love potions. It was highly sought-after, harvested, and sold across Europe, and "knock-offs" were also traded—fakes derived from other roots that resembled the mandrake.

The ancient Greek herbalists reported that the mandrake would shriek when uprooted, and that anyone who unearthed it would die if he heard its scream. It was thus said that the only way to harvest a mandrake safely was to tether it to a dog: the dog, tempted with meat, would yank the plant out of the ground, and the mandrake's demon would be transferred to the sacrificial animal.

Myths, folklore, and cultural associations with wildflowers date back to ancient Greek and Chinese, Roman, and Indigenous American mythology, and proliferated in Europe during the Middle Ages—a period rich in folklore.

THE LANGUAGE OF FLOWERS

As plants were transported from one country to another, they took on new associations, uses, and meanings. Floriography describes the Victorian practice of assigning wildflowers symbolic meanings, creating the so-called Language of Flowers. Some of these have survived: roses denoting love and passion, for example. Many wildflowers also feature prominently in literary works. Dozens are mentioned in Shakespeare's plays, reflecting an affinity for plants that has been attributed to the playwright's country upbringing. Here are some plants with strong historical associations in folklore, culture, and literature:

- **Cherry blossom** *Sakura* (Japanese for cherry blossom) heralds the start of spring in Japan. The white or pink clouds of blossoms also resonate with the historical Japanese belief that living beauty is ephemeral.
- **Daffodil** The scientific name *Narcissus* comes from the mythical Greek man who fell in love with his reflection—a legacy that influenced the flower's association with egotism in the Victorian Language of Flowers. Daffodils are also a symbol of rebirth and have long been associated with Easter. They feature in Shakespeare's *The Winter's Tale* and later inspired the poetry of William Wordsworth.
- **Rose** Roses feature prominently in Greek mythology. Rose garlands were also made for Roman festivals, where they were offered to the deities. According to Islamic tradition, the highly fragrant damask rose sprang from the sweat of the Prophet Muhammad, conferring the plant's essence as rosewater or oil, as well as its spiritual significance.
- **Madonna lily** Adored for its large, trumpet-shaped white flowers and strong perfume, the Madonna lily (*Lilium candidum*) has long symbolized purity. By 1300 the flower had become associated with the Virgin Mary, and it featured in paintings of the Virgin for the next 500 years, for instance in Renaissance works depicting the Annunciation.

Flower symbolism
Roses (opposite, top) feature prominently in Greek mythology, while Madonna lilies (bottom) symbolize purity and commonly feature in artwork depicting the Annunciation.

Lawrence Alma-Tadema, *The Roses of Heliogabalus* (1888)

Leonardo da Vinci, *The Annunciation* (c. 1472)

Nature study
In *Spring Spreads One Green Lap of Flowers* (1910) by John William Waterhouse, the artist depicts wildflowers, such as daffodils (*Narcissus*), with lifelike accuracy.

Wildflowers have been a popular subject in art for centuries. They have been used to symbolize religious or spiritual themes, and to represent the beauty of nature.

WILDFLOWERS IN ART

Just as wildflowers have featured prominently in literature over the centuries, artists too have long been inspired by their symbolism. They traced the meaning of lilies, roses, irises, and daffodils—alongside many more—and captured them in paint.

Wildflowers appear everywhere in Pre-Raphaelite paintings, and indeed flowers were intrinsic to these artists' style and themes. The Pre-Raphaelite Brotherhood was a group of English painters and poets founded in the mid-nineteenth century. Known for their penchant for detail, intense colors, and complex compositions, they depicted wildflowers with great accuracy and in a very lifelike way.

In 1851–1852 John Everett Millais depicted the death of Shakespeare's character Ophelia in painstaking detail that reputedly shocked the critics of his time. The withering wildflowers in the painting symbolize her doom, and each plant is clearly discernible: willow, nettle, and daisy, representing mourning, pain, and innocence respectively.

The painting *Echo and Narcissus* (1903) by John William Waterhouse illustrates the myth of Echo and Narcissus from Ovid's *Metamorphoses*. Near the nymph Echo, yellow flag irises (*Iris pseudacorus*) spring up from the waterside in lifelike detail. A yellow water lily (*Nuphar lutea*) is shown in the water, while white daffodils (*Narcissus*) can be seen emerging in the grass beside Narcissus's left foot. *Narcissus* flowers feature in several of Waterhouse's works, including *Spring Spreads One Green Lap of Flowers* (1910; opposite); here, again, they are depicted with lifelike accuracy.

Wildflowers are intrinsically interconnected with human culture, and always have been. Ethnobotany examines how people of a particular culture and/or region make use of indigenous plants.

ETHNOBOTANY

Ethnobotany is a field in which the natural and social sciences intersect. It examines the interaction and interrelationships between people and plants that have been shaped by religion, local culture, and sociopolitical context.

Naturalists began collecting local ethnobotanical knowledge during the European colonial expansion in the fifteenth century, when they were searching for new commodities including medicinal plants. More recently, "bioprospecting" has involved the commercialization of plants and traditional medicinal knowledge in drug discovery. When such knowledge belonging to Indigenous or local communities is exploited—used unfairly, without the sharing of any benefits that arise—this is known as "biopiracy."

Here are some plants that have ethnobotanical significance:

- **Coneflower (*Echinacea*)** is native to North America, where nine species are recognized, of which three are used medicinally. Traditional knowledge of the use of this wildflower drew the attention of European settlers, leading to commercial preparations for rheumatism and other ailments in the nineteenth century.
- **Witch hazel (*Hamamelis*)** was used by Indigenous American peoples as a plant medicine to treat such ailments as eye and skin irritation. In the mid-nineteenth century the first patent medicine was developed from this wild plant, and today extract of witch hazel is sold around the world.

LOST LANGUAGE OF PLANTS

Researchers have identified a strong correlation between a richness in local languages and areas that are high in biodiversity. Languages and local knowledge of plants are at risk of extinction, as well as the plants themselves.

- **Peyote (*Lophophora williamsii*)** derives its name from the Nahuatl word for silk cocoon, referring to the woolly nature of this small, spineless cactus. The ritual use of peyote by Indigenous peoples of Mexico is ancient and derives from the pre-Columbian practices of earlier peoples. Wild populations of this plant are under significant threat from illegal and over-harvesting.
- **Baobab (*Adansonia*)** is an iconic wild tree of the African bush. It develops a swollen, bottle-shaped trunk and produces large, creamy-white flowers. In some African cultures this tree is considered a dwelling place of ancestral spirits. The lives of many African peoples have been and still are interwoven with this extraordinary tree.

Ethnobotany as a discipline is a relatively ***modern*** *concept, but people have been using their* ***indigenous plants*** *since* ***antiquity****.*

There has always been a thin line between botany and alchemy. Over the centuries, folklore and superstition have built a complex and fascinating history of plant lore—and magic.

WILDFLOWERS AND MAGIC

From the hemlock used to poison Socrates, the olive branches used as prizes in the ancient Olympic Games, and the laurel wreathes used to crown Roman emperors, to the chocolate drunk for virility and power by the Aztec, plants were considered gifts from the gods and were used in every possible way by the people of ancient civilizations. It is little surprise, then, that they have left such a rich legacy—one that predates written accounts.

Herbals are important resources for plant historians. The *Herball* by John Gerard (1545–1612) is a volume of plant lore firmly rooted in sixteenth-century magical thinking. Gerard was curator of the physic garden belonging to the College of Physicians in London, and he grew a miscellany of plants, including some that were rare in Britain at the time. His herbal became a popular English gardening reference in the seventeenth century, although it is in fact a largely plagiarized translation of a Latin herbal from 1554 by the Flemish botanist Rembert Dodoens.

Witches and faith healers required a good working knowledge of plants to be able to cure people's ills and work with the spirits. Before the advent of clinical evidence and scientific thinking, elaborate rituals for plant-based healing emerged. Life was hard and short and any intervention welcome, so magic was entirely plausible. Wise women held important medical learning within the community, and worked with knowledge of local plants and potions handed down through the generations.

Contrary to healing, curses, jinxes, and hexes were dark spells intended to do harm, and these too involved plants. Hanging the seaweed known as bladder wrack in the right place could curse someone's urinary tract, for example. Staffs or wands cut from yew, hawthorn, or rowan were effective for channeling magical powers, while witches' broom handles were made from ash wood, for protection.

The Three Witches (or Weird Sisters) in William Shakespeare's play *Macbeth* famously added to their cauldron "Eye of newt, and toe of frog,/ Wool of bat, and tongue of dog,/ Adder's fork, and blind-worm's sting." This may well have referred to mustard seeds, buttercup, hounds-tongue, and adder's tongue—all of which are in fact wildflowers.

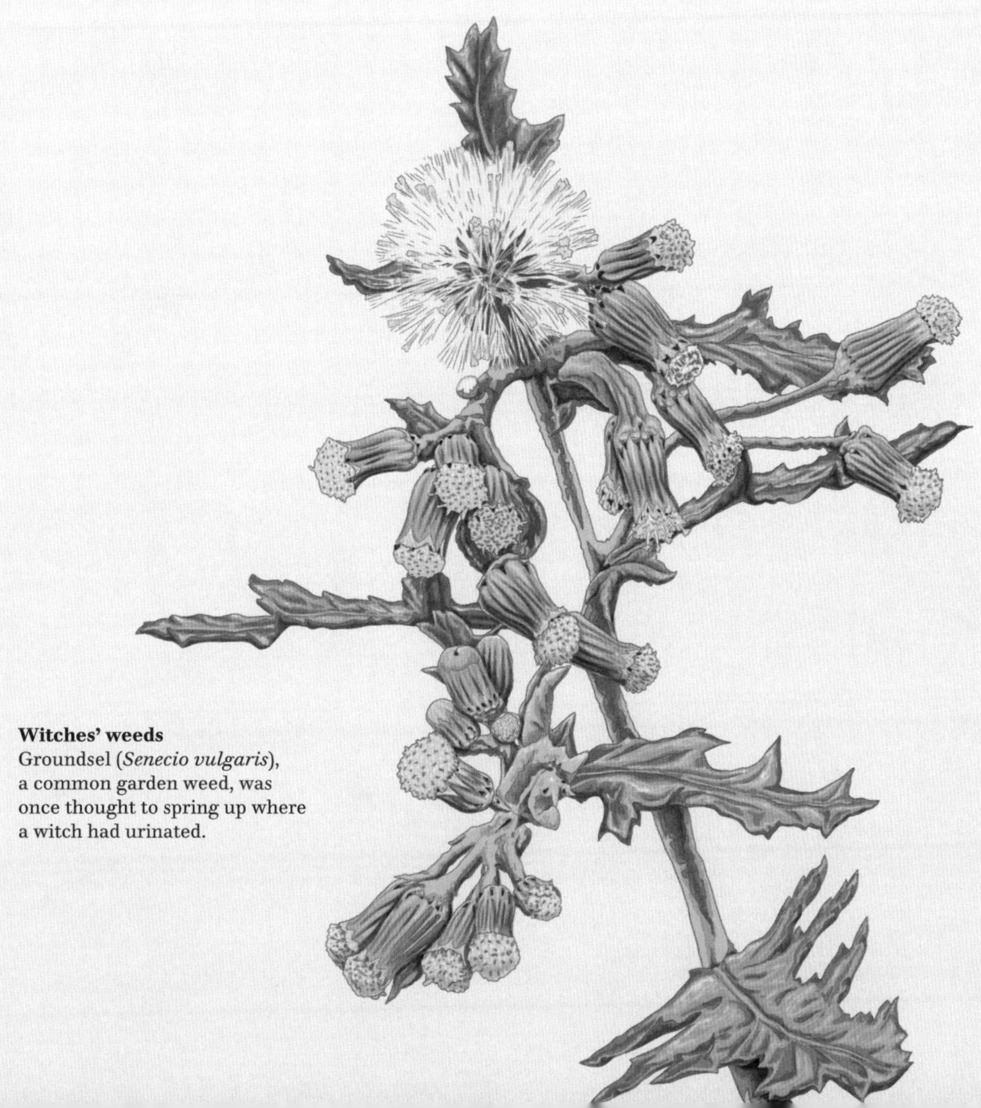

Witches' weeds
Groundsel (*Senecio vulgaris*), a common garden weed, was once thought to spring up where a witch had urinated.

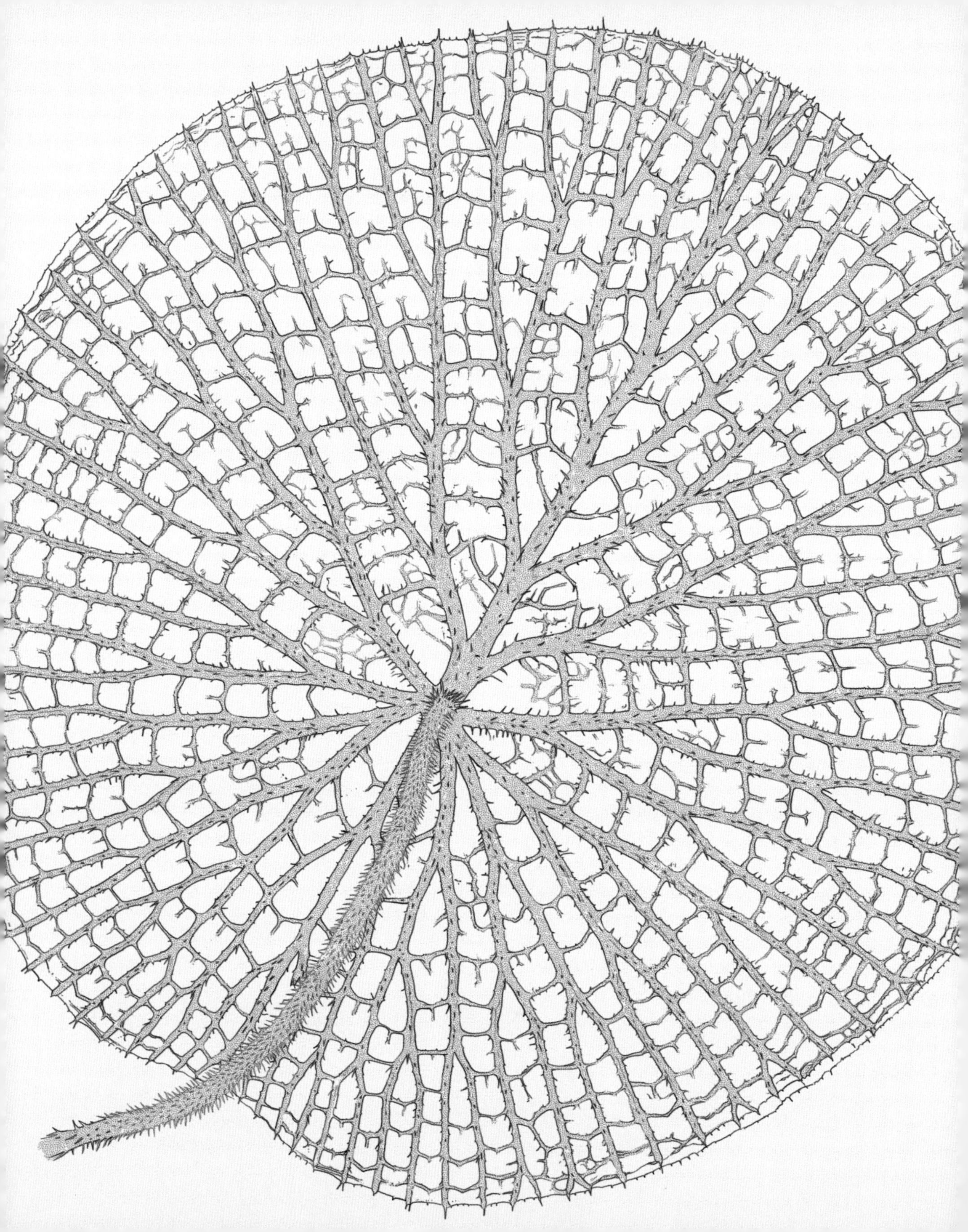

Biomimetics describes the application of biological structures, systems, and processes in technology. There's a lot we can learn from wildflowers.

BIOMIMETICS

Living organisms have inspired biomimetic applications of all kinds, from buildings to microfluidics (the movement of tiny amounts of liquid through channels in devices, such as inkjet printers). Here are some structures and technologies that have been informed by plants over the centuries:

- Joseph Paxton's Crystal Palace in London in the mid-nineteenth century was inspired by the leaf structure of the giant Amazonian water lily (*Victoria amazonica*). Scientists have recently shown that the leaf structure is highly economical, using the minimum amount of biomass that can cover a large surface area efficiently for photosynthesis. This could inspire the design of floating offshore solar panels.
- Burdock (*Arctium lappa*) is a common European wildflower that grows along riverbanks and in woods. It produces sticky fruit that cling to the fur of passing animals (and the clothes of passing humans) as a means of dispersal. In 1941 a Swiss engineer discovered that his dog's fur was covered in these burrs. He examined them under the microscope, found that they had tiny hooks that catch on to hair and fabric, and designed the synthetic replica, Velcro, that we now use every day.
- Liquid-manipulating technology has been optimized by examining the functional surfaces of living organisms, such as water-repellent lotus leaves (see p.192). This technology is used in architecture, medical devices, and household products.
- Plants can be particularly useful in informing the physics of wetting (lubrication) technology. Lubricated surface structures lock in water and create a self-cleaning surface on metal, plastic, and textiles, to repel contaminants. They have been optimized by examining the surfaces of carnivorous pitcher plants (*Nepenthes*; see pp.152–155), on which water condenses and forms a slippery film, driving insects into the trap.

Giant Amazonian water lily (*Victoria amazonica*)
The structure of this remarkable plant inspired Joseph Paxton in his design for the Crystal Palace in London.

Botanical illustration has always been important in preserving knowledge about wildflowers. Besides their beauty, many botanical illustrations have been used in the description of new plant species, so they hold immense scientific value.

BOTANICAL ILLUSTRATION

Wildflower illustrations feature in the first herbals, where they were closely associated with medicine. Later, in the sixteenth century, botanical illustration offering a truer likeness to the plants they depicted featured prominently in printed books. Then, herbaria (archives of dried, pressed plants; see pp.220–221) around the world began to amass vast collections of botanical illustrations. Many of these were used in the description of new species and have intrinsic historic and scientific as well as illustrative importance. Botanical illustration is still alive and well. Botanical illustrations for use in books or scientific papers are usually created in pen and ink or in watercolor, and depict the minute features of plants.

Some historical illustrations of plants and the natural world were highly interpretive, for example the artwork of the German zoologist Ernst Haeckel, who famously depicted many stylized sea creatures. Others illustrated their subjects more accurately and in minute detail, for example the prolific eighteenth-century Austrian botanical artist Ferdinand Bauer, who illustrated the *Flora Graeca*, a 10-volume publication of the plants of Greece by the English botanist John Sibthorp. Bauer's botanical illustrations became highly valued and sought-after both for their scientific and horticultural interest, and for their beauty. The *Flora Graeca* has been described as one of the most magnificent floras ever created.

TURNING OVER A NEW LEAF

Early botanical illustrations were transferred, in reverse, from paper to blocks of wood, so they could be carved, inked, and then printed. Later, copperplate engraving enabled larger images to be made, with more finely cut lines allowing greater detail.

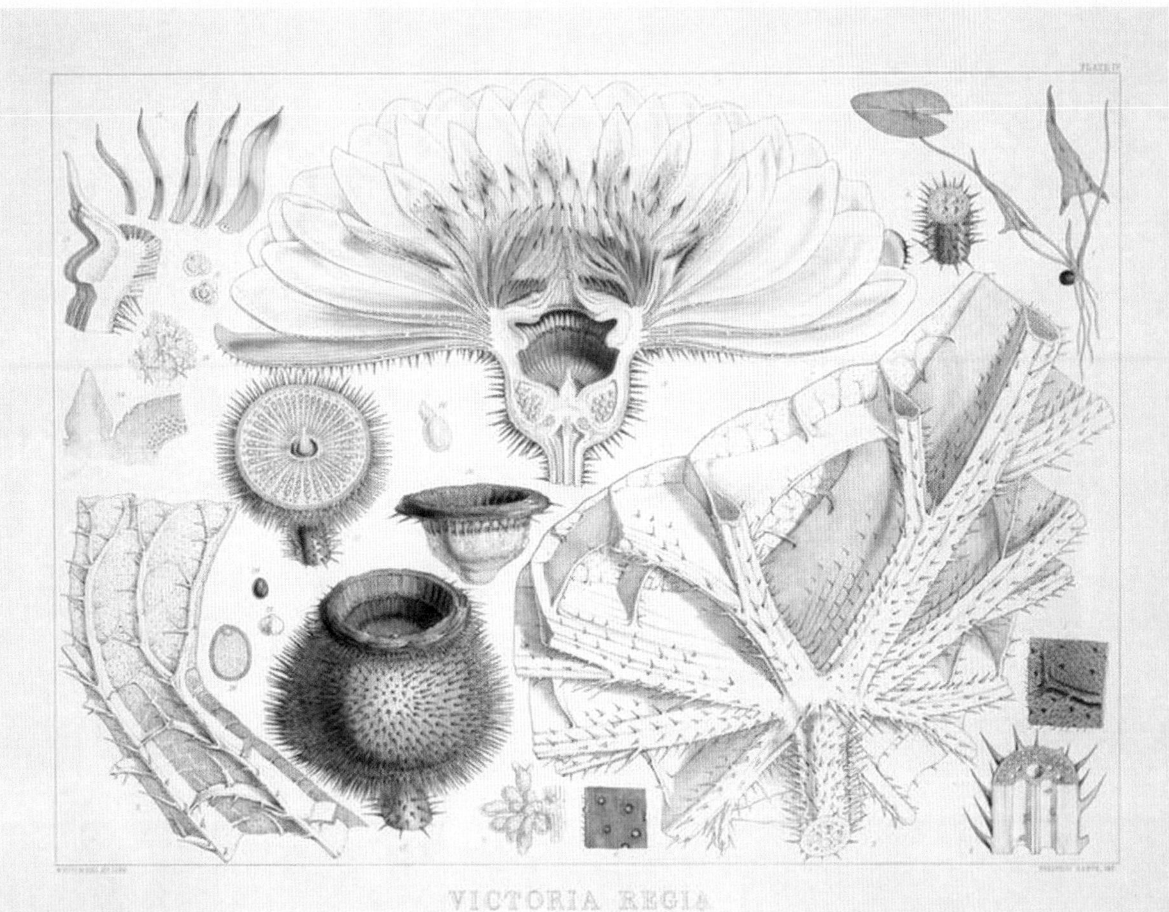

The royal water lily
Victoria Regia: or, Illustrations of the Royal Water-Lily, from the series *Specimens Flowering at Syon and Kew*, with descriptions by Sir William Jackson Hooker, 1851. Typical of traditional botanical illustration, this color lithograph depicts various aspects of the plant's anatomy and life cycle.

Dracula simia

CHAPTER IX

GROW

IN A FAST-CHANGING WORLD we are increasingly recognizing the importance of plants and biodiversity to the health of our planet. Wild plants give us the air we breathe, the food we eat, and the clothes we wear, as well as offering solutions to great challenges, from identifying new medicines to ensuring food security. They are also fundamental to our mental health and well-being.

Purple prairie clover (*Dalea purpurea*)
This wildflower is a perennial native to high-elevation grasslands of North America. Its spikes of purple flowers attract a variety of pollinators, such as bees and butterflies, and as a legume it has nitrogen-fixing properties, making it ideal for restoring prairie plantings (see also pp. 186–187).

Yellow rattle (*Rhinanthus minor*)
After the flowers of yellow rattle fall, the papery brown calyces rattle in the wind, hence the plant's name. This is an annual that siphons food from the roots of grasses, suppressing the grasses' dominance and thereby enabling other wildflowers to thrive (see also pp.56–57).

Corncockle (*Agrostemma githago*)
This flower was common in wheat fields in Northern Europe in the nineteenth century, when its seeds were inadvertently mixed with harvested seed and resown every year. It was introduced into the US, Canada, Australia, and New Zealand. Corncockle decreased with the introduction of herbicides, but it is making a resurgence as a component of seed mixes used in municipal roadside plantings.

Most of the world's wildflower meadows have been lost over the last century. Introducing a combination of wildflowers and grasses into a garden is a small way to help make up for the loss of this habitat, providing food and shelter for a diversity of animal life.

GROW YOUR OWN WILDFLOWERS

There are many ways to grow wildflowers, for example laying wildflower-seeded turf, planting wildflower plugs, or simply sowing seed onto existing turf or bare earth. You can create a mini-meadow or sow wildflowers in gaps in your borders, and if you don't have a garden, you can grow wildflowers in a container.

First, consider whether you want an annual or perennial wildflower meadow. Annuals (poppies, for example) complete their life cycle in one year and tend to thrive with disturbance; perennials (such as wild Shasta daisies) reappear each year and require more stable conditions. Avoid sowing seed on nutrient-rich soils or adding fertilizer, since rich soil is likely to encourage weeds and fast-growing grasses that will outcompete most establishing wildflowers. Planting wildflowers is an effective way to introduce a colorful, wildlife-friendly display to your plot, whatever size it may be.

Rewilding cities can be a powerful way of ***restoring biodiversity****. Urban green spaces—such as* ***parks and gardens****—can improve biodiversity as well as* ***human well-being****.*

Rewilding can be defined as the large-scale restoration of ecosystems and natural processes in a designated area to promote biodiversity and resilience.

REWILDING

Humans have profoundly influenced every habitat on Earth, and driven a nature and biodiversity crisis; indeed, most wildflowers now face possible extinction. We must find new ways to conserve biodiversity.

The generally accepted meaning of rewilding is to return "wildness" to landscapes that have been harmed, altered, or nature-depleted. Initially, the concept emphasized protecting vast areas with a focus on animal predators, but latterly ecosystem restoration (or rewilding) has taken a more holistic, process-orientated approach, and at different scales—even in yards.

Unlike "conservation" in a conventional sense, rewilding places emphasis on restoration with minimal human intervention. It doesn't mean abandoning land; some level of intervention is required, for example introducing herds of free-roaming herbivores to create sufficient disturbance to support wildflower diversity. Without adequate disturbance, most wildflowers are eventually outcompeted by grasses, shrubs, and trees.

Rewilding at scale is usually carried out in conjunction with landowners and organizations. In some cases it first requires a proactive approach in, for example, reducing the nutrients in the soil, controlling competitive agricultural weeds, and facilitating plant establishment through sowing seed. Wildflowers are key to the rewilding process; where flora leads, other wildlife will follow.

NATURE BOUNCE-BACK Afforestation is the establishment of forest ecosystems in areas from which forests have been absent for a long time. It involves planting trees, often over large areas, to mitigate the effects of land degradation and the impact of climate change. Reforestation, on the other hand, is the establishment of trees in areas that are already forested or have been recently deforested, to offset the effects of the trees' removal.

Humans live in a fast-changing world. We are increasingly recognizing the importance of plants and biodiversity to the future health of our planet—and also to our own mental health and well-being.

FLOURISHING

We are discovering more and more not only that can we reintroduce nature and biodiversity, including wildflowers, where they have been lost, but also that green and natural spaces have a positive impact on brain health. A wealth of scientific research and literature now demonstrates the role the natural environment plays in our mental well-being. Spending time in nature, engaging with nature, and a sense of connectedness with the natural environment all have a positive impact on our lives. Now, more than ever before, landscape architects and town planners are considering using wildflowers in landscape design to promote therapeutic responses.

SEEING PLANTS Our very existence depends on plants, yet to many of us they are invisible, a phenomenon that has metaphorically been called "plant blindness." We, as a species, have evolved to hunt or flee—in other words, to notice—other animals. Plants, on the other hand, often fall into the shadows; they are the green backdrop against which our lives play out. Even in wildlife documentaries, all too often plants simply make up the scenery. Two in five of the world's wildflower species are threatened with extinction, and plants hold many of the answers to the global challenges we face. Noticing plants is important.

Astonishing people with unusual or surprising plants is one way to get them noticed. Opposite are two species that are hard to miss.

HOUSEPLANTS TAKING OVER OUR HOMES

People have grown potted plants since ancient times, and today, more than ever, houseplants are growing in popularity. Plants are scientifically proven to clean and purify the air, so bringing the wild indoors can help create a healthy environment.

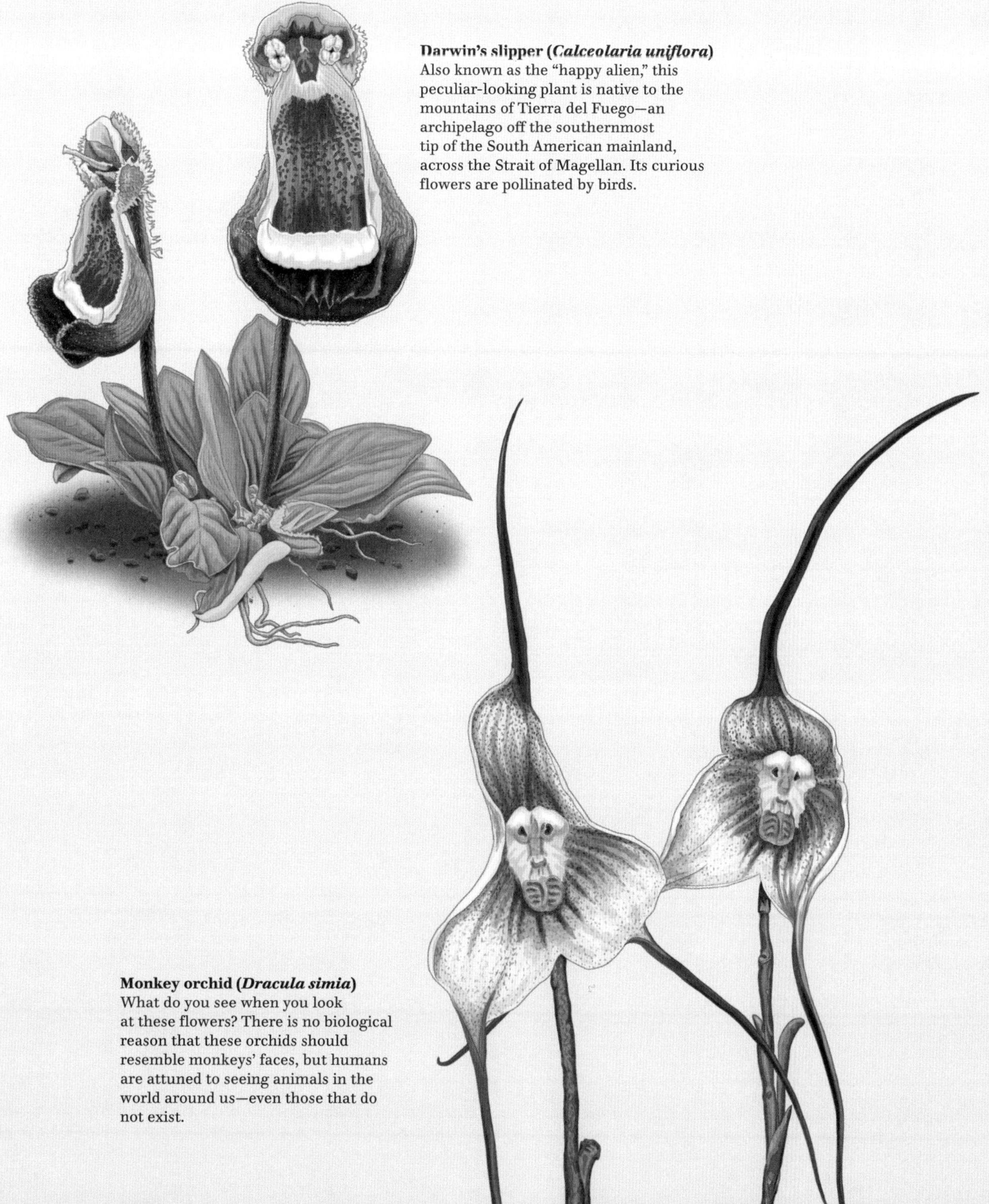

Darwin's slipper (*Calceolaria uniflora*)
Also known as the "happy alien," this peculiar-looking plant is native to the mountains of Tierra del Fuego—an archipelago off the southernmost tip of the South American mainland, across the Strait of Magellan. Its curious flowers are pollinated by birds.

Monkey orchid (*Dracula simia*)
What do you see when you look at these flowers? There is no biological reason that these orchids should resemble monkeys' faces, but humans are attuned to seeing animals in the world around us—even those that do not exist.

REFERENCES

pp.16–17 The Rise of Plants Sauquet, Hervé, et al. (2017). "The Ancestral Flower of Angiosperms and its Early Diversification." *Nature Communications* 8, www.nature.com/articles/ncomms16047.

pp.20–21 Wild Water Weeds Prestianni, Cyrille, and Robert W. Gess (2019). "*Rinistachya hilleri* gen. et sp. nov. (Sphenophyllales), from the Upper Devonian of South Africa." *Organisms Diversity & Evolution* 19: 1–11, https://link.springer.com/article/10.1007/s13127-018-0385-3.

pp.72–73 Darwin's Orchids Darwin, Charles R. (1862). *On the Various Contrivances by Which British and Foreign Orchids are Fertilised by Insects, and on the Good Effects of Intercrossing.* London: John Murray.

pp.76–77 Nectar Cheats Ehlers, B. K., and J. M. Olesen (1997). "The Fruit-Wasp Route to Toxic Nectar in *Epipactis* Orchids?" *Flora* 192/3: 223–229.

pp.90–91 Trappings and Droppings Chin, Lijin, Jonathan A. Moran, and Charles Clarke (2010). "Trap Geometry in Three Giant Montane Pitcher Plant Species from Borneo Is a Function of Tree Shrew Body Size." *New Phytologist* 186/2 (April): 461–470, https://nph.onlinelibrary.wiley.com/doi/10.1111/j.1469-8137.2009.03166.x.

pp.160–163 Fairy Lanterns Siti-Munirah, Mat Yunoh, Nikong Dome, and Chris Thorogood (2021). "*Thismia sitimeriamiae* (Thismiaceae), an Extraordinary New Species from Terengganu, Peninsular Malaysia." *PhytoKeys* 179: 75–89, https://phytokeys.pensoft.net/article/68300.

Sochor, Michal, et al. (2018). "Recovery of *Thismia neptunis* (Thismiaceae) after 151 Years." *Phytotaxa* 340/1 (February), https://doi.org/10.11646/phytotaxa.340.1.5.

pp.206–207 Life on the Rails Harris, S. A. (2002). "Introduction of Oxford Ragwort, *Senecio squalidus* L. (Asteraceae), to the United Kingdom." *Watsonia* 24: 31–43, http://archive.bsbi.org.uk/Wats24p31.pdf.

pp.218–219 Threatened Species Begum, Shabana (2022). "Scientists Swim across Muddy River Monthly to Confirm Existence of New Peat Tree Species." *Straits Times*, November 30, www.straitstimes.com/singapore/scientists-swim-across-muddy-river-monthly-to-confirm-existence-of-new-peat-tree-species.

Swanepoel, Wessel, et al. (2020). "From the Frying Pan: An Unusual Dwarf Shrub from Namibia Turns Out to Be a New Brassicalean Family." *Phytotaxa* 439/3: 171–185, www.doi.org/10.11646/phytotaxa.439.3.1.

Tobias, Adriane B., Chris J. Thorogood, and Pastor L. Malabrigo Jr. (2023). "The Reinstatement of *Rafflesia banaoana* (Rafflesiaceae), and Implications for Assessing Species Diversity and Conservation Requirements of the World's Largest Flowers." *Phytotaxa* 612/2, https://phytotaxa.mapress.com/pt/article/view/phytotaxa.612.2.5.

Zubov, Dimitri, Anna Trias Blasi, and Ruslan Mishustin (2022). "*Sternbergia mishustinii* (Amaryllidaceae): A New Species from the Mersin Province in Southern Turkey." *Kew Bulletin* 77: 317–323, https://link.springer.com/article/10.1007/s12225-022-10013-8.

pp.244–245 Roman Herbs Andrews, Alfred C. (1948). "The Use of Rue as a Spice by the Greeks and Romans." *Classical Journal* 43/6 (March): 371–373, www.jstor.org/stable/3293587.

Briggs, Lisa, and Jens Jakobsson (2022). "Searching for Silphium: An Updated Review." *Heritage* 5/2: 936–955, www.doi.org/10.3390/heritage5020051.

Davies, R. W. (1970). "Some Roman Medicine." *Medical History*, 14/1 (January): 101–106, www.doi.org/10.1017/S0025727300015192.

Kumbaric, Alma, Valentina Savo, and Giulia Caneva (2013). "Orchids in the Roman Culture and Iconography: Evidence for the First Representations in Antiquity." *Journal of Cultural Heritage*, 14/4 (July–August): 311–316, www.doi.org/10.1016/j.culher.2012.09.002.

Tosun, Fatma, et al. (2023). "Biological Activities of the Fruit Essential Oil, Fruit, and Root Extracts of *Ferula drudeana* Korovin, the Putative Anatolian Ecotype of the Silphion Plant." *Plants* 12/4: 830, www.doi.org/10.3390/plants12040830.

pp.252–253 The Language of Flowers Dobbs, Liz (2022). *The Secret Language of Flowers: The Historical Symbolism and Spiritual Properties of Flowers Throughout Time* (DK Secret Histories). London: DK.

pp.254–255 Wildflowers in Art Mancoff, Debra N. (2003). *Flora symbolica: Flowers in Pre-Raphaelite Art.* Munich, London, and New York: Prestel.

pp.256–257 Ethnobotany Edwards, Sarah E. (2023). *The Ethnobotanical.* London: Kew Publishing.

pp.258–259 Wildflowers and Magic Lawrence, Sandra (2020). *Witch's Garden.* London: Kew Publishing.

pp.260–261 Biomimetics Box, Finn, Chris Thorogood, and Jian Hui Guan (2019). "Guided Droplet Transport on Synthetic Slippery Surfaces Inspired by a Pitcher Plant." *Journal of the Royal Society Interface* 16/158 (September), www.royalsocietypublishing.org/doi/10.1098/rsif.2019.0323.

Box, Finn, et al. (2022). "Gigantic Floating Leaves Occupy a Large Surface Area at an Economical Material Cost." *Science Advances* 8/6 (February), www.science.org/doi/10.1126/sciadv.abg3790.

Sánchez-Galván, Gloria, Francisco J. Mercado, and Eugenia J. Olguín (2013). "Leaves and Roots of *Pistia stratiotes* as Sorbent Materials for the Removal of Crude Oil from Saline Solutions." *Water, Air, & Soil Pollution* 224 (10 January), https://link.springer.com/article/10.1007/s11270-012-1421-0.

pp.262–263 Botanical Illustration Simblet, Sarah (2020). *Botany for the Artist: An Inspirational Guide to Drawing Plants.* London: DK.

FURTHER READING & RESOURCES

General Reading

Antonelli, Alexandre, *The Hidden Universe: Adventures in Biodiversity*, Chicago: University of Chicago Press/London: Witness Books, 2022

Drori, Jonathan, *Around the World in 80 Plants*, London: Laurence King, 2021

Harris, Stephen A., *Roots to Seeds: 400 Years of Oxford Botany*, Oxford: Bodleian Library, 2021

Mabey, Richard, *The Cabaret of Plants: Botany and the Imagination*, New York: W. W. Norton, 2015

Stafford, Fiona, *The Long, Long Life of Trees*. New Haven, CT, and London: Yale University Press, 2016

Thorogood, Chris, *When Plants Took Over the Planet: The Amazing Story of Plant Evolution*, London: Quarto Publishing, 2021

Regional Guides

Brandenburg, David M., *National Wildlife Federation Field Guide to Wildflowers of North America*, New York: Union Square & Co., 2012

Niering, William A., *National Audubon Society Field Guide to North American Wildflowers: Eastern Region*, New York: Knopf Doubleday Publishing Group, 2001

——, *National Audubon Society Field Guide to North American Wildflowers: Western Region*. Knopf Doubleday Publishing Group, 2001

Stace, Clive, *New Flora of the British Isles*, Middlewood Green, Suffolk: C&M Floristics, 2021

——, *Concise Flora of the British Isles*. Middlewood Green, Suffilk: C&M Floristics, 2022

Thorogood, Chris, *Field Guide to the Wild Flowers of the Eastern Mediterranean*, London: Kew Publishing, 2019

——, *Field Guide to the Wild Flowers of the Western Mediterranean*, 2nd ed, Kew Publishing, 2021

Online Resources

Alpine Garden Society (UK): www.alpinegardensociety.net

American Fern Society: www.amerfernsoc.org

American Horticultural Society: www.ahsgardening.org

American Orchid Society: www.aos.org

Association for the Taxonomic Study of the Flora of Tropical Africa: www.aetfat.org

Australasian Plant Society: www.anzplantsoc.org.uk

Botanic Gardens Conservation International: www.bgci.org

Botanical Society of America: www.botany.org

Botanical Society of Britain & Ireland: www.bsbi.org

Botanical Society of South Africa: www.botanicalsociety.org.za

British Bryological Society: www.britishbryologicalsociety.org.uk

Canadian Botanical Association: www.cba-abc.ca

The Carnivorous Plant Society: www.thecps.org.uk

Field Studies Council (UK): www.field-studies-council.org

German Society for Plant Sciences: www.deutsche-botanische-gesellschaft.de

International Carnivorous Plant Society (US): www.carnivorousplants.org

International Parasitic Plant Society: www.parasiticplants.org

The Orchid Society of Great Britain: www.osgb.org.uk

Plant Heritage (UK): www.plantheritage.org.uk

Plant Network (UK and Ireland): www.plantnetwork.org

Plants of the World Online (Royal Botanic Gardens, Kew): https://powo.science.kew.org

Royal Horticultural Society (UK): www.rhs.org.uk

Société botanique de France: https://societebotaniquedefrance.fr

GLOSSARY

actinomorphic radially symmetrical; compare **zygomorphic**

androecium the collective male sex organs of a flower; compare **gynoecium**

angiosperm a flowering plant

annual a plant that completes its life cycle within a single year

biennial a plant that completes its life cycle over two years

biodiversity the variety of all living **species**, genes, and **ecosystems**

bract a modified (usually reduced), leaflike structure, most commonly in the **inflorescence**

bulb a swollen underground stem surrounded by fleshy layers

calyx (pl. **calyces**) the lowermost whorl of **sepals** in a flower

capitulum (pl. **capitula**) a group of tiny flowers united in a single structure

carpel the floral organ that bears the ovules in flowering plants (a unit of a pistil)

corm an underground stem that acts as a storage organ

corolla the whorl of petals above the **sepals** (**calyx**)

co-sexual describes a flower that contains both male and female parts

cross-fertilization the fusion of male and female sex cells following **pollination**, leading to the development of seeds

cultivar a plant produced artificially by selective breeding

cyanobacteria a group of bacteria that were the first organisms known to have produced oxygen by photosynthesis

cyme an **inflorescence** in which the central or terminal flower opens first, followed by the peripheral or lower flowers

dioecious describes a species in which male and female flowers are borne on separate plants; compare **monoecious**

ecosystem a biological community, or network, of interacting species and their physical environment as part of a complex system

endemic describes a plant that is found in only one place

epiphyte a plant that lives in the branches of trees and obtains moisture and nutrients from rainwater runoff

exudate a fluid exuded by an organism, e.g. from a root

floral tube a **corolla** that is tubular

floret a tiny flower

form the taxonomic rank below a **variety**

genus (pl. **genera**) a **taxonomic** term used in biology; organisms in the same genus all derive from a common ancestor. Wildflowers have two-word scientific names: the first is the name of the genus and the second the name of the species, e.g. *Bellis perennis* (lawn daisy), *Epipogium aphyllum* (ghost orchid), and *Echinocereus coccineus* (scarlet hedgehog cactus)

geophyte a plant that produces underground storage organs (**bulbs**, **corms**, or **rhizomes**) to survive a period of dormancy

gymnosperm an ancient **lineage** of seed-producing, nonflowering plants including conifers and cycads

gynoecium the collective female sex organs of a flower; compare **androecium**

herbal a book containing the names and descriptions of plants, typically with their uses

herbarium a collection of preserved (e.g. pressed and dried) plant specimens and associated information

inflorescence a group or cluster of flowers on a plant

invasive describes a species that establishes and spreads with adverse impact on native **biodiversity**, **ecosystems**, **species** and, in some cases, people

legume peas, beans, and their relatives. Also refers to the seed pod produced by such a plant

liana a plant that climbs, e.g. into the tree canopy. Also known as a vine

lineage a group of related plants that are all descended from a common ancestor

lithophyte a plant that is adapted to growing out of rock

monoecious describes a species in which male and female flowers are borne on the same plant; compare **dioecious**

morphology the study of the structure and form (e.g. anatomy) of plants

ovatc cgg-shaped (e.g. of a leaf)

perennial a plant that completes its life cycle over the course of several years, usually flowering annually; may be short-lived or long-lived

perianth the **calyx** and **corolla** combined

photosynthesis the process by which a green plant converts sunlight and carbon dioxide into energy for growth and reproduction

pollination the process by which pollen grains are transferred from the male anther to the female stigma of a flower, leading to its fertilization

raceme an unbranched **inflorescence** in which each flower has a short stalk, and the flowers open in sequence from bottom to top

relict a plant or **lineage** that has survived from an ancient form

rhizome a creeping, rootlike underground stem

sepal a leafy structure protecting a flower (a unit of the **calyx**)

spadix a spike-like flowering structure

spathe an enlarged **bract** enclosing the **inflorescence** in some families (e.g. Araceae)

species the basic **taxonomic** unit; individuals in a species share the same name

spore a minute (single-cell) reproductive unit, often wind-dispersed

succulent a plant with a fleshy, water-retentive habit (e.g. of leaves or stems) that confers an advantage under dry conditions

symbiosis the close association of different life forms that confers an advantage to both (e.g. ants living in ant plants)

taxonomy the science of describing and naming organisms, and grouping related organisms (classifying them)

tendril a specialized threadlike structure (e.g. of a stem or leaf), sometimes coiled, that enables a plant to climb

trichome a small hair e.g. on a flower or leaf

tuber a modified stem that acts as an underground storage organ

umbel a cluster of flowers with short stalks arising from a single point

variety the **taxonomic** rank above a **form**

vascular describes a plant that has specialized tissues for the transportation of water and nutrients

zygomorphic bilaterally symmetrical; compare **actinomorphic**

INDEX

INDEX OF FLOWERS

T

U

V

W

Z

Dactylorhiza maculata

Sunbird on an aloe

ABOUT THE AUTHOR

Chris Thorogood is a plant biologist at the University of Oxford. He is a lecturer of biology and holds the position of Deputy Director and Head of Science of the University of Oxford Botanic Garden and Arboretum. Chris is a visiting professor at the University of the Philippines, where he teaches botany and forestry and carries out fieldwork and conservation, with a focus on the world's largest flowers (genus *Rafflesia*). He has also carried out fieldwork in Japan, West Asia, and the Mediterranean, where he taught field botany for more than a decade.

Chris's current research focuses on evolution, conservation, floras in biodiversity hot spots, and biomimetics—the interdisciplinary field in which adaptations from living organisms are applied to the synthesis of materials, systems, or machines, for example solar panels inspired by water lilies. He is a Fellow of the Linnean Society of London, an editor for the journal *Plants People Planet* of the New Phytologist Trust, and a Fellow of the Society of Botanical Artists.

As well as being a plant biologist and author, Chris makes regular appearances on TV and radio, and is also an award-winning botanical illustrator and wildlife artist. Obsessed with plants, he is on a mission to make us see them differently, and realize how we, they, and our planet are all connected.

ACKNOWLEDGMENTS

I owe a debt of thanks to the many botanists around the world who, over the years, have tirelessly shared their flora with me one plant at a time; many feature in these pages. My sincere thanks also go to the DK team, whose significant effort made this book possible: Rosanna Fairhead, the copy-editor; senior editors Lucy Sienkowska and Alastair Laing; Barbara Zuniga, who oversaw the design, Giulia Garbin, who designed the concept, Vicky Read, who designed the pages, and Izzy Poulson, who designed the jacket; and the talented illustrators Dan Crisp, Jessica Ip, and Stuart Jackson-Carter, who brought the whole thing to life.

PUBLISHER'S ACKNOWLEDGMENTS

DK would like to thank Kathy Steer for proofreading and Ruth Ellis for indexing.

Editorial Manager Ruth O'Rourke
Senior Editors Lucy Sienkowska, Alastair Laing
Senior US Editor Megan Douglass
Senior Designer Barbara Zuniga
Production Editor David Almond
Senior Production Controller Samantha Cross
DTP and Design Coordinator Heather Blagden
Publishing Assistant Emily Cannings
Jacket Designer Izzy Poulson
Art Director Maxine Pedliham

Editorial Rosanna Fairhead
Design Vicky Read
Illustration Dan Crisp, Jessica Ip,
Stuart Jackson-Carter
Design styling concept Giulia Garbin

First American Edition, 2025
Published in the United States by DK Publishing,
a division of Penguin Random House LLC
1745 Broadway, 20th Floor, New York, NY 10019

25 26 27 28 29 10 9 8 7 6 5 4 3 2 1
001–341259–Mar/2025

Published in Great Britain by Dorling Kindersley Limited

A catalog record for this book
is available from the Library of Congress.
ISBN: 978-0-7440-9987-4

Printed and bound in China
www.dk.com

This book was made with Forest Stewardship Council™ certified paper—one small step in DK's commitment to a sustainable future.
Learn more at **www.dk.com/uk/information/sustainability**

PICTURE CREDITS

The publisher would like to thank the following for their kind permission to reproduce their photographs:

(Key: a-above; b-below/bottom; c-center; f-far; l-left; r-right; t-top)

Alamy Stock Photo: Album 253t, ARTGEN 254, PictureLux/The Hollywood Archive 253b, The History Collection 263

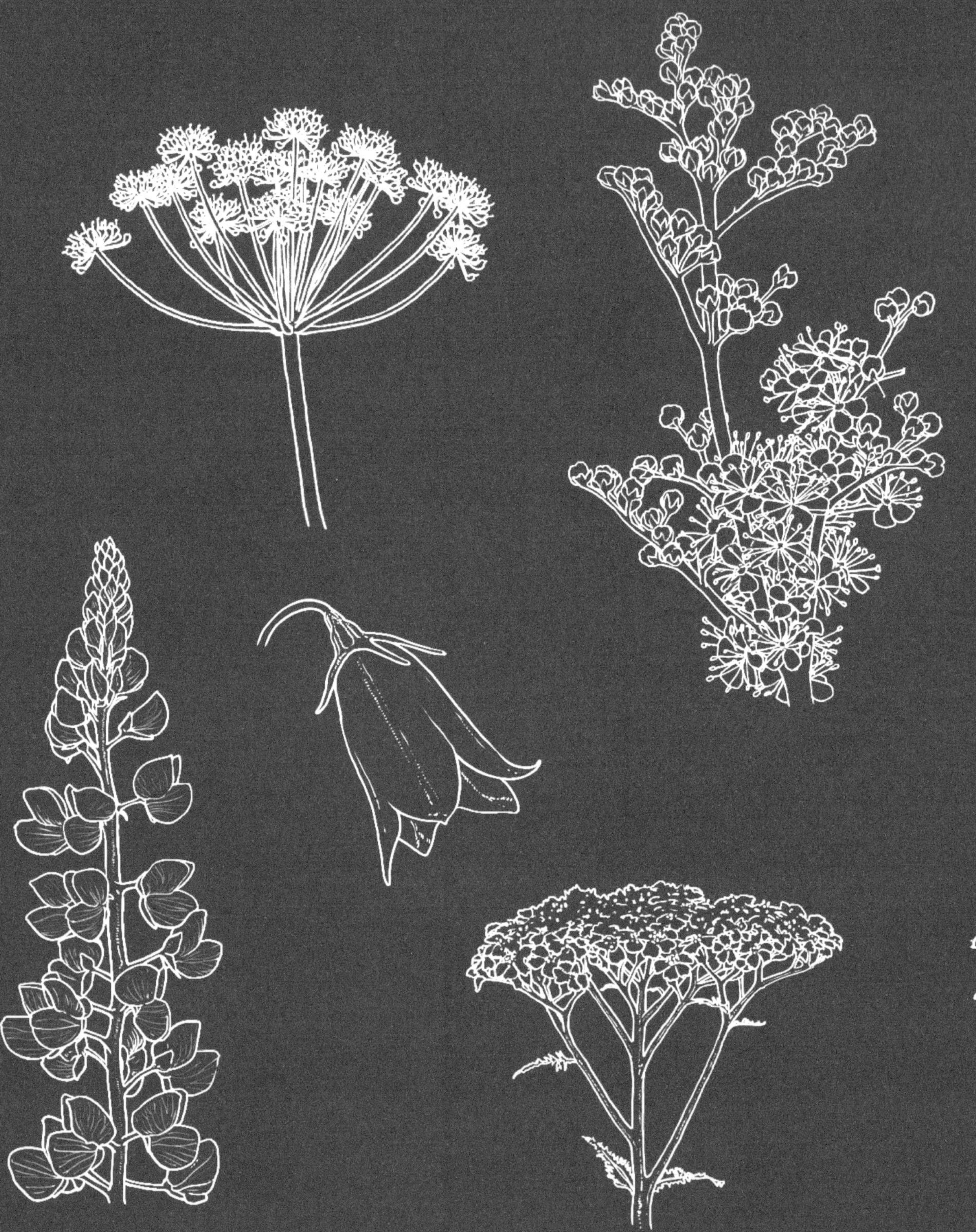